'But, do you not see, gentlemen, it is absolutely nothing to me, I console myself that I am the man I am and will remain so, whether you praise me to the skies or throw no matter how much dirt at me.'

ALBERT BONNIER, 1841.

———

'I took you because you were the most fearless.'

**AUGUST STRINDBERG
TO ALBERT BONNIER, 1884.**

ALBERT BONNIER

ALBERT BONNIER

HIS LIFE AND TIMES

PER T. OHLSSON

MANILLA
PRESS

First published with the title *Albert Bonnier och hans tid* by Albert Bonniers Förlag,
Sweden, in 2020

First published in the UK by Manilla Press
an imprint of Bonnier Books UK
4th Floor, Victoria House
Bloomsbury Square
London, WC1B 4DA
England

facebook.com/bonnierbooksuk/
twitter.com/bonnierbooksuk

Hardback – 9781786581969

A CIP catalogue of this book is available from the British Library.

Typeset by Envy Design Ltd
Printed and bound by Clays Ltd, Elcograf S.p.A

1 3 5 7 9 10 8 6 4 2

Every reasonable effort has been made to trace copyright holders of
material reproduced in this book, but if any have been inadvertently
overlooked the publishers would be glad to hear from them.

Manilla Press is an imprint of Bonnier Books UK
www.bonnierbooks.co.uk

CONTENTS

FOREWORD AND ACKNOWLEDGEMENTS

When Albert Bonnier, my publisher, phoned me in late 2016 and asked whether I would consider writing a book about his ancestor and namesake, I was assailed by a slightly panicked sense of doubt. What did I know about old Albert Bonnier, founder of the great publishing house? Little more than that he was born into a Jewish family in Copenhagen, that he came to Sweden as a young man and started publishing books early on, that he became the publisher of many of Sweden's most celebrated authors and that he was subjected to hate campaigns, often with antisemitic overtones.

Nevertheless, I had no hesitation in setting about working on the first biography of Albert Bonnier.

There were three deciding factors.

Firstly, my interest in the formative nineteenth century, which was kindled in earnest when I wrote *100 år av tillväxt* (*100 Years of Growth*), the biography of Sweden's Minister for Finance, Johan August Gripenstedt.

Secondly, my interest in the significance of immigration, reflected in *Konservkungen* (*The King of Preserves*), my book about Herbert Felix, a refugee of Jewish descent who volunteered to serve in the Second World War in an attempt to rescue his condemned family and who later built up one of Sweden's largest food companies.

And above all, thirdly:

During my most preliminary research, I realised this was an exciting and fascinating story that should be told, as Albert Bonnier was revealed to be one of the most important figures in, and for, Sweden's modern public life.

* * *

It took just over three years to put this book together, but had it not been for the energies of many helpful people, it would probably have taken thirty.

My main sources include the extensive Bonnier publishing and family archive, now held by Sweden's Centre for Business History in Bromma. Eva and Albert Bonnier gave me unfettered access to this material and I would like to express my great thanks to them and to the Centre for Business History's staff. Another important source was Swedish newspapers from the time of Albert Bonnier, now digitalised by the National Library of Sweden.

Numerous literary studies and theses have been extremely important. I would particularly like to mention Gunnel Furuland's well-written *Romanen som vardagsvara* (*The Novel as Everyday Commodity*) and Gundel Söderholm's thorough *Svea* on Albert Bonnier's literary annual.

When it comes to the general development of the Swedish book industry, particularly the conflicts within the Swedish Publishers' Association, Sven Rinman's history from the 1950s has proved invaluable, followed by works from authors including Johan Svedjedal.

Among the many biographical contributions to the picture of Albert Bonnier, the books of writer and publisher Per I. Gedin, a colossus of scholarship, have played a key role, especially *Litteraturens örtagårdsmästare* (*A Gardener of Literature*), his biography of Albert's son, Karl Otto Bonnier.

Karl Otto Bonnier in particular has a special place in this book. He died in 1941, but I am especially grateful to his four-part history of the Bonnier family, *En bokhandlarefamilj* (*A Family of Booksellers*). These volumes have served as a map, helping me to navigate my way through an otherwise impenetrable forest of material. His painstaking interpretations of what the Bonnier brothers wrote and thought, in their not always easily interpreted correspondence with each other and with different authors, is an endeavour in the field of literary history from which I have benefitted greatly.

As far as possible, I have used the original nineteenth-century spellings when quoting letters and other documents, apart from on occasions where I am relying on evidence from a later date, e.g. Gustav Fröding's letter in an edition from the 1930s.

Regarding August Strindberg's correspondence with Albert and Karl Otto, among others, I have based the quotes on the collections of Strindberg's correspondence edited by and with a commentary by Torsten Eklund.

* * *

During the course of this work, a number of people have served as assistants, sounding boards and advisers. Sofia Murray, librarian at Malmö City Library, once more helped me to find relevant literature, which I often obtained via the outstanding services of the second-hand bookseller h:ström in Umeå. Kim Salomon, emeritus professor of history at Lund University, accompanied the process throughout, as did Bengt Braun, CEO of the Bonnier Group for many years. Carl Henrik Carlsson of the Hugo Valentin Centre at the University of Uppsala has helped me with important information. Daniel Sandström, editorial director at Albert Bonniers Förlag, who holds a PhD in literature, has guided me through the world of books. In Christian Manfred I have had an eminent editor and in Nina Ulmaja a superb designer.

With great patience, those closest to me – Mia, Lukas, my friends, my colleagues – have once more put up with the wild-eyed self-obsession of authorship. Thank you.

* * *

And last, but truly not least:

My warmest thanks to my friend Bo Bergman, language expert and educator *par excellence*, who, yet again, has taken the time to read a manuscript chapter by chapter, his eagle-eyed colleague Ingrid H. Fredriksson and – above all – my ever-enthusiastic and supportive publisher, Albert Bonnier, in so many ways reminiscent of his namesake and the subject of this biography.

Malmö and Vomb, March 2020
Per T Ohlsson

STOCKHOLM 1838

On the last nights of August 1838, as the gentle dusk of late summer fell over Stockholm, the peace was broken by a howling mob streaming through Gamla Stan, the old town. Marinated in spirits, free-flowing in early nineteenth-century Sweden, where home distilling was legal, they threw stones, fought and shouted taunts.

The unrest was a by-product of what were known as the Crusenstolpe riots, or the Rabulist riots, earlier that summer.

Tensions had been growing for some time, fuelled by social wrongs and the authoritarian rule of King Karl XIV Johan. It all exploded when the popular radical ('rabulist') writer Magnus Jacob Crusenstolpe, one of Karl Johan's most outspoken critics, was condemned to three years' imprisonment for having accused the King and the Government of Sabbath-breaking because an appointment decision was signed on a Sunday. Indignation tipped over into violence, which reached a peak on 19 July. Troops were called in and two demonstrators were killed.

A nervous calm subsequently settled over the capital but

as August turned to September unrest flared up again. This time the fury was not only directed towards those in power. Instead, the main target was a small religious minority of a few hundred people in Stockholm, a city with a population of approximately 80,000. They were termed adherents of the Mosaic faith, in other words, Jews. In Sweden, they numbered approximately 900 people, divided, with a few exceptions, between only four cities in which they were permitted to settle and work. Among them were three brothers, originally from Copenhagen: Adolf, Albert and David Felix Bonnier.

Albert, the middle brother, in particular, was to make quite a name for himself.

At the age of barely fifteen, he had arrived in Stockholm in 1835 to work as an assistant in Adolf's bookshop at Storkyrkobrinken 12 in Gamla Stan. However, Albert's real interest was in publishing and as early as 1837 he had saved up enough coppers to publish his first publication, a satirical pamphlet translated from French, *Bevis att Napoleon aldrig har existerat. Stort erratum. (Proof that Napoleon Never Existed. Major Erratum).* It was a minor success and the slim volume went into a second edition. Everything looked promising. But just a year later he was forced to experience at close quarters an unusually violent outbreak of the antisemitic atmosphere that was to shadow his life and his deeds, albeit in more muted forms.

Sweden has never come so close to a pogrom.

* * *

On the evening of Tuesday 28 August and the following night, Jewish homes on Stora Nygatan, Västerlånggatan and on Järntorget were attacked by an angry mob. The sound of breaking glass echoed down the streets and alleyways of Gamla Stan.

The rioting intensified and on 30 August, Governor of Stockholm, Axel Johan Adam Möllerhjelm, the highest ranking official in the city's administration, feared the situation was on the verge of disintegrating entirely. He warned of 'an attempt to employ powerful and deliberate persecution against the Jews in the city'.

Terrified Jewish families turned to the authorities requesting protection, which they received.

The fact that this protection could be a little haphazard was shown by *Aftonbladet*, Sweden's largest newspaper, founded by Lars Johan Hierta in the wake of the bourgeois Paris Revolution of 1830.

On 31 August, the newspaper told of a certain Mr Rossbach who had come off badly in an encounter with dragoons called in to restore order. On his way home, Rossbach had requested permission to pass a patrol and been authorised to proceed. He and his party had hardly started walking when one of the dragoons gave chase:

> He then ran down a street but was followed by the horseman, who started to strike him with his sabre; and continued long to do so, notwithstanding the whole neighbourhood hearing Rossbach shout loudly: 'What in the Lord's name do you want? I have said nothing and done nothing, etc.' Finally in a stroke Rossbach lost his hat and when he attempted to lean down and pick it up, he received a slice in the arm, followed by more.

The next day *Aftonbladet* published, slightly apologetically, a clarification on a point that the newspaper had neglected to mention:

> Mr Rossbach is a member of the Jewish congregation; which should not be left unsaid, in particular because (...) he, who furthermore is an older man with a family, cannot be claimed in the slightest way to have attacked the guard, but was utterly innocently persecuted and abused for no reason whatsoever.

The factor that had unleashed the storm was what was known as the Edict of Emancipation, a royal decree of 30 June 'regarding the obligations and rights of adherents of the Mosaic faith in the Kingdom of Sweden'. In practice, this abolished *Judereglementet*, a statute dating from May 1782 setting out restrictions on Jews wishing to settle in Sweden. The new edict expanded the rights of the Jewish minority, not least in opening up more choice in terms of place of residence.

When in the 1770s Gustav III allowed the Jewish merchant, seal engraver and stonemason Aron Isak from Brandenburg to settle in Stockholm without demanding he convert to Lutheranism, Isak managed to convince central holders of power, among them Governor of Stockholm Carl Sparre, that he be allowed to bring relatives and friends with him to his new homeland. This was the start of Jewish immigration to Sweden, albeit to an extremely limited extent.

Jews were permitted to practise their religion in strictly Lutheran Sweden, but a special regulation was issued, along Prussian lines, regulating their existence. Jews were able to build synagogues and undertake a limited number of occupations. The restrictions were narrow. *How* narrow was shown by the detailed list of the crafts that Jews were allowed to pursue:

> A Jew may otherwise earn a living by Art painting, engraving, Seal engraving, polishing Diamonds and other gemstones, Optical glass polishing, and production of all manner of Mathematical and Mechanical Instruments, drawing Plans and Patterns, Embroidery and other artistic stitching, Lacquer manufacture, Penmaking, Cork cutting and similar work that is not within the purview of the Guilds.

Jews were only allowed to settle in Stockholm, Gothenburg, Norrköping and later also in Karlskrona. They were permitted to operate businesses only in these towns. They were prohibited from marrying anyone of the Christian faith. And they had no political rights.

As the number of Jews increased and many became successful, moves were made, with the support of more liberal tides of opinion, to petition the authorities to lift the restrictions imposed in a regulation that seemed increasingly out of date. The edict of 30 June 1838 was the result.

The first section prescribed that Jews who were Swedish citizens 'were hereinafter in all respects to enjoy equal legal status with other Swedish subjects'. Nowhere was the authoritarian sounding term 'regulation' mentioned. Nevertheless, several restrictions remained; for example, Jews were not allowed to purchase real estate in rural areas without the permission of the King and had to take responsibility for care of the poor within their own community. However, it looked as though the position of Sweden's Jews would be considerably improved in terms of everything from freedom of movement to business activity.

The edict was published in the official gazette, *Statstidningen*, better known as *Posttidningen*, on 10 August.

* * *

Soon opinion started to seethe, first in the opposition press, which objected to the edict not having been brought before the Riksdag of the Estates (the Diet), whereupon discontent spread through the populace. Jewish businesses were particularly felt to pose a threat to the ability of Christian Swedes to earn a living.

Finally, emotions bubbled over.

Much of the anger was directed towards a person who was not of Jewish descent, but who was considered to be responsible for the Edict of Emancipation: State Secretary Carl David Skogman. It was Skogman who had brought the matter before the Council, i.e. the King and the Government. In his capacity as acting president of the National Board of Trade, he had also played a key role in the preparatory work of drafting the edict. The windows of Skogman's home on Skeppsbron were smashed, according to newspaper *Dagligt Allehanda*, to the accompaniment of 'loud and unrestrained expressions of dissatisfaction at the emancipation of the Jews'.

But it was the Jews as a group that were the focus of the mob's inflamed attention. One of the Jewish-owned properties that suffered the worst damage was, significantly enough, the home of Aron Levi Lamm, the head of Stockholm's Jewish congregation.

After a few days, the situation quietened down. Stockholm's Mosaic congregation donated 3,000 riksdaler towards maintaining order. Incitement continued in the press critical of the Government and a rumour began to spread that the King imported from France, born Jean Baptiste Bernadotte, was in fact Jewish.

One of the more aggressive organs was called *Freja*. On 4 September *Freja* warned of the consequences of 'Unleashing the Jews over the whole Kingdom':

> Experience has hitherto shown, we have heard people say, that the Jews, despite the restrictions with which the Regulation encircled them, have been *above the law*; and how much more powerful might not these strangers become in the country now that these restrictions have largely been removed.

Six days later, on 10 September, the violence flared up again. Lamm's house was attacked once more and the anger was also directed at Aron Isak's daughter-in-law, one of the most respected members of the Jewish congregation. When the newspapers stated the names of the people whose homes had been damaged, the nature of the protests stood plain and clear: Schück, Schneider, Glosemeyer, Scharp, Schön, Nachmanson.

Now the King and the members of the Government grew nervous. Had the edict of 30 June gone too far?

The city elders of Stockholm submitted a document to Karl Johan in which they expressed their concern that the edict would make it easier for Jews to immigrate to Sweden and that Swedish businessmen would then 'be completely squeezed out' by adherents of the Mosaic faith via 'trading connections with their compatriots in faith in foreign lands'. The King's response was conciliatory.

The most striking retreat from the June edict, however, concerned the right of Jews to settle outside Stockholm, Gothenburg, Norrköping and Karlskrona. On 21 September, a supplementary statute was adopted on the application of the June edict 'in certain cases'. Foreign adherents of the Mosaic faith with a residence permit were only to be allowed to settle in one of these four towns. Adherents of the Mosaic faith who were born in Sweden or who had become Swedish subjects had to apply for royal permission if they wished to settle elsewhere. An announcement on the edict was published in *Statstidningen* on 25 September.

In the still indispensable work *Judarnas historia i Sverige (The History of the Jews in Sweden)*, published for the first time in 1924 by Albert Bonniers Förlag, Uppsala University historian Hugo Valentin stated:

> So the Government, to pour oil on troubled waters, had sacrificed one of the most important provisions of the June edict, that on the right of Jews to settle freely anywhere in Sweden.

This restriction remained in force until 1854 and Jewish emancipation was not fully achieved until a Riksdag decision was passed in 1870. Step by step, Jewish rights were expanded, a slow but inexorable process that ran in parallel with Albert Bonnier's growing publishing business.

* * *

The outbreak of antisemitism in 1838 was a setback in the Jewish struggle for emancipation, but whether the disorder directly affected young Albert is unclear. The correspondence preserved from this period is limited and addresses other concerns. Nor does anything indicate that the bookshop on Storkyrkobrinken suffered damage; perhaps it was thought to be too insignificant. However, Albert, with his memories of the more tolerant environment of Copenhagen, must have found the fury frightening, a brutal omen of the difficulties he had to reckon with, now that he was seeking to build a future in this new country.

Of the antisemitic vitriol that would later be directed at him personally – peaking with the court case surrounding the publication of August Strindberg's *Getting Married*, the subsequent battle within the Swedish Publishers' Association, and the freedom of the press case against Gustaf Fröding – he was fortunately unaware.

Over time, it nevertheless became clear that Albert Bonnier had arrived in Sweden at precisely the right moment. The renowned critic and literature expert Karl Warburg, later Albert's good friend, was to describe the 1830s with an apt phrase:

The time of melting ice appeared to be past, a time of spring had arrived for Swedish liberalism.

* * *

When the teenaged Albert landed on Swedish soil in 1835 with eight shillings in his pocket, he was also stepping over the threshold of a new age in one of the poorest and most backward countries in Europe, a wounded former great power that, through ill-fated wars abroad and internal mismanagement, had lost both territory and status.

Despite this inauspicious starting position, it is strange how many threads from Albert's later successes can be traced back to these miserable years, and how they shaped his life and actions.

The world was a scene of violent upheaval. The Poles were rising against the Russians, the Italians against the Austrians, and in the British Empire slavery was abolished. In Sweden not that much was happening, at least not on the surface.

The major political issue of the day, representational reform to abolish the mediaeval Riksdag of the Estates with its nobles, priests, burghers and peasants, had ground to a halt despite the hopes raised after the overthrow of Gustav IV Adolf in 1809, the end of Gustavian autocracy and the implementation of the new Instrument of Government. Industrialisation, which had made its breakthrough in England, had not yet reached the mainly agrarian Sweden, which applied a restrictive and mercantilist trade policy. To the extent that Sweden was open to the outside world, this concerned infectious diseases rather than exchange of goods; a cholera epidemic in 1834 wiped out about 13,000 people. There was talk of 'feeble' times.

Two men in the opposition, Carl Henrik Anckarsvärd and Gabriel Richert, summarised the lethargy in a pamphlet on the issue of representation:

We feel the slowness, the costs, the wearing down and weakening of vigour; we are aware of no notable improvement in laws, in public management, in the internal state and welfare of the country: everything halts in ambiguous half measures, if not something worse; and after years of fighting one sinks back into the same apathy and the same numbness as before.

But under the surface, processes were being set in motion that would revolutionise life in Sweden and create completely unique conditions for a publisher in tune with the times.

The breakthrough of steam power was starting to make it easier to transport goods by sea. Sending heavy shipments of books between different destinations in Sweden was now considerably faster; previously it could take months for a parcel to reach Stockholm from Lund or Malmö by horse and cart. Steamers were only reliable in the warmer months of the year, however. Once the ice formed, one was still reliant on transport by horse. Even here, efficiency improvements were achieved with the introduction of a State-subsidised stage coach system, initially between Ystad and Stockholm, and between Gothenburg and Stockholm. However, the major revolution came with the railways, which started to undergo serious expansion in the 1860s, precisely at the time that the publishing company Albert Bonniers Förlag was in an expansive phase of its own; Albert bought his own printworks in 1856.

Hardly surprisingly, a heart-felt plea for Swedish railway construction was published as early as in the 1846 edition of *Svea*, the literary '*folkkalender*' or 'people's annual' which Albert Bonnier had started to publish a few years earlier, and which he was to edit until his death in 1900, a combined test bed and recruitment base for literary talents, from August Blanche and August Strindberg to Gustaf Fröding and Selma Lagerlöf.

Doubts have been voiced regarding the need for or the opportunity to lay railways in Sweden. The need for such routes seems, however, to be clear as day in a country as sparsely populated as ours, and where the distances are so great that the individual provinces might well need to be brought closer the one to the other.

The expansion of the railways increased travel in Sweden. One typical example of Albert's capacity to exploit the revolutions and innovations of the age for commercial purposes was that he then started to publish a new form of informative literature, what today would be called travel guides. In 1866, the readers of *Dagens Nyheter*, a newspaper he was involved in setting up, would have seen an advertisement, personally signed by Albert, addressed 'To Gentlemen Hoteliers, Restaurant owners, et cetera' urging them to provide information about prices, standards of rooms, and so on for his *Illustrerad Reshandbok genom Sverige (An Illustrated Travel Guide through Sweden)*, 'intended to be of service to domestic travellers and foreigners alike'.

Another significant change was the abolition of the power of withdrawal, the section in the 1812 Freedom of the Press Act which made it possible for the Court Chancellor, one of the Ministers of State, to prevent the publication of a periodical considered to be 'harmful to public safety'. The provision was applied over and over again, not least against the newspaper *Aftonbladet*, which circumvented it by numbering its editions. Ultimately, the power of withdrawal became ineffectual and almost ridiculous. It ceased to be applied in 1838, although it was not formally abolished until seven years later. The air became slightly easier to breathe.

It also became easier to start and run businesses. The Manufacturers and Tradesman's Ordinance of 1846 abolished compulsory guilds, Sweden's first limited liability company was formed in 1848, and freedom to establish and conduct a business was introduced in 1864. Interest rates were liberated, leading to the emergence of a modern and more flexible credit system, and Sweden joined the European free trade system. Many of these reforms were pushed through by the liberal Minister for Finance Johann August Gripenstedt, whose brochures were marketed approvingly by the Bonnier bookshop.

The same year in which the antisemitic protests occurred, 1838, also saw a public transformation that heralded a new era: Erik Gustaf Geijer's 'apostasy' from conservatism to liberalism. A historian, writer, philosopher, composer and member of the Swedish Academy, Geijer was one of the central figures in Swedish public life. In the January issue of his new periodical, *Litteratur-Bladet*, he made a kind of personal and political declaration of independence that echoed across the nation:

> In actual fact I have never belonged to any party, not even my own, if such a party had existed. But should someone find particular value in reproaching me with apostasy, so be it! I am an apostate to myself; which also involves no injury.'

What Geijer was signalling was a break from the suffocating dependence on norms and conventions of personality, while he, more clearly than most of his contemporaries, saw how a new social class, that in the long term would come to set the tone, was emerging with justified demands for freedom and development opportunities. And this class, the middle class, could read. Gathering around the lamp in the evening and listening to a book being read out loud became an increasingly common evening entertainment in the homes of the Swedish bourgeoisie.

Literacy was relatively widespread in Sweden thanks to the priests testing the members of their parish on Martin Luther's Small Catechism every year. Further improvements in literacy came with the Swedish Elementary School Act of 1842, although it took time for schools to be built everywhere. However, the most important aspect for Albert Bonnier's business was that the emergence of this reading middle class coincided with the breakthrough of a literary genre that was to define his publishing company more than any other: the novel.

The impetus came from outside, mainly from Britain and France, and from popular authors such as Walter Scott, Edward Bulwer-Lytton, Eugène Sue and, a little later, Alexandre Dumas and Charles Dickens. Their novels were translated and often published in pamphlets available at a reasonable price on subscription. In this area too, Lars Johan Hierta was a pioneer with his *Läsebibliothek af den nyaste utländska litteraturen* (Readers' Library of the Newest Foreign Literature) in 1833 and Albert Bonnier would soon jump on the bandwagon with his own *Europeiska följetongen* (European Series).

Things were also moving on the Swedish literary fiction scene. Carl Jonas Love Almqvist started publication of the suite *Törnrosens bok* (*The Book of the Thorn-Rose*) in 1832 and the very end of the decade saw his novel critical of marriage *Det går an*, (published in English in 1919 as *Sara Videbeck and the Chapel*) where the message of equality between the sexes caused an uproar.

In a patriarchally oppressive age, where women lacked the

most elementary rights, it was nevertheless a female author, Emilie Flygare-Carlén, who achieved the greatest success with her stories of the Bohuslän archipelago in western Sweden, including her breakthrough novel *Rosen på Tistelön* (*The Rose of Tistelön*) of 1842 and *Enslingen på Johannisskäret* (*The Hermit*) four years later.

With the decision in 1858 that unmarried women could be granted legal majority, one of the first tentative little steps was taken towards citizens' rights for the subordinate half of the country's population. The process was spurred on by another female writer, Fredrika Bremer. Her publisher was Adolf Bonnier, Albert's older brother and forerunner.

* * *

Albert Bonnier's arrival in Sweden thus happened to coincide with the winds of change sweeping across the poverty-stricken country on the northern periphery of Europe: technically, politically, socially, economically – and in terms of literature.

And then there was Stockholm, the city that was to become his new home.

In the highly dramatic year of 1838 a construction project was carried out that was to change the lives of the Bonnier brothers.

Norrbro, the bridge across Helgeandsholmen, from the island on which Gamla Stan, the old town, stood to Norrmalm, opened to traffic in 1807 after twenty years of construction; the foundation stone had been laid by Gustav III in 1787. It was an imposing structure, 190 metres long and 19 metres wide, and the first bridge in Stockholm to have pavements and be laid with flagstones. This pedestrian-friendly bridge became a popular place to walk and over time the idea came about to build what was termed a 'bazaar' on the bridge, the closest equivalent today being a shopping mall. And so the bazaar took shape.

Along the western side of the bridge a row of shops and restaurants was formed, known as *Norrbrobasaren*, or sometimes *Bazaren*. It opened in 1839 and was an instant success. It was a place where the more fashionable people of Stockholm could show off and those who made a habit of strutting about on the bridge were dubbed 'Norrbro lions'.

On both the south and the north side, the bazaar complex was supplemented by larger premises, described as pavilions. Adolf Bonnier, the eldest of the Bonnier brothers and the head of the family in Sweden, instantly realised that a move from the cramped shop on Storkyrkobrinken to the open and easily accessible Norrbro Bazaar would open up new sales opportunities for his books, as all the signs indicated that Norrmalm was set to become the city's new commercial centre. Adolf managed to secure a lease in the southern pavilion and in October 1839 'Bonniers bokhandel, Bazaren, Norrbro', opened, as sung of in August Strindberg's collection of poems *Sömngångarnätter på vakna dagar* (*Sleepwalking Nights in Broad Daylight*) from 1884.

Strindberg, who at the time was in more or less self-imposed exile, had walked past the window of a butchers in Paris and clearly been gripped by nostalgia, despite a not entirely uncomplicated relationship to the name of Bonnier:

Then my thoughts took flight
to the old Norrbro bazaar,
where the gleaming rows of windows
are viewed by women and children.

There in a bookshop's window
Hangs a little calfskin book.
It is a torn-out heart
dangling there on its hook.

And so the story of Albert Bonnier can begin, with a year that might have spelt disaster for him, his family and his fellow Jews, but which instead heralded success that he could not have imagined in his wildest dreams, when the cobbled streets of Gamla Stan were littered with crushed glass during the nights of turmoil in the late summer of 1838.

CHAPTER I

ARRIVAL

**From Dresden to Copenhagen.
A revolutionary family tree? Disaster in Denmark.
To Sweden! A book sector lying fallow.
By the 'Grace' of the King. Albert lands on Swedish shores
The first book.**

———

When Albert Bonnier stepped off the boat onto Riddarholmen quay in Stockholm in 1835, he was not the first in his family to have made his way to Sweden to seek his fortune. Two of his relatives, his older brother Adolf and his father Gerhard, were ahead of him. One had succeeded; the other had failed. Dating the start of the Bonnier family's activities in Sweden to Albert's arrival in 1835, or to the publication of his first book in 1837, may therefore seem slightly misleading. While Albert was to make a major success as a literary entrepreneur and innovator, he was not the pioneer. That credit goes to Adolf Bonnier.

Considering Albert's meagre finances and his youth – he would be fifteen in the October – there was no talk of arranging separate accommodation for him. He lodged in Adolf's home, which adjoined the bookshop on Storkyrkobrinken. Fourteen years older than Albert, Adolf was by this point relatively established in Stockholm and a year earlier had married Esther, née Philip. They had met in Karlskrona, where Esther and her family belonged to the small Jewish group permitted to settle in the naval town. A loving relationship seems to have immediately developed between Albert and Esther; she became something of a surrogate mother to her young brother-in-law.

* * *

Along with all the actual trunks and boxes shipped to Sweden from Copenhagen in this period, there came a lot of family baggage.

The Bonnier brothers' father, Gerhard Bonnier, was born in 1778 as Gutkind Hirschel in Dresden, the capital of the Electorate of Saxony, which had suffered severe damage in the Seven Years' War of 1756–63. Here, as in many places in Europe, there was a long tradition of antisemitic oppression which curbed the opportunities of the Jewish minority to earn a living. Gutkind Hirschel seems nevertheless to have grown up in a relatively well-off family, which was also a large one. His parents, jeweller Hirschel Löbel and his wife Feile Srasser, had ten children, eight of whom lived to adulthood.

Little is known of Gutkind Hirschel's youth; the total destruction of Dresden in an Allied bombing raid in February 1945 has made research difficult. Thanks to his grandson Karl Otto Bonnier's family history and – above all – the complex jigsaw puzzle of fragments that Svante Hansson put together in his biography *Den förste Bonnier* (*The First Bonnier*) it is nevertheless possible to establish the main features of the story.

Gutkind must have been offered what was for Jews an unusually thorough education in worldly topics, because he was later able to earn a living as a language teacher – isolated and oppressed, the Jews of Dresden mainly spoke only Yiddish. Besides German, Gutkind spoke French and some English. Where he gained this education is not entirely clear, but there is much to indicate that it was obtained in Prague in the Austrian province of Bohemia, where the Holy Roman Emperor Joseph II's Edict of Toleration in 1781 had given Jews expanded rights with the aim of making them 'useful to the state'.

It is probable that all the restrictions to which Jews were subjected at home in Dresden prompted Gutkind to head north, towards Copenhagen. After a stay in Hamburg where he earned his living as a language teacher, he arrived in the Danish capital, via Lübeck, in October 1801 with the aim of working as a teacher. Two and a half years later he was granted a Danish residence permit. Gutkind titled himself *sprogmester* (language master) and to judge from letters and other documents, he seems to have learnt at least the basics of the Danish language astonishingly quickly. By this point he had also married a Dane, Ester Elkan.

Denmark was already a relatively tolerant country in terms of Jewish rights, and in 1814 this approach was to culminate in what was termed the Letter of Freedom of the Jews, a law that gave Jews the opportunity to participate in society on relatively equal terms. The choice of Copenhagen as a place to settle therefore seems to make sense for a young, ambitious and well-educated Jew from Dresden who adopted the French-sounding name Gerhard Bonnier.

* * *

It is here, in Copenhagen, that the story of the Bonnier family of booksellers and publishers begins. For little came of Gerhard's plans as a teacher and *sprogmester* in the Danish capital. He was leaning more towards the world of books.

At the time of his marriage in 1803, Gerhard bought a lending library, which he moved to Kronprinsensgade where his home was situated. But the most important factor was that in 1805 he was granted the right to work as a bookseller, in other words a permit to sell books. Like the library, the bookshop had an international focus, with an emphasis on non-fiction and scientific literature, and a notably large proportion of Swedish authors, including the two botanists Elias Fries in Lund and Carl Peter Thunberg in Uppsala.

A year earlier Gerhard had started a publishing business, whose first work was a translation from German with the title *Underfulde og sandfærdige Kriminalhistorier* (*Wonderful and True Stories of Crime*), making it the first book to be published under the name of Bonnier. As with the library and the bookshop, the book publisher Gerhard Bonnier concentrated more on translations of foreign non-fiction titles than on Danish literature. He was keen to forge international contacts, where his language skills naturally smoothed the way, and made several trips abroad. These international ambitions were to be inherited by his sons Adolf and Albert. However, out of respect for his new homeland, Gerhard's catalogue also included a couple of works by the biggest names in Danish literature in the first half of the nineteenth century: Adam Oehlenschläger and N. F. S. Grundtvig.

But what was going on with the publisher's own name? In Denmark, Gutkind Hirschel had somehow become Gerhard Bonnier.

The change of name is one of the more bizarre elements in Bonnier family history, built on a pure fabrication that would not be out of place in the publishing house's most imaginative novels.

According to a Danish *Litteraturlexicon* from 1827, in an article written by Gerhard himself, he was not born in Dresden at all but in Besançon in eastern France. This article also stated that 'the famous French representative Bonnier (...) was his uncle'.

This reference was to nobleman Antoine Bonnier d'Alco, who, after the French Revolution in 1789, was a member of France's Legislative Assembly and the National Convention. He was among the majority who voted for Louis XVI to be sent to the guillotine. Bonnier d'Alco made a diplomatic career during the French Revolutionary Wars and was appointed French emissary to the Second Congress of Rastatt in Germany in 1799. He left the peace deliberations in protest at the treatment of France by its enemies and was attacked and murdered on his way home. The murder attracted a great deal of attention across Europe, a *cause célèbre* that made Bonnier d'Alco something of a revolutionary martyr.

However, the story of the 'uncle' was pure invention on Gerhard's part. No family relationship between him and Antoine Bonnier d'Alco can be proved whatsoever. But the tall tale lived on and must have been retold by his son Albert, because it reappeared in an obituary of him, written by his friend Frans Hedberg and published in *Svea* in 1901. In it, Albert's liberal and free-thinking inclinations were explained by the fact that he 'was the descendant of a French revolutionary and presumably born a radical'.

The name Bonnier had been introduced into the Hirschel

family by a circuitous route, as Karl Otto Bonnier later recounted in his family history. The background was that Gerhard's eldest sister Breindel had married a banker named Lazarus Lehmann, whose family had long had Francophile sympathies, which apparently grew after the revolution. An ancestor who had been a banker for the Elector of Saxony, Augustus the Strong in the early eighteenth century was called variously Bunner, Bonner – and Bonnier. When Breindel had twin boys in 1801, she immediately started to call one of them Bonnier, despite the fact that, like his mother's brother, his name was actually Gutkind. Karl Otto Bonnier seized on this:

> Perhaps it is too daring a hypothesis to assume that – after Breindel Hirschel-Lehmann introduced the name Bonnier to the family in March 1801, several of her siblings decided in consultation firstly – as Breindel had done – to Frenchify the name Gutkind to Bonnier, and secondly to go even further and – abandoning the name Hirschel – adopt the beautiful French-sounding name as their surname?

There is much to indicate that this may have been where Gerhard's first impulse to use the name Bonnier came from, but it is a long way from there to claiming a family relationship with a French revolutionary.

The explanation for Gerhard choosing to introduce himself as a descendant of the renowned Antoine Bonnier d'Alco is shrouded in mystery. Over the years, he also asserted from time to time that he was originally a French citizen, which he was not.

Although information about Gerhard's personality is scarce,

there are no traces of fraudulent tendencies or psychological disturbance. And his purpose was not to hide or to tone down his Jewish identity; that was something he was proud of throughout his life. Perhaps the tall story about Bonnier d'Alco was part of his marketing in a new country, a way to make his brand more exciting, particularly as Gerhard had initially intended to earn a living as a teacher of languages, including French. Or perhaps it merely reflected a more or less conscious desire to appear at least slightly remarkable. A retouching of the past was transformed into a self-experienced truth. And Gerhard Bonnier was – and is – hardly alone in that.

* * *

Initially, Gerhard's business went well and was supplemented in 1816 by a newspaper, *Dagsposten*, and a printworks. One clear sign of success was that in 1813 Gerhard bought a property on the corner of Købmagergade and Silkegade, having outgrown the premises on Kronprinsensgade.

Over time his family grew. First came a daughter Frederikke in 1804, followed by a son Adolf in 1806 and then daughters Henriette, known as Jette, in 1808, Julie in 1809 and Bolette in 1811. After a brief pause, which coincided with his expanding business, another six offspring came into the world; Hanne in 1813, twins Salvador, known as Sally, and Philippine in 1816, Albert on 22 October 1820 and finally David Felix in 1822. In between, in 1818, a son Emanuel was born who lived only to the age of eight months.

Originally the children were given Jewish names, which were then replaced with names that were more practical in a non-Jewish context. In the Jewish congregation of Copenhagen, little Albert was first registered as Elkan Bonnier, the Yiddish version of the Hebrew Elkanah, after his mother's paternal grandfather, whose name was Elkan Abraham.

Very little is known about the conditions in which the Bonnier children grew up or their education. Education was compulsory for both boys and girls in Denmark from 1814, with the restriction for Jewish children that the Mosaic congregations were not allowed to determine the teaching, which, in other words, had to be provided in the customary Danish manner.

After a period of school attendance, at least the two youngest sons, Albert and David Felix, were sent for private tutoring under the supervision of a teacher named Isaak Levin, who according to Karl Otto Bonnier 'equipped both the boys with a respectable store of knowledge in various subjects, mainly foreign languages'. At the start of the nineteenth century, special schools had been established for Jewish boys and girls but it is not known whether the older Bonnier children attended them. Certainly Gerhard, with his experience as a language teacher, would have contributed to the children's acquisition of languages where time and opportunity allowed. With his background and his knowledge, he could undoubtedly be categorised as a *maskil*, a term with Hebrew roots that refers to educated and reform-minded Jews. Giving the children a broad, worldly education was entirely in line with these values.

One moving detail from the Bonnier home in Copenhagen was that the oldest daughter Frederikke seems to have acted as a kind of third parent to her younger siblings, particularly since Gerhard and Ester had started to be weighed down by financial problems. Frederikke died in 1828, at the age of only twenty-three. Albert took her death hard and the loss left a deep scar. 'Many times in the autumn of his years my grandfather Albert Bonnier talked about his older sister who had been like a loving mother to him,' his grandson Åke Bonnier remembered many years later.

One can merely speculate, but perhaps here lies part of the explanation as to why Albert so quickly took to Adolf's wife Esther when he arrived in Stockholm and why, in that patriarchal age, he does not seem to have had any problems with encountering strong, self-confident women. This applied in his social life as well as in his interactions with prominent female authors and is also reflected in his relaxed relationship with his highly gifted but headstrong daughter Eva, who sought to forge her own path to become a talented artist.

* * *

When Albert Bonnier was just one year old, his father's Danish success story came to an end. It was the start of a long drawn-out failure that was partly due to Gerhard himself. He had over-reached himself and spread himself too thin. Events outside his control also had a part to play. For several years, Denmark had found itself in what could almost be compared to an economic depression, ultimately caused by the country's unfortunate alliance with France in the Napoleonic Wars. In 1807, the British Navy had bombarded and destroyed parts of Copenhagen, and the Continental System, Napoleon's attempt to starve out the British by means of blockades, had severe consequences for the previously open trading nation of Denmark, which in 1813 was forced to declare state bankruptcy.

Supplies of goods, including books, had to pass through French-controlled territory, affecting Gerhard, who had developed business connections in England and with German towns such as Leipzig, where he had been able to obtain literature of interest at the Leipzig Book Fair. The French censors also confiscated writing considered to be politically dangerous. The Danish book market shrank, competition became tougher and the value of money depreciated at the same time as Gerhard acquired more and more children to support.

Gerhard was unwilling to accept the severity of the situation. 'New branches of business were added and the first years following the state bankruptcy were in fact the height of his career, although it became evident that the Colossus stood on feet of clay,' said Svante Hansson in *Den förste Bonnier*. Finally, the bubble burst. '*Le temps est terrible*', times are terrible, sighed Gerhard in a letter to one of his contacts in Sweden; he often corresponded in French.

In December 1821, Gerhard Bonnier had to sell the printworks and his property, and cut back on the bookshop business. Soon he started to look towards the neighbouring country on the other side of the Sound. Might the future lie there?

* * *

Compared with England, the large countries on the continent and even Denmark, the Swedish book market was lagging behind. For a long time, the books that were widely disseminated in large editions had tended to be religious in nature, and, for understandable reasons, scientific literature such as the work of Linnaeus only reached a limited readership. In practice, making a living as a poet was impossible. In the seventeenth century, Georg Stiernhielm, 'the father of Swedish poetry', was entirely dependent on royal patronage and on his income as a civil servant. Carl Michael Bellman's fate a hundred years later is well known; he died penniless.

Neither bookshops nor a publishing industry existed in any real sense. In the mid-eighteenth century, in Sweden's Age of Liberty, book printers had gained greater opportunities to sell books. Previously, for example, the bookbinders' guild had had a monopoly on selling bound printed products. However, this change was of only limited significance as there was not yet a broad reading public.

One important change occurred with the 1810 Freedom of the Press Act, a result of the coup a year earlier in which King Gustav IV Adolf was deposed. The act abolished censorship and laid down the right of authors to their works, stating: 'Each piece of writing shall be the property of the author or the legal holder of its rights.'

However, progress was slow.

There were a dozen bookshops in Stockholm in the mid-1820s, but outside the capital such shops were a virtually unknown phenomenon. Books were sold in rural areas, but via representatives, *kommissionär*, usually priests or teachers who, to use a more modern expression, sold books as a side hustle. A contemporary observer sighed at the state of affairs:

> One must, if one is to obtain a book, be fortunate enough to catch the bookseller at home; sometimes one finds oneself seeking him out more than once in vain.

The leading book company in about 1820 was N. M. Lindh in Örebro, whose business included printing and publishing what were termed 'robber novels'. Popular in early nineteenth-century Sweden, this genre – tales of outlaws and bandits – was imported from Germany following the example of Schiller's play *Die Räuber* (*The Robbers*), and could be described as an early predecessor of pulp fiction. When a new owner dropped the novel publication side of the business, the publisher lost its special position.

This was the situation in Sweden when Adolf Bonnier, who had become Gerhard's right-hand man, made several business trips to the neighbouring country in the mid-1820s, visits that also had an element of reconnaissance about them. What would it take for a move to Sweden to be capable of compensating for the losses in Denmark? After a period of consideration and influenced by weighty financial problems at home, father and son concluded that Sweden did in fact offer opportunities for a bookseller with sufficient skills to exploit them.

In summer 1827, Adolf, then twenty-one, went to Gothenburg. His luggage included several large boxes of books in different languages which might be of interest to a Swedish audience. The initial plan seems to have been for Adolf to attract new customers to order from the bookshop in Copenhagen and to act as a travelling representative, but soon he started to consider a more permanent presence in Gothenburg.

The fact that Gerhard and Adolf's choice fell on Gothenburg rather than Stockholm – both cities were open to Jews after all – was not only due to Gothenburg being closer to Copenhagen in purely geographical terms. Gothenburg, Sweden's second city, had no proper bookshop. The city was virgin territory, in other words. But Adolf and Gerhard were not alone in recognising this gap in the market.

A Danish competitor, Christian Wilhelm Kyhl Gleerup, had started a bookshop in the Swedish university town of Lund a year earlier. Now he was expanding his business to Gothenburg. This meant Adolf had to hurry to get his business established in Gothenburg before Gleerup managed to capture the local market.

In late August, Adolf advertised 'a good and complete Lending Library here in Gothenburg, in which neighbouring Towns may also participate'. The library was to offer 'the best of the older books, German, French, English, Danish and Swedish literature'.

It was the start of a new era for the Bonnier family.

* * *

Adolf Bonnier's business in Gothenburg got off to a flying start. Initially he concentrated on developing the lending library, but, as time went on, proper bookselling also took off. In 1828 he earned just over 2,000 riksdaler and was able to send remittances back to Gerhard, who was keenly in need of money. When Adolf went home to Copenhagen in May that year due to the death of his sister Frederikke, he took with him a bill of exchange for a hundred Danish rigsdaler for Gerhard and a salmon for his mother Ester. In Gothenburg he lived in lodgings but according to notes he left, he treated himself to the odd extravagance, including a new coat which he was able to show off at 'Mamsell Åberg's balls'.

It was at this time, after returning from Copenhagen, that

Adolf decided to settle in Sweden. However it was Stockholm, not Gothenburg, that appealed to him most. In spring 1829 he travelled to Stockholm via Örebro and Arboga, equipped with a box of books and a domestic passport; free movement within the Kingdom of Sweden had not yet been introduced. Adolf also decided to apply for Swedish citizenship.

With the help of advertisements in the Stockholm press, he got a bookselling business off the ground, but citizenship was a tougher prospect; the restrictions of *Judereglementet* were a major obstacle. In July, his application was rejected by a decision signed by King Karl XIV Johan, which did, however, grant him permission 'by Our Grace (...) to reside here in the Kingdom until further notice'. The slightly patronising tone must have angered him; it is clear from various evidence that Adolf was more conscious of his Jewish identity – and integrity – than his younger brothers Albert and David Felix.

In his book about the family, *Bonniers – en släktkrönika 1778–1941* (*Bonniers – a Family Chronicle 1778–1941*), Åke Bonnier, as Albert's son Karl Otto had done previously, drew the presumably correct conclusion that Adolf felt insulted and that this explains why it took twenty more years before he reapplied for citizenship. By that point, Sweden had gained a more liberally minded king in Oscar I, who succeeded Karl Johan in 1844. His second application was granted.

Adolf did not stay long in Gothenburg after his visit to Stockholm. He travelled back to Copenhagen to assist Gerhard, who was now in tougher financial straits than ever before. It is likely that Adolf received a grateful welcome because this time too he brought with him money for Gerhard and fish for Ester.

In Copenhagen, the entire business was on the verge of

collapse and Gerhard was forced to write to his creditors and beg to defer his loan repayments. The situation was not eased by the fact that eight children, including Albert, were still living at home. Together, Adolf and Gerhard finally reached the conclusion that both the bookshop and the publishing company had to be sold. But they could not find a buyer. Instead they made the bold decision that Gerhard should move to Stockholm, open a bookshop there and then bring the whole family over. Gerhard arrived in Gothenburg in November 1830 and then continued on to the Swedish capital.

At the same time, Adolf took an initiative that established him even more firmly in Gothenburg. Once more it was a reaction to the spectre of the ambitious C. W. K. Gleerup. One telling detail, by the way, is that Gleerup, originally from Aalborg in Denmark, had had no problem becoming a Swedish citizen; he did so in 1828.

The thirty-year-old Gleerup, who had now become bookseller to the university in Lund, moved his Gothenburg subsidiary to new and better premises. Adolf realised he needed to keep pace with his competitor. In the autumn of 1830 he opened a bookshop on the corner of Kungsgatan and Östra Hamngatan, two bustling streets in the heart of the city.

In all events things continued to go well for Adolf in Gothenburg.

For Gerhard in Stockholm it was a different story.

* * *

Having installed himself in Stockholm and made contact with his own and Adolf's business connections, in April 1831 Gerhard Bonnier submitted an application to the King, written in French, to open a bookshop and for a residence permit. He emphasised his international connections and his experiences of publishing Swedish scientific literature. A certificate from the Head of the Institute of Technology, today Stockholm's Royal Institute of Technology, and from the Director of the National Library of Sweden were appended to his application. Both had bought books from Gerhard and vouched for his character. The former, Gustaf Magnus Schwartz, considered it desirable to have someone capable of 'providing us with a true foreign bookshop'. The latter, Per Adam Wallmark, emphasised Gerhard Bonnier's 'speed, accuracy and cheap prices for the Book Commissions he has undertaken'. The Governor of Stockholm, based on Gerhard being 'born a French citizen', recommended that the application be approved. Nevertheless on 14 May, the answer was a simple no, without further explanation. The King 'found no reason to grant His benevolent approval to this humble Application'.

In his family history, Karl Otto Bonnier speculated that the reason for this practically brusque rejection of a carefully prepared application was that it might have been due to Gerhard's claim to be related to Antoine Bonnier d'Alco. Over the years, and since accepting the Swedish throne, the former revolutionary general Bernadotte had grown more reactionary and may, according to Karl Otto Bonnier, have reacted to the name with instinctive negativity:

The King thinks: So who is this Frenchman who now wishes to settle in the country as a bookseller? Naturally a descendant of the old 'king murderer'. And highly likely to be a Jacobin himself! No thank you!

We don't want any *sans culottes* here! Hence rejection 'sans phrases'.

This exciting explanation naturally has an irresistible appeal, but is still pure, unsubstantiated speculation. Only a couple of years earlier Karl Johan had granted permission to Adolf, with the same surname as Gerhard, to stay in Sweden. Why would the King have allowed this if he felt such an aversion to the name of Bonnier? A much more likely explanation is that Gerhard was simply a victim of the extremely strict restrictions of *Judereglementet*. In 1815–38, no more than twenty-five adherents of the Mosaic faith were granted permits to settle in Sweden.

Despite this miscalculation, Gerhard stayed on in Stockholm, where he rented premises on Västerlånggatan in Gamla Stan and opened a lending library and a bookshop in Adolf's name. He did not return to Copenhagen until early spring 1832, where an impatient Ester was waiting for him.

Ester was acutely aware of the situation at home and seems to have taken an active part in running the bookshop and publishing company while Gerhard was in Sweden, but she was highly doubtful about relocating to a new country. In a moving letter written to Gerhard in Stockholm in 1831 – written in the Hebrew alphabet in Yiddish and transcribed by Svante Hansson – Ester said that she was having difficulties paying in shops but still thought it would be better to remain in Copenhagen, even though everything was expensive there. Because it is hard to get started in a new place and there is not much to be gained by it:

[B]esser veren es ja ven du hir bleybe kantest, gevist kost alles fil hir, aber van man alles oyf eyne neye shtel

zol anfangen zo ist es zer shver und er alles im gang
komt, zo izt vol oykh nikht fil tzu ferdinen.

After his failure in Sweden, Gerhard Bonnier slipped into the
margins of family history. Ester died in 1838 but Gerhard led
a long life, although beset by financial pressures in his last
decades. He was only able to survive with the help of the
money his sons sent from Sweden. Despite scarce resources,
he travelled often and at the age of seventy-eight visited his
childhood town of Dresden, where, according to a letter to
Adolf, he enjoyed 'unforgettably happy Days'.

Gerhard Bonnier's efforts in the Danish and Swedish book
market should not be underestimated. Perhaps he built a house
of cards that collapsed, but for a few years in the 1810s, he
was a leading actor, almost alone in Scandinavia in having an
international outlook and foreign contacts. In this sense he was
undoubtedly an inspiration to Albert, who would become the
most successful of his sons, and who introduced major foreign
authors such as Dickens, Zola and Tolstoy to a broader Swedish
audience. But to this second youngest son, it seems that Gerhard
mainly served as a warning. This can be deduced from Albert's
determined but at the same time cautious construction of his
publishing and other businesses: invest only when you have
sufficient capital of your own, avoid taking out large loans and
take no risks purely for the sake of risk-taking.

Gerhard Bonnier died in 1862. His eldest son Adolf informed
his brother Albert that their father would now 'be able to
enjoy the long deserved rest that his inexhaustible industry
and restless enthusiasm have not indulged him with in life'.

* * *

With Gerhard back in Copenhagen, Adolf concentrated on building up the business in Stockholm, where he arrived in spring 1832, leaving the day-to-day operation of the shop in Gothenburg to an employee named Lauritz Kamp. However, on inspecting the dark, cramped premises on Västerlånggatan, Adolf was disappointed and soon signed a lease on a shop on the ground floor of Storkyrkobrinken 12. This better location boosted trade and from this base Adolf forged links with publishers such as Lars Johan Hierta, P. A. Norstedt & Söner and N. M. Lindh in Örebro, as well as with popular authors who were publishing their own work, including Erik Gustaf Geijer in Uppsala.

Adolf was working at fever pitch. He supplied books to institutions such as the Royal Swedish Academy of Sciences and the National Library of Sweden and even to the Court, where his customers included Queen Desideria and Princess Joséphine. The first of many business trips abroad was made to the Book Fair in Leipzig, true to his father's habit.

In the early 1830s he started a publishing business, whose first published work was a translation of a curious German children's book entitled *Wie Heinrich von Eichenfels zur Erkenntnis Gottes kam*, in Swedish *Barndoms-hjertat, eller huru Henrik af Eichenfels lärde känna Gud* (published in English in 1847 as *Henry of Eichenfels or How a child learned to know that there is a God*). This was thus the first printed item in Swedish to have Bonnier as the publisher.

Adolf's foremost move as a publisher, however, was the series *Klassiska Författare i Svenska Vitterheten* (*Classical Authors in Swedish Literature*) published in more than fifty volumes up to 1842. The authors included Georg Stiernhielm and Lasse Lucidor. The most significant action for the future was that Adolf, through the heirs of Anna Maria Lenngren, obtained the rights to her posthumously published collection *Skalde-försök* (*Attempts at Poetry*), which despite its modest title is an epoch-making work in Swedish literature with its perspective on female education, for example in the satirically ironic poem 'Some words to my dear daughter, if I had one' from 1798:

Our sex has little need, my dear,
of wasting time with books.
And should you read, be brief for fear
the sauce pot over-cooks!

Skalde-försök has since been printed in countless editions.

In January 1835, Adolf also started to publish a political and literary weekly magazine, *Panorama*. It was short-lived, but, like Gerhard's earlier *Dagsposten* in Copenhagen, was a sign that the publishing family of Bonnier was not only interested in books but also in periodicals.

The greater the success Adolf had in Sweden, the more he considered the possibility of easing the burden on his parents in Copenhagen by bringing his younger brothers to Stockholm where they could help in the bookshop. He had already brought the then thirteen-year-old Salvador to Gothenburg in 1830. Salvador, known as Sally, came to Stockholm in September 1833 but the experiment did not end well. After just over a year, Sally was sent back to Denmark and packed off to study agriculture.

Very little is known of Sally Bonnier, but he was evidently conscientious and helpful. When Adolf applied for Sally to be registered in Gothenburg in 1831, the County Governor attested that 'during his stay in the city the young Bonnier consistently distinguished himself as being obedient, respectable and hardworking'. But Sally was, in the words of Karl Otto Bonnier, 'very poorly equipped in the head'; today he would probably have described him as having a learning disability. It was the start of a tragedy that was to end in misery in a mental hospital in the United States.

* * *

After the failure with Sally, it was natural to have the next son in the family, Albert, come to Sweden.

On 15 August 1835, Albert collected a passport from Copenhagen police court that guaranteed him free passage and certified that he was not carrying any infectious diseases. Adolf had travelled down to Copenhagen to accompany his brother to Stockholm. They departed in early September and arrived in Stockholm, via Gothenburg, probably on 11 September, because Adolf noted in his cashbook that this was when Albert's luggage was collected.

What did the city that was now to be Albert's new home look like?

Presumably, he gained quite a mixed impression after growing up in Copenhagen, a somewhat larger metropolis in terms of population, which had started to lift itself out of the devastation caused by the British bombardment and the state bankruptcy of 1813.

Stockholm must have seemed relatively undeveloped and peripheral compared with the more continental Copenhagen, which was in fact on the verge of what has subsequently been called a golden age, a culturally vigorous period linked with names such as storyteller Hans Christian Andersen, philosopher Søren Kierkegaard and painter Christen Købke.

A few years earlier another foreign observer had depicted the Stockholm milieu. This was the British hunting enthusiast Llewellyn Lloyd, who had made his home in Sweden, first in Värmland and later in the area around Vänersborg, where he wrote books about Sweden's customs and fauna which became popular in his homeland and in his new country. In *The Field Sports of the North of Europe* from 1830 he drew a picture of Stockholm. Lloyd found that the city was 'singularly and romantically situated' with many 'handsome public edifices', among them the Palace and Riddarholm Church. But 'the streets are in general narrow, and the pavement is not the best possible: there are no flag-stones for foot-passengers.' His main objection was of a sanitary nature:

> One would be inclined to imagine Stockholm must be a healthy place: But I have more than my doubts as to this being the case. Indeed, I am inclined to think fevers and other disorders are usually more prevalent in that capital than in many parts of Sweden. Possibly, this may be partly owing to the water, as this, in some parts of the town is very bad.

Albert was immediately put to work on simple tasks in the bookshop on Storkyrkobrinken, where Adolf concentrated on teaching his younger brother everything about the bookselling profession step by step. It went extremely well – so well that a couple of years later Adolf decided to also welcome David Felix to Stockholm.

Albert had greater ambitions than unpacking, sorting and

selling books. Undoubtedly inspired by both Gerhard and Adolf's examples, he too wanted to launch himself into a publishing career.

In autumn 1837 Albert took his first tentative steps as a publisher with *Bevis att Napoleon aldrig har existerat*, printed in the compact format that Adolf used for his series of Swedish classics. Albert financed the project with money he had saved from two years of working in the bookshop on Storkyrkobrinken, an elementary principle that was to guide him throughout his life and that was presumably founded in lessons learned from Gerhard's bankruptcy.

The small volume was a French satire on an originally German work, *Das Leben Jesu* (*The Life of Jesus, Critically Examined*), by theologian David Friedrich Strauss, which had caused a great deal of uproar. Strauss claimed that the story of the life of Jesus was built on myth, not on fact.

With his very first publication, Albert thus showed that he was not reluctant to challenge the conventions of the day. This became even clearer the following year, the tumultuous 1838, when he published his next work, *Pepparkorn för hvar och en i allmänhet och vederbörande i synnerhet* (*Peppercorn for each and every one in general and to whom it concerns in particular*) by Gotthilf August von Maltitz, a German 'rabulist' who had achieved considerable popularity with his satirical aphorisms, originally published as *Pfefferkörner*. The term 'rabulism' referred to different strains of opinion that advocated change by means of social upheaval.

Maltitz also wrote a comedy, *Das Pasquill*, translated into Swedish as *Pasquillet*, which became a major success at Djurgårdsteatern in Stockholm the same year. One of the speeches, made by a police spy, has become a classic: 'Don't argue, just arrest.'

His son Karl Otto's verdict was no rose-tinted description with the benefit of hindsight but a statement of fact:

> In these uncertain years of revolution the eighteen year-old bookshop assistant stood – as he would later throughout his life – fully and wholly on the side of the liberal opposition.

There is something both stubborn and precocious about young Albert Bonnier's entrance onto the Swedish publishing stage: a newly arrived Jew from Copenhagen who almost immediately made common cause with the critics of Karl XIV Johan's authoritarian rule. The radical tendencies would be tempered over the years but from the very start, Albert was marking where he stood. Out of this slightly headstrong self-confidence there emerged a trait that was to make his actions distinctive, but sometimes also provocative to representatives of the established order. This was summed up by Frans Hedberg in *Svea* more than sixty years later when Albert's life had drawn to a close:

> Free-thinking as he himself was, he was never afraid of allowing his printing presses to spread free-thinking opinions and audacious views, and while the prosecutions over freedom of the press that he suffered for the work of Strindberg and Fröding brought him much unpleasantness, they could not dislodge his opinion that the publisher is a *disseminator* and not a *judge*.

CHAPTER 2

YOUNG MAN ON THE MOVE

Three brothers in Stockholm. No heavenly peace.
A gathering place on Norrbro bridge. A cruel fate.
Albert's European adventure.
A disappointment. Homewards with new ideas.
A fashion journal. *Stockholms Figaro*.

———

The same autumn that Albert arrived in Stockholm, 1835, Adolf upgraded his accommodation. Initially, he and Esther had lived in quite cramped conditions next to the bookshop, but now Adolf signed a lease on a spacious five-room flat three floors up in the property, with an adjoining box-room in the attic. The household grew, first with the addition of Albert and then of David Felix. Perhaps Adolf also harboured hopes that he and Esther would start a family, but, according to Karl Otto Bonnier, he had been convinced at an early stage that their marriage would be childless, which presumably made him feel even greater motivation to look after his younger brothers. He also rented out a room to a friend, the poet Karl August Nicander, who died in 1839.

The fact that Adolf had, one might say, gone up in the

world, is shown by the fact that he could afford servants, to whit, a maid and a shop boy.

It was in this by all accounts well-organised environment that Albert started to realise his publishing dreams with the satire on Napoleon in 1837. In 1838 he had only one piece published, Maltitz's *Pepparkorn*, but the bookshop's move to the newly built Norrbro Bazaar the following year seems to have spurred him on. The shop opened its doors on 1 October 1839. At about this time Albert published an ABC, song pamphlets, a comedy by the Austrian dramatist Eduard von Bauernfeld, and, just in time for Christmas, a title that hinted at social aspirations on the part of its nineteen-year-old publisher: *Den bildade verldsmannen (l'homme comme il faut) eller anvisning att göra sig omtyckt i sällskaper och af det täcka könet. (The Educated Man of the World (l'homme comme il faut) or Guidance in making oneself Popular in Company and with the Fairer Sex).*

During these years, their sister Hanne came to visit from Copenhagen; after Frederikke's death she seems to have become the brothers' favourite. Adolf considered allowing Hanne to move to Stockholm, but Esther begged him not to disrupt their 'heavenly peace': '[W]e both know that it is so difficult for you to deny anyone anything – but *do not* do it'. Adolf shelved his plans.

Heavenly peace was not always easy to come by in the Bonnier household, however. When David Felix came to Stockholm in summer 1837, he and Esther instantly rubbed each other up the wrong way. The contrast with Albert and Esther's warm relationship could not have been greater.

David Felix was a happy-go-lucky chap, although something of a scamp. He was clearly highly intelligent, according to Karl Otto Bonnier the most intelligent of the brothers, but could also be condescendingly arrogant. He disliked the fact that Esther imposed rules and he also thought, to add insult to injury, that she was painfully ugly. A preserved letter that David Felix sent to his sisters in Copenhagen in 1838, says pretty much everything about his bottomless contempt for Adolf's wife, but perhaps also something about the sixteen-year-old scapegrace's talent for precisely worded sarcasm and spitefulness. After calling Esther 'Corpus delicti', i.e. physical evidence of a crime, he worked himself up into a veritable cascade of insults:

> Imagine a small, thin Woman, no taller than Hanne, a wrinkled *dreadful* Figure, a small, round, fat, red face that sits deep down between her shoulders, a round little reddish Nose, *thick bushy eyebrows*, reasonably decent grey eyes, ugly brown Hair and *completely Bald* on one side of the head.

He concluded his harangue by stating that Esther could have served as a 'Drum major for the lifeguards' and that Hanne 'was scratched by her Beard' when she kissed her.

The situation escalated to mutual hatred and the whole debacle ended in 1842 with David Felix being sent to Gothenburg, where he took over the running of Adolf's bookshop and then started both a publishing business and a new newspaper, *Göteborgs-Posten*.

The conflicts between Esther and David Felix must have placed Albert in an awkward position between the two, but failed to curb his publishing ambitions, however.

The number of political titles he published at this early stage is remarkable. *Väckelse på nya året* (*New Year Awakening*) took the form of an open letter to Magnus Jacob Crusenstolpe and *Tablå öfver Dagens frågor vid 1840 års riksdag* (*Tableau of Issues of the Day at the Riksdag of the Year 1840*) reflected the hopes for reform associated with this Riksdag. There, the twenty-six-year-old debutant at Riddarhuset, Johan August Gripenstedt, held a meritocratic oration that might have been made for an upwardly mobile young man like Albert Bonnier:

> History seems to demonstrate the truth of the statement that the fate of humanity proceeds following a certain law, and that this law is that of progress (...) Through a thousand years of conflict this principle has striven to 'level the heights and fill the depths' among classes in society, and has from a few, solely ruling nobility seized the prerogative of power and reputation, to demonstrate and declare the right of ability hereto over that of birth.

Gripenstedt was to advance to the post of Minister for Finance and in that role drive through a number of epoch-making liberal and modernising reforms, keenly supported by Albert Bonnier.

* * *

Following its move to the southern pavilion of Norrbro Bazaar, Bonnier's bookshop soon became a meeting point where various prominent persons liked to stop off, perhaps on their way to or from the establishment in the northern pavilion, the *Pavillon du Bazar*, which was what was termed a *schweizeri*, run by the German-born pâtissier Frederick W. F. De la Croix, Stockholm's restaurant king.

Schweizeri was the contemporary term for fine restaurants with rights to serve alcohol, a type of establishment brought to Sweden by Swiss bakers. The *Pavillon du Bazar* was to become a watering hole for the Bonnier brothers. Here they forged contacts and gathered over food, drink and cigars with friends like Stockholm's boisterous poseur August Blanche, over the years one of the more popular Bonnier authors, with works such as *Sonen af Söder och Nord* (*The Son of South and North*), a thriller with a revolutionary theme.

A glimpse into the work of the bookshop on Norrbro was later provided by the renowned actor and director Ludvig Josephson, who worked as an assistant to Adolf Bonnier in his younger years. Josephson, who was also a member of a Jewish family, was later to become artistic director of Stockholm's Royal Dramatic Theatre, and in 1879–87, of the New Theatre in Stockholm, where he put on brilliant performances of plays by writers including August Strindberg.

He remembered his years on Norrbro:

> Mainly I remember his old Excellency Count Trolle Bonde, the master of Säfstaholm, where he owned one of the largest public libraries in the Kingdom (...) The blind old Count could not make out the bindings of the impressive works he bought, but he enjoyed the heft of the volume and when one described the finesses of the binding (...) In those days one saw from time to time von Hartmansdorff and other great political men, the highest military personalities, courtiers and Riksdag celebrities, etc. (...) Crown Prince Carl himself stepped over the bookshop's threshold more than once (...) Among prominent and popular authors

and figures of literature, one saw quite frequently C. J. L. Almqvist, August Blanche, Mrs Carlén with her husband (he usually came alone), Fredrika Bremer, C. A. Adlersparre, Nils Arfvidsson. L. J. Hierta (...) It was not unusual for many of these experts on and champions of different social issues to be listened to with great interest by other customers. And there were many of these conversations, which sowed educational seeds among office boys and apprentices in this, Stockholm's foremost bookshop.

The manager, Adolf Bonnier, was described by Josephson as 'a good-natured and popular man' who, however, does not seem to have demonstrated any great talent for administration; Adolf was constantly looking for papers that he had lost. But his journalistic activity continued at a frantic pace.

At Christmas 1840 Adolf started to publish a Sunday magazine that, appropriately enough, he entitled *Bazaren*. It was short-lived but was the start of a connection with a liberal journalist, aged twenty-nine at the time, his mind as sharp as his pen, who was to become one of the Bonnier brothers' closest and most loyal friends. The editor appointed was Oscar Patric Sturzen-Becker, who wrote under the pen name Orvar Odd. Well-known from the columns of *Aftonbladet*, he was later to become a poet in the footsteps of Heinrich Heine, a devoted Scandinavianist and the founder of the *Öresunds-Posten* newspaper in Helsingborg.

Bazaren broke a minor floodgate. Up until then, no Swedish newspapers had been published on a Sunday. With hindsight, Adolf's manifesto in the first edition can be seen as a harbinger of the weekly or popular press of a future age.

With this newspaper, which in no case steps out as any rival to the other journals of the capital, all of which are more or less political sheets, the intention is, to the best of our ability, to fill the gap that is found in our newspaper literature regarding a paper solely for the salons and so also for Sunday, a paper of playful and easily digested content, to read over the teacups, during conversation, when one has a headache and finds parliamentary negotiations too weighty, and advertisements too lacking in creativity but would like a little reading to divert oneself with.

* * *

After just over five years of hard work as an assistant to Adolf, where he helped to establish the bookshop on Norrbro and learned the rudiments of the business, an impatient Albert started to long for new challenges abroad. It was only there that he could develop further as a bookseller and a publisher. Germany was particularly attractive. The fact that the initiative behind this idea was his own is shown by a letter of recommendation in German which Adolf signed on 28 April 1841. Adolf vouched for Albert's hard work and loyalty and emphasised that his younger brother now needed to gain experience from larger booksellers, adding:

With pain I can do nothing other than accept my brother's fervent desire and give him the best re-commendations to my gentleman colleagues.

A few days later, Albert left Stockholm with Berlin as his first stop.

Albert's departure was at the same time the prelude to a cruelly tragic episode in the Bonnier family's history, perhaps the most tragic of all. To replace Albert in the bookshop, Adolf brought their brother Salvador, Sally, to Stockholm for a second try. This too ended badly. In a letter to Albert, dated in July, David Felix wrote:

> Sally has come here. What shall I say of him? He is as he always is, quite the same as before; there can therefore be little to say about him. I now want to take him and slice his head in half to see what is inside it and then sew it back together again. But what is there inside? Nothing; it is empty, quite empty, not a thought, not one, and no facility to get a thought into it either.

After failed attempts to send Sally to learn bookbinding, first in Stockholm and then in Denmark, the brothers agreed that he should travel to America. Sally arrived in New Orleans in 1847 on the ship *Virginia* from Gothenburg. Contact between the brothers ceased. David Felix wrote to the captain of the *Virginia* for information about Sally and received a sad message in August 1848. Adolf took it upon himself to inform Albert, who happened to be visiting Gerhard in Copenhagen.

> In a gentle way you should tell father and the family that Sally ended his days in America (according to information that has reached us) in a Madhouse – may God have mercy on his soul.

* * *

For Albert Bonnier, the future looked brighter. He was twenty years old when he left Sweden for what can almost be described as a grand tour, clearly with the object not only of improving himself but of enjoying life. In later years, he grew slightly tubby and compensated for incipient thinning hair with a well-cut beard, but the young Albert was what one might call a stylish young man, richly gifted with social talents.

In Berlin he met, through an acquaintance, a young, beautiful singer and seemed to capture her interest. According to this acquaintance, she had explained that 'if there were nothing but boys like that in Stockholm, she would certainly like to undertake an artistic trip there'.

From Berlin, Albert then continued to Leipzig and to a placement with one of Adolf's business contacts or representatives, Karl Franz Koehler. After a couple of months in Leipzig, where he made many friends on happy evenings in restaurants, he travelled on to Vienna, where he was offered a place in Peter Rohrmann's large bookshop on Wallnerstrasse. On the way he fell into the company of both a celebrated Danish cello virtuoso, Christian Kellermann, who he immediately became good friends with, and naturally a lady, only referred to as 'Fräulein W'.

The post working unpaid for Rohrmann proved to be a miscalculation. In a letter to one of his Leipzig friends, Albert complained that he was only allowed to perform simple, monotonous tasks such as 'copying inventories and entering German invoices'. He had hardly anything to do with books. He soon wanted to leave and expressed his dissatisfaction in a draft letter that was presumably never sent, but which illustrates a self-confidence that today would probably be termed cockiness. Albert explained that the managers at Rohrmann made him feel like a 'forward street urchin' and continued:

> But do you not see, gentlemen, it is absolutely nothing to me, I console myself that I am the man I am and will remain so, whether you praise me to the skies or throw no matter how much dirt at me – and allow me also to have my own opinions about you.

The correspondence between Albert, his family and friends was frequent in the 1840s, but many letters from Albert are missing in the Bonnier family archive, which otherwise contains plenty of material from that time. The letters may simply have been lost or been weeded out for reasons that remain unclear. However, with the help of the preserved letters sent to Albert, it is nevertheless possible to gain an idea of his experiences in these formative years.

In autumn 1841 he evidently wrote a letter to Adolf and his sister-in-law Esther in which he complained about his situation at Rohrmann's. This is clear from Esther's consoling answer:

> We send you our most tender greetings, we have read your letter with sympathy, but, truly, I have not been sad, as you needed these experiences; with God's help you will become a chastened person. Here you were travelling quite blind, which was a great pity, as God has given you such unusually great reason and such great capacity for work.

While awaiting a new post – which he eagerly sought – and to dispel his discontentedness, Albert flung himself into a life of entertainment and socialising. Just as in Leipzig, he made new friends and wrote to one of them that Vienna, despite everything, was a place 'where one can really enjoy oneself'.

These years in the early 1840s were when Albert's reputation as an eligible bachelor was formed, a reputation he does not seem to have had anything against. One illuminating detail when it came to his outward appearance, which he was careful to cultivate, was that after his stay in Leipzig, he considered he needed a new jacket. He wrote to a friend and asked him to check the measurements with Albert's old tailor in Leipzig. His friend answered that it did not matter whether the measurements were saved or not, as 'it would be impossible for an aesthetically minded tailor to have failed to remember such a Junoesque figure'.

* * *

Rescue came in early January in the form of Adolf's good friend Karl Franz Koehler in Leipzig; Koehler seems to have acted as a kind of mentor for Albert during his continental travels. Koehler arranged a place for him with the well-known bookseller Carl Geibel in Pest, which was not merged with Buda to form Budapest, the capital of Hungary on the Danube, until 1873.

Albert immediately set off and began his placement with Geibel on 1 February 1842. He then stayed in Pest for eight months, a time that was to have a major impact on his development. His son Karl Otto remembered how in his older days his father referred to his 'highly pleasant position' with

Geibel and that this period 'became extremely fruitful for his later work as a bookseller and as a publisher'.

A brief attempt on the impatient Albert's part to keep a diary in August and September is a particularly interesting document.

His political sympathies are shown by a note from August 1842 when he witnessed the impressive opening of a new bridge:

> The city was illuminated with a torchlit procession for Széchenyi and Kossuth. However, it was clearly apparent that everything was done to order – the impulse had not come from the people.

Mentioning István Széchenyi and Lajos Kossuth by name is interesting in this context. Széchenyi implemented liberal reforms and Kossuth was a prominent agitator for the Magyar, or Hungarian, liberation movement which sought to break the dominance of the Austrian Habsburgs. A little later, in the aftermath of the revolutions of 1848, Kossuth was to take the lead in a short-lived bid for Hungarian independence, before being forced into exile following Russian intervention.

The notes in his diary show that Albert had learned to command his new Swedish mother tongue, but he was also battling to learn English, albeit a slightly strange ambition in Pest in Central Europe.

> I sweated like a dog just now to speak English with a travelling couple. It is so rarely that one needs it here so in the end one finds it very difficult. The Englishmen who make their way here generally speak

broken German or French and do not at all require that one should entertain them in their mother tongue (...) God knows that I really need to hear a great deal – before anything stays in my Brain.

There was also time for entertainment and excursions. And Albert enjoyed life:

Yesterday I was invited by some good Friends to join them on an excursion into the countryside. We travelled after midday out to Auwinkel or to be exact out to the Buda Hills, where firstly dinner was taken in the best of comfort so that we did not break up until about half past three. We then walked on through wonderful green valleys, where everywhere the trees stood laden with the most ripe and most wonderful fruit and climbed several mountaintops from where we had the most wonderful views across Buda and Pest (...) while the Danube shimmered and flowed gleaming between both cities and gave the most heavenly prospect one can desire.

However, Albert's European adventure was nearing its end. This was due to the ever worsening conflict at home in Stockholm between Esther and David Felix. As early as Boxing Day 1841, David Felix had written to Albert that 'Esther is always the same, unfortunately, as you know, not to her advantage' and that she 'finally' had realised how much he hated her. A complete breach between them was unavoidable, but how would the easily disorganised Adolf then manage to run a bookshop and the publishing business in Stockholm on his own?

Adolf was quite simply in the process of working himself to death.

In spring and summer 1842 Esther sent several letters to Albert in Pest begging him to come home to help his older brother:

> The poor Angel good Adolph is working more of course, and even more than he need, but still disorder prevails and Adolph has many worries, which makes me mournful and melancholic, as is it not heavy and hard to see an object we love more than ourselves suffer and have troubles.

Some months after this letter, on 24 June, Esther made her wish even more plain:

> I see you in my thoughts, how you with God's help return, and simply pray to God that I may not become too proud to have such a close relative (...) When I think of you, it is as you were the first year you came to us, so angelically innocent and childish – I would do much to have some of those past years back again.

Esther's verdict on David Felix was as harsh as his about her:

> Poor David, I feel sorry for him, as he does what is within his power to make himself hated by us, but we truly do not do so – as to hate someone, one must first have loved them – and him we have truly never loved.

The definitive break came in August. David Felix was sent, or banished, to Gothenburg where he was to take over operation of Adolf's bookshop. In what appears to have been a brutally unsentimental manoeuvre, the loyal Lauritz Kamp was sacked to make room for the youngest Bonnier brother.

Albert had to come home.

It was a terrible disappointment for Albert Bonnier. In his diary he called the news from home 'a complete revolution in my undertakings and thoughts'. He had great plans to stay in Pest over the New Year and then travel to Leipzig and attend the Book Fair. Most of all he harboured a desire to go to Paris and perhaps spend a year there. To a Swedish friend in Paris he wrote complaining: 'Had I been able to, how dearly would I have stayed longer, much longer.'

In a letter he told Adolf and Esther that he was prepared to travel back to Stockholm. They were clearly moved by his self-sacrificial decision and in October sent an answer in which they nevertheless kept an opportunity open for Albert to stay abroad a while longer. Despite all the strains that this would involve, they could consider, albeit temporarily, calling David Felix back home to Stockholm. Adolf wrote:

> So dear it would have been to me had you come home now in the autumn, but still that is by the by, and you may extend your stay with Geibel half a year and then travel to the fair in Leipzig.

Esther agreed and ended with a motherly greeting: 'Live well my son, whatever you decide, may He protect and preserve you.'

Nothing came of this fairly veiled offer. When the letter

arrived in Pest, Albert had already left, with fulsome credentials from Carl Geibel in his pocket.

Albert took his time. On his way home he stopped off in Leipzig, Prague and Berlin, where he saw old friends, and then he paid a visit to the family in Copenhagen. He finally arrived in Stockholm at the end of November or early December, in time for the Christmas rush.

* * *

Once at home, Albert was fully occupied helping Adolf run the bookshop and had little time to spare for his publishing business, but from his time on the continent he had brought with him ideas for journalism that he decided to attempt to realise in Sweden.

The first was to launch a fashion magazine. Such publications existed in several European cities, including Leipzig, but not Stockholm. When Albert stopped off in Leipzig on his way home, he took the opportunity to buy a collection of colour fashion plates from a newspaper publisher in the city. Thanks to these preparations, by New Year 1843 he was able to publish the first issue of *Stockholms Mode-Journal – Tidskrift för den eleganta verlden* (*Stockholm's Fashion Journal – Magazine for the Elegant World*). The announcement did not hide *Mode-Journal's* naked commercial ambition:

> One fine day you come strutting with a coiffure, a costume, that you have been assured is utterly modern, you attract everyone's attention, a thousand lorgnettes are turned in your direction, and both proud and shy at the same time you want both to be seen and to hide;

then – the horror! – one newly returned from Paris
meets you, takes you aside and whispers: 'Heavens!
That was on the way out when I left Paris.'

To spare 'all in the general public (...) this great insult' Albert
now offered *Mode-Journalen*. The reference to the general public
can hardly hide the fact that the prime target of the magazine
was women in the higher echelons of society. Nevertheless, a
glimpse of Albert the 'rabulist' came through in a summarising
comment: 'Whether we hit the right note, the public's own
verdict will tell; as the voice of the people is the voice of God'.
The name of the editor was not stated, but according to Karl
Otto Bonnier it was undoubtedly Wilhelmina Stålberg who
took on that task. Stålberg was one of Sweden's most read and
printed writers in the 1840s, but critics associated her with
'bad literature', which possibly explains her covert role. To
posterity she is best known for the text of the song 'Hjalmar
och Hulda'.

Mode-Journalen came out once a month at a quite reasonable
subscription price of three riksdaler per year. It must have
done good business because the magazine remained in print
for ten years, until 1853, when *Mode-Journalen* was merged with
a competitor entitled *Illustrerad tidning för fruntimmer* (*Illustrated
Magazine for Women*).

Alongside *Mode-Journalen* Albert also had slightly more
literary plans. In autumn 1844 he published translations of
Hans Christian Andersen's fairy tales and Charles Dickens' *A
Christmas Carol*. But the most important question on his mind
was how to align himself with Sweden's most talented writers.

In purely competitive terms, he faced a formidable obstacle
in the form of Niklas Hans Thomson, a significant but today

relatively overlooked figure in early Swedish publishing history. N. H. Thomson, born in Malmö in 1793, moved to Stockholm and established himself in the 1830s as the leading publisher of Swedish literature, with authors such as Carl Jonas Love Almqvist, Emilie Flygare-Carlén and August Blanche. Karl Otto Bonnier described the situation as Albert initially having to be content with 'the crumbs from Thomson's rich table'.

Albert's long-term plan was to attract the sharpest pens in the country by publishing periodicals. At Christmas 1844 he launched *Stockholms Figaro*, an illustrated, literary, weekly paper with Albert himself as the editor. It was clearly inspired by *Bazaren*, and was to be quick-witted and cutting. Albert persuaded August Blanche to write the introduction:

> The name Figaro is a guarantee of cheerfulness and mad tricks. Therefore, it is self-evident that a paper that bears the same name, must also be madly entertaining.

Another mission statement for the paper, which encapsulated the young Albert Bonnier's radical attitudes to an even greater degree, read:

> However, should it ever happen that one chin or another happens to come into contact with our Barber's razors, that is, after all, just as it should be (...) As to throats, however, we shall proceed with caution.

On the threshold of a dizzying period of reform with railways, freedom of trade and the abolition of the Riksdag of the Estates, the paper took a generally progressive attitude, sometimes worded with crushing irony against the sleepy state of affairs. In the first edition of 1846 it greeted the New Year – and its readers – with the following message:

> May the proposed railways, in the event they ever move from the imagination into the area of reality, not put excessive life and movement into our good countrymen and disturb their happy equilibrium (...) May our priests be a model to the people in the acquisition of this worldly good and our burghers never forget that guild regulations constitute the primary condition for the existence and well-being of the trades and crafts!

Stockholms Figaro only survived until 1847, but it strengthened Albert's connections with rising authors. Contributors not only included Blanche, but also Johan Gabriel Carlén (Emilie Flygare-Carlén's husband), Fredrika Bremer, Carl Vilhelm August Strandberg – better known by the pseudonym Talis Qualis, meaning 'I am such as I am' – and Carl August Adlersparre, pen name Albano, the son of general Georg Adlersparre who played a key role in the coup of 1809. Like *Mode-Journalen*, *Stockholms Figaro* was printed at Hörbergska tryckeriet in Stockholm, which was to be bought out by Albert just over ten years later.

Among the publishing projects that Albert launched after returning home from his European adventure, however, nothing was to prove as important as the literary 'people's annual' he started to publish at Christmas 1844. Following the model of the German *Volkskalender*, it blended short stories, essays and poetry with factual information. He would continue to edit and publish this annual every year until his death.

To use a slightly disrespectful term, Albert Bonnier made himself a testbed for writing talent. The title of the annual bore witness to his ambition to become a publisher not merely *in* but also *for* his new homeland: *Svea.*

CHAPTER 3

MOTHER SVEA

A literary annual. A modern publisher.
Scandinavian passions and plans. A family tragedy.
'Water over his head'. The novel library.
Citizenship. To revolutionary Paris.

––––

The relationship between Adolf and Albert Bonnier was close and deeply devoted. Considering their differences in age and experience, it could basically be described as similar to a father-son relationship. Glimpses of this can be seen in Ludvig Josephson's unpublished memoirs, in which he describes his time in the bookshop on Norrbro and a recurring morning ritual.

In summer 1845 Adolf had signed a lease on a seven-room flat on Ankargränd. It was so spacious that he let some rooms to his young assistants, Josephson among them:

Towards me, the old firm's manager, the man of the house, was particularly friendly and gave me personal lessons in the English language every morning, once he had begun by giving his brother Albert his customary lecture for lying too long in bed.

Adolf and Albert successfully ran the bookshop on Norrbro together. But after his return to Stockholm, armed with plenty of ideas for the future, Albert was careful to distance himself from what he saw as his older brother's tendency to take fanciful risks. Towards the booksellers, Albert used the business name 'Förlagsbyrån', while the printed materials themselves mainly bore his own name as the publisher, sometimes abbreviated to Alb. Bonnier.

Albert also gained entry to the Swedish Publishers' Association, formed in 1843 to protect the interests of the industry. The influence of members in the association was ranked by the size of their publishing business. A voting list from January 1844 shows that the newly admitted Albert Bonnier was placed last. He had two votes; Adolf six. Presumably at that point the thought that, more than thirty years later, he would be the organisation's chair barely crossed his mind.

Adolf thought they should merge their publishing businesses but Albert refused, explaining later in a letter to David Felix, in which one can trace a fear of repeating Gerhard's mistakes:

> One reason why I refused my approval was also – that I disliked Adolf's inclination to play fast and loose without sufficient taste and discrimination just as long as it is obtained for a cheap fee and ideally on long credit – that I did not want to launch my small boat on those choppy waters in which his publishing ship constantly rolls, but instead seek to sail my little vessel on short journeys close to the shore to a near and safe harbour.

Albert now wanted to go his own way, systematically and cautiously. This plan was highly bound up with the annual, *Svea*, which over time was to become a widely disseminated forum for several new authors, including August Strindberg, Gustaf af Geijerstam, Oscar Levertin and Victoria Benedictsson, writing under the pseudonym Ernst Ahlgren. Later, *Svea*'s columns would be opened to names such as Gustaf Fröding and Selma Lagerlöf.

One of Albert's colleagues, the German-born bookseller and publisher Carl Eduard Fritze, advised him against the venture after a failed annual attempt of his own, but Albert had made up his mind. At Christmas 1844, in parallel with *Stockholms Figaro*, the first edition of *Svea* was published, intended for the year 1845.

The introduction was impressive, if not to say bombastic:

> This experiment in popular reading is dedicated by the publisher to the noble and high-minded Swedish Nation.

It is in such choices of phrasing that one detects the immigrant Albert Bonnier's vehement desire to be seen as and respected as Swedish. In the discussion on the conditions for Jewish emancipation taking place in Mosaic circles, on preserving distinction versus assimilation, Albert was a keen advocate of the latter.

Svea's political profile was not as clear as that of *Stockholms Figaro*, but it had liberal sensibilities. For his time, Albert was also remarkably supportive of female authors. One of the annual's early writers was Jeanette Granberg Stjernström, a social reformer, dramatist and translator.

Albert had hunted far and wide for an editor for *Svea*, but had failed to find anyone he considered suitable. Instead he took on the role himself, although he had help from author and translator Gustaf Thomée, at that time one of Albert's most trusted employees. This proved to be a stroke of genius.

In a look back at *Svea* fifty years later, Karl Warburg wrote:

> Perhaps, however, the circumstance that *Svea* did not have a 'literary' editor was precisely what contributed to its unusual success. The writers in Sweden at that time were then, as is almost always the case, divided into groups of different party colours, and it was therefore not unlikely that involvement from different sides could be gained more easily by a neutral publisher who was 'outside the guild'.

Over time, *Svea* gained a circulation of 10,000 and the fact that Albert Bonnier used the annual to expand his network of contacts with talented Swedish writers is confirmed in his extensive correspondence with different contributors on everything from ideas for articles to fees. This has been analysed and summarised in literature researcher Gundel Söderholm's thesis on *Svea*. Here the picture emerges of a determined and methodical editor:

> One (...) characteristic feature is that he constantly encouraged or provided flattering comments. Partly, this could of course have been genuine on his account, but it was also a means of getting busy authors on board. When it came to works he wanted very much, he sent many patient reminders if contributions were delayed.

Albert's social ease was highly characteristic. Many of the authors who contributed to *Svea* over the years also became his personal friends and to them his tone was highly informal and relaxed, a precursor of the closeness he was to develop with great figures such as Zacharias Topelius and Viktor Rydberg.

It was a method of building loyalty that Albert Bonnier was alone in practising at that time. Up until then, relationships between author and publisher had been reasonably promiscuous, if one may use such an expression. In the 1840s, for example, Carl Jonas Love Almqvist published about twenty books — with eleven different publishers. In this sense, as in many others, Albert Bonnier was 'the first modern publisher' writes Per I. Gedin in *Litteraturens örtagårdsmästare*, (*A Gardener of Literature*) his biography of Albert's son Karl Otto.

In connections with authors with whom he never succeeded in forging close links, despite persistent attempts, Albert made sure to maintain a correct and respectful tone. This was the case, for example, with his contacts with Anne Charlotte Leffler, a central figure in the modernisation of Swedish literature in the second half of the nineteenth century. She never became one of the Bonnier publishing company's big names. With his good friend Frans Hedberg, one of *Svea*'s keenest contributors and the originator of popular plays such as *Rospiggarna*, on the other hand, Albert could engage in unbridled arguments without it disrupting their relationship in any way.

The first annual edition of *Svea*, for 1845, contained a portrait of King Oscar I and Queen Josefina, texts about Gustav Vasa and Erik XIV and a long essay by Thomée entitled *En blick på Sveriges nuvarande ställning* (A *Look at Sweden's Present Position*). The nationalistic approach was clear, in other words, but in *Svea*'s early volumes, the perspective was also Scandinavian.

The first edition contained a 'Scandinavian folk song' by poet
Johan Nybom:

> What is the Scandinavians' land?
> Svea-land? Tronda-land?
> Is it where the Sound embraces
> Happy, beautiful Copenhagen?
> O yes, yes, yes!
> All − all are Scandinavia.

For this was the age of Scandinavianism. And the Bonnier
brothers, born in Denmark but working in Sweden, were
dedicated to the cause.

* * *

Scandinavianism, an extension of the national liberal ideas
of romanticism, started to make itself felt in the 1830s. The
symbolic starting point came in 1829, when Sweden's national
poet Esaias Tegnér placed a laurel wreath on the head of his
Danish counterpart Adam Oehlenschläger at a doctoral degree
ceremony in Lund, declaring: 'The time of division is past.' A
more practical and prosaic reason for these ideas taking root
was the establishment of the first regular steamer connection
between Malmö and Copenhagen that same year.

Scandinavianism was built on the assumption of a deeper
historical and cultural friendship between the Scandinavian
peoples, attitudes that particularly struck a chord with the old
hereditary enemies Sweden and Denmark. The Norwegians,
tied with Sweden in a problematic personal union, were
more wary. Scandinavianism was also directed against what

were felt to be external threats, in Sweden's case Russia, in Denmark's Germany.

Students, young academics and cultural figures were the driving force. In the arctic winter of 1838, students from Lund and Copenhagen marched across the ice of the Öresund to greet each other and the following year a first cross-border student meeting was held in the Danish capital. This was followed in 1842 by another student meeting in the same city, where Danish author Frederik Barfod spoke on the topic 'Nordic unity is Nordic freedom'. The next meeting, in 1843, took place in Uppsala, and was attended by a small group of students from Finland. In some places in Sweden there were hopes that a concerted Scandinavian effort might lead to reunification with Finland, which had been lost to Russia in 1809.

At Midsummer 1845 it was time for yet another student meeting in Copenhagen. Albert Bonnier went, not only encouraged by his Danish background but undoubtedly by his circle of writing friends. Both Oscar Patric Sturzen-Becker and C. V. A. Strandberg, who wrote under the pen names Orvar Odd and Talis Qualis respectively, were ardent Scandinavianists.

Emotions ran high in *Stockholms Figaro*. According to the paper, the meeting in Copenhagen would 'mark an epoch in the history of the whole Nordic region'. And it went further than that. *Figaro's* editor, Albert Bonnier, took on the role of foreign correspondent on the ground in Copenhagen, from where he sent back enthusiastic reports:

The importance of the meeting has not solely made a deep impression on every participant; its consequences are incalculable, and the whole of Europe shall listen with attention to its deliberations.

However, it was Adolf who was to contract the most severe dose of Scandinavian fever. The background was tragic.

* * *

Finally, after eleven years of marriage to Adolf, Esther had become pregnant. It can be deduced that it was the expected expansion of his family that led Adolf to move to a new, bigger home. To give Esther peace and quiet, he also rented a summer residence on Djurgården. He was clearly worried about her health and about how she would cope with the strain of pregnancy. His worries were justified. After a difficult labour, on 3 October 1845 Esther's baby was delivered stillborn, and she died herself just hours later.

Initially, making the funeral arrangements and dealing with other practical details enabled Adolf to keep the worst of his desolation under control, but as time went on the grief started to overwhelm him. Supported by Albert, who agreed without hesitation to keep the business in Stockholm going, Adolf went to Copenhagen to seek consolation and come to terms with his loss with fewer distractions. During this stay, which lasted more than three months, he began to ponder an idea which rang warning bells for the more cautious Albert.

In Copenhagen, Adolf was gripped by the passions of Scandinavianism, partly influenced by two Swedish acquaintances who were also in Denmark. These were Sturzen-Becker and Carl Jonas Love Almqvist, the latter controversial in Sweden and increasingly spending time outside the country. In early February 1846, Almqvist delivered a well-attended lecture in Copenhagen entitled *Om skandinavismens utförbarhet* (*The Practicability of Scandinavianism*). Adolf was also adopted as a member of the illustrious *Skandinavisk Selskab* (Scandinavian Society), which attracted a long list of Danish luminaries.

Immediately on arriving in Copenhagen in November, Adolf hinted in a letter to Albert that he had 'numerous ideas for the future', and continued: 'The book trade here is *highly, highly* profitable, but, although there are so many of them here now, it is run *dreadfully* and miserably by *every one of them*.'

Adolf had noticed a lack of Swedish books in the Danish shops and saw an opportunity not only to help 'promote the *Scandinavian* Idea' but also to strike a blow for Swedish literature, and French, German and English literature too. His idea was that he himself, Albert and David Felix would become partners with shops in Copenhagen, Stockholm and Gothenburg.

In January 1846 he wrote to Albert, asking his opinion.

> An *association* on a larger or smaller scale I am willing to enter into, to promote the *Establishments* in Stockholm, Gothenburg and *Copenhagen* together with you and to an extent David, regarding which we would consider and plan together in more detail in the future.

In the same letter Adolf highlighted the 'wonderful location' of Copenhagen 'for being able to obtain in haste items from Germany, France and England' and expressed a hope for 'a shop in *Norway*'. Nor did he hide an ambition to 'force out G', in other words C. W. K. Gleerup.

What Adolf seems to have had in mind was an international chain of bookshops with a Scandinavian profile. Albert and David Felix were highly doubtful. It appears that they sensed their father Gerhard's tendency towards flights of fancy in their older brother's magnificent plans, a feeling that was hardly assuaged by the fact that Adolf thought Gerhard would be able to help out in the Copenhagen branch where necessary. David Felix was the firmest in his rejection of the idea: 'The plan may be thought about and hoped for, but not carried out.'

Albert's answer, which has not been preserved, seems to have been worded more cautiously but nevertheless clearly, because Adolf, with certain circumlocutions, admitted that it had given him doubts.

> Your response regarding *the great plan* – or *the castle in the air* as it pleases you to more rightly call it – was dearly welcome to me and quite reassuring – as a firm *decision* for or *aversion* against the project was all I could want or expect, and I can assure you that I have slept and thought even more upon this than I had then, without even at this moment being fully agreed with myself on which decision one is to take.

In March Adolf was back in Sweden and the Scandinavian bookshop idea was shelved, but only temporarily. In late summer, in a new visit from Adolf to Copenhagen, it flared up again, what he in a letter to Albert called 'the long and often chewed over and spoken of Idea'. This time Adolf even managed to talk round David Felix, who was also in Copenhagen for their sister Bolette's wedding. David Felix had reached the conclusion that they might as well let Adolf try out his idea, as long as it was done quickly and resolutely: 'If it's war, so let it be war! This eternal discussing and pondering ought to lead to some result.'

Albert's opposition seems to have wavered for a few days, possibly due to his younger brother's changed attitude, but to judge from Adolf's answer to a letter from 12 September, Albert had finally put his foot down with a rejecting comment that clearly made an impression – 'being in water over one's head'.

Adolf's capitulation came a few weeks later on 2 October. Albert had, he wrote, brought him 'to a resolution to allow everything to remain *in statu quo*'.

Exactly what would have happened had Adolf Bonnier's plans been realised is impossible to say, but it seems highly likely that the history of the Bonnier bookshop – and in the long run the publishing company – would have taken an entirely different turn.

* * *

In many letters and documents from the mid-nineteenth century the picture emerges of a huge, almost manic, capacity for work on the part of Albert Bonnier. Despite the most stressful circumstances – Esther's death, responsibility for running Adolf's business during his absence, plus his own business – it was during these hardworking years that Albert managed to lay the foundations of his great success. *Svea* was an important tool, but in 1846 he started a project that more than any other was to pave the way for his future position as Sweden's pre-eminent publisher of literary fiction: *Den europeiska följetongen. Nytt romanbibliothek*, (*The European Series.*

New Novel Library) a title that was soon changed to *Den europeiska följetongen. Tidskrift för Utländsk Romanlitteratur* (*The European Series. Periodical for Foreign Novels*).

As a literary genre, the novel can be traced back to the ancient world, then developing through the tales of chivalry of the medieval period and, in the seventeenth and eighteenth centuries via works of storytelling such as Miguel de Cervantes' *Don Quixote* and Daniel Defoe's *Robinson Crusoe*. But it was not until the early nineteenth century that the novel in a more modern sense captured the public imagination through the author of *Ivanhoe*, Walter Scott and, a little later, Eugène Sue, Alexandre Dumas *père*, Honoré de Balzac, George Sand, William Thackeray and Charles Dickens. This went hand in hand with the emergence of a growing – and reading – middle class in the wake of industrialisation in countries such as Britain and France. This new and relatively well-off bourgeoisie demanded cultural entertainment. The novel, often published in serialised form, was the perfect means of providing it.

Sweden lagged behind in this trend, but in around 1840, at the time of Albert Bonnier's entry onto the Swedish publishing scene, the novel was introduced in Sweden too. Carl Jonas Love Almqvist had a special role to play in the popularisation of the novel, with *Drottningens juvelsmycke* (*The Queen's Tiara*), *Törnrosens bok* (*The Book of the Thorn-Rose*) and *Det går an* (*Sara Videbeck and the Chapel*). Two female authors were also of great importance: Fredrika Bremer with novels such as *Grannarne* (*The Neighbours*) and *Hemmet* (*The Home*), and the bestselling Emilie Flygare-Carlén, whose breakthrough novel *Rosen på Tistelön* (*The Rose of Tistelön*) had a documentary background. In the mid-nineteenth century, Flygare-Carlén's literary salon in Stockholm served as a kind of epicentre for Swedish literature.

Something new was starting to break through. Albert Bonnier recognised this and decided to seize the moment.

* * *

'Novel libraries', simply produced pamphlets sold to subscribers at a reasonable price, became popular in Sweden in the 1830s. First out of the gate, as was so often the case, was Lars Johan Hierta with *Läsebibliothek af den nyaste utländska litteraturen* (Readers' Library of the Newest Foreign Literature) in 1833, later known merely as *LäseBibliothek* (Readers' Library) and *Nytt LäseBibliothek* (New Readers' Library). Two years later N. H. Thomson responded with *Kabinettsbibliothek af den nyaste litteraturen* (Home Library of the Newest Literature). Both mainly focused on translations of foreign novels, although Thomson was more inclined than Hierta to promote Swedish authors such as Emilie Flygare-Carlén, while Hierta's key selling point was the immeasurably popular Englishman Edward Bulwer-Lytton. Another important player was Östlund & Berling, a printing firm in Norrköping, who in 1845 started to publish their own *Originalbibliothek* (Original Library), to which they attracted Flygare-Carlén.

It was total anarchy. There was no regulated copyright for translations and they were produced randomly without the original authors receiving any payment. It was not until the international Berne Convention for the Protection of Literary and Artistic Works in 1886 that the situation began to be regulated, but it took until 1904 for Sweden to sign up.

Instead, between Swedish book publishers there prevailed

a kind of 'gentleman's agreement' that they would announce planned translations in advance to avoid clashes. This was not always successful and Albert was soon to be dragged into a festering conflict with Lars Johan Hierta.

The market was ripe for exploitation. A contemporary observer reported how on Saturdays there was 'a certain anxious waiting' in educated Stockholm families. What they were waiting for was the delivery of 'a small greyish pamphlet bearing the quite curious title *Läsebibliothek*'. As soon as it was delivered by a postman – the leaflets came by mail – one sought out 'a quiet corner in the house, and the lucky holder of the pamphlet was forced to share the contents by reading it aloud'.

This increasing interest in fiction led to a veritable explosion of printed works. In the period 1830–60, the production of printed material in Sweden more than doubled. 'From books in general being seen as a relatively expensive and exclusive product, the novel published in pamphlet form had in reality become an everyday commodity,' says literature researcher Gunnel Furuland in her thesis on the novel libraries of the nineteenth century.

For the twenty-five-year-old Albert Bonnier, entering this growing publishing market must have seemed irresistible. In summer 1846 he started the weekly publication of the series of pamphlets *Europeiska följetongen* which, in its first few years, was to introduce several major European novels to a broad Swedish public, including Thackeray's *Vanity Fair* and Alexandre Dumas *fils' La Dame aux camélias* (*Camille*). Later, in the 1850s, came works including Dickens' *David Copperfield* and from the USA Harriet Beecher Stowe's anti-slavery novel *Uncle Tom's Cabin*. The same year as the French original, 1862,

Victor Hugo's *Les Misérables* was published in *Följetongen* under the Swedish title *Det menskliga eländet.*

Följetongen's very first edition, however, was a translation of the now forgotten French author Eugène Sue's *Martin, hittebarnet,* (*Martin, l'enfant trouvé; Martin the Foundling*) which had been published in the French periodical *Le Constitutionnel.* Once more, it was Adolf who supported his younger brother. He was in Paris and sent home issue after issue of *Le Constitutionnel,* which Albert then had quickly translated.

Albert kept himself informed of new literary phenomena by reading foreign newspapers and through his own contacts. And as with *Svea,* he read through practically everything printed in *Följetongen,* often including the proofs.

* * *

The Swedish publishing giant of the day was Lars Johan Hierta, the founder of *Aftonbladet,* a successful entrepreneur and former of liberal opinion who had grown considerably wealthy. This unavoidably led to conflicts between the established Hierta and the young newcomer Albert Bonnier.

The first crossing of swords concerned the translation of Alexandre Dumas *père*'s *Mémoires d'un médecin* (*Memoirs of a Physician*). Albert chose to sound the retreat 'to avoid collision, which in a country with so small a number of readers as Sweden would undoubtedly be damaging to the Competitors'. But then the battle moved up a gear. In 1847 Albert announced that he intended to publish a translation of Edward Bulwer-Lytton's new novel *Lucretia or The Children of Night.* Hierta responded to the challenge by immediately starting to publish a translation in *Aftonbladet.* Albert responded in *Stockholms Figaro:*

We have always considered it to be, to put it in the mildest form, less than chivalrous, for a publisher to use his newspaper as a vehicle for his other businesses.

This was hardly Albert Bonnier's finest hour. Publishing Bulwer-Lytton broke the tacit agreement that publishers respected each other's favoured authors. And criticism against Hierta for having used his own newspaper in the conflict lacked credibility now that Albert himself was using *Stockholms Figaro*.

There was a sense of enjoying picking a quarrel about Albert's behaviour. Perhaps he was seeking to mark his presence on the publishing stage by attacking the foremost name in the industry. In all events, Albert escalated things by launching ironically contemptuous attacks on Hierta in retorts that hint at a slight inferiority complex:

The modern giant (...) stands roaring terribly while he in fact has become aware that people dislike him and fear him greatly. Although against the old fighter *Figaro* is a mere youngster, and brings no other weapons than a few smooth stones from the river, the battle must be waged.

The conflict between Lars Johan Hierta and Albert Bonnier continued into the 1850s, when the former stopped publishing his series of novels; Bonnier's continued to be published until 1910, with a brief interruption in 1855–57.

In a literary sense, there was no winner. In the rush to publish first, translations were often produced that were substandard. 'Neither can be said to be the real victor in the race, but both were losers in terms of translation quality,' Gunnel Furuland sums up the situation. The battle showed, however, that Albert Bonnier was a fearless actor, hungry for success – and quite shameless when the need arose.

One reason why Albert Bonnier's novel pamphlets outlived Hierta's – and also Thomson's – was superior marketing that, with hindsight, takes on a strikingly modern hue. Besides announcements of cultural novelties, Bonnier's pamphlets contained attractive presentations of the authors and their future publications, what today are usually termed puff pieces. Nor was he shy about shamelessly promoting the benefits of his own serials compared with those of his competitors, for example in the first issue in 1847:

The advantages that distinguish this library are as follows: A comfortable and handy format, and economical yet not eyestrain-inducing print, accurate translations and a cheap price.

Although Albert initially concentrated on foreign authors, both *Svea* and the publication of *Den europeiska följetongen*, later with the title *Nya följetongen*, facilitated contact between him and several of the most notable names among Swedish authors of the day. Here were established authors such as August Blanche with *Taflor och berättelser ur Stockholmslifvet* (*Pictures and Tales of Stockholm Life*) and Johan Gabriel Carlén with *Romanser ur svenska folklifvet* (*Romances from Swedish Folk Life*), here were forgers of political opinion such as Emil Key with *Om Skandinaviens framtid* (*On the Future of Scandinavia*) and quick-witted newspapermen such as Henrik Bernhard Palmær, the founder of *Östgöta Correspondenten*, with *En liten lustresa*

(*A Little Journey*) and *Aftonbladet's* Karl Anders af Kullberg with *Det otroliga* (*The Unbelievable*).

There is every reason here to dwell on son Karl Otto Bonnier's account in his family history, partly based on his own memories of his father:

> In older days, when interest in new, larger companies started to fade and he often handed over running of connections with the younger generation of authors to his son and fellow partners in the publishing company, it was always, however, the two enterprises from his youth, '*Följetongen*' and '*Svea*' that remained close to Albert Bonnier's heart and to which he dedicated his last energies.

* * *

The late 1840s were a hectic time for the three Bonnier brothers. Albert was working intensely on *Den europeiska följetongen* and *Svea*. Adolf was expanding his publishing company and had found a new wife in Sophie Hirsch, sister of one of the brothers' closest friends, music publisher Abraham Hirsch; in November 1848 they had a son Isidor Adolf. David Felix, who had started to only use the name Felix, had married and started a publishing business in Gothenburg. Adolf Bonnier also gained the status of academic bookseller in Uppsala, an honourable assignment that required Swedish citizenship.

Adolf's promotion to bookseller to the university seems to have been the main reason why the brothers applied to become Swedish citizens in summer 1849. Even Felix was keen to have the question resolved, because he had great plans for his business in Gothenburg and wanted to avoid anyone being able to 'impugn' him. Albert, on the other hand, seems to have viewed the whole thing more as a formality that needed to be organised sooner or later.

On 11 September 1849 the brothers' citizenship applications were granted and they were thus released from an inconvenience that had hung over them even since their arrival in Sweden; as adherents of the Mosaic faith they merely had permits to stay in the Kingdom of Sweden until further notice and could be deported at any time. Nothing indicates that they experienced any impending danger, but recurring manifestations of antisemitic opinion, at their most violent in 1838, naturally made them aware of the risks.

The brothers' coordinated applications for citizenship confirm how closely intertwined they were, but some friction arose between them now that all three were engaged in phases of expansion.

Much seems to have been rooted in Felix's desire to emerge from his older brothers' shadow. Felix wanted to take over the bookshop in Gothenburg entirely, under his own business name, which Adolf accepted after quite an acrimonious exchange of letters. And in 1849 a conflict arose between Felix and Albert on an impressive work of lithographs, *Sverige, framställdt i taflor* (*Sweden in Pictures*), which they initially intended to publish jointly. Felix changed his mind and demanded sole rights, to which Albert agreed, provided that he was able to have the name of his publishing firm on the title page. Felix refused.

After a sharp exchange of words, in which an angry Felix called Albert a 'dog Turk', Albert disengaged from all further involvement in the project, which became a success in the first half of the 1850s.

None of this had any lasting consequences for the brothers' relationship. Despite skirmishes, they remained close friends, often prepared to give each other a helping hand when needed.

* * *

For Albert Bonnier, the most disruptive event in these years was the revolution of 1848 or rather revolutions. It all began in Paris on 22 February, before spreading across much of Europe, albeit in varied forms. In France, where the bourgeois July Monarchy from 1830 was replaced by the Second Republic, the uprising was caused by poor harvests, social misery and unemployment and had socialist overtones. In Germany, Italy and Habsburg Austria, the revolts had a nationalist character. When the ripples reached Sweden in March, they led to demands for suffrage, representational reform and a republic.

After violent disorder in Stockholm and other cities, with about thirty deaths, a jittery Oscar I reformed the Government in a slightly more liberal direction. One of the new ministers was Johan August Gripenstedt, only thirty-four years old.

The revolutions came to nothing, beaten down practically everywhere, and have been called 'an overture without an opera', but still with hindsight can be seen as an expression of a popular awakening that over time was to transform Europe politically and nationally.

Albert Bonnier's sympathies were obvious and in this year of revolution, 1848, he joined an organisation in Stockholm, *Reformvännerna* (*The Friends of Reform*), which was formed at a 'simple dinner for heroes of freedom of all classes' with the aim of 'awakening the dying Rabulism to life'. The more than six hundred members of the society also included his rival Lars Johan Hierta. Politically they were close, which made Albert's fixation on Hierta as his sworn enemy-in-chief even more incomprehensible.

Albert went even further than that. As early as 1842 he had had dreams of being able to conclude his European journey with a longer stay in Paris, but loyalty to the exhausted Adolf had seen him instead return home to Stockholm. Now he felt an irresistible urge to go to the French capital and feel the winds of change sweep across his brow. He asked Adolf for two months' leave from the bookshop and made his way abroad in early July 1848. Felix, who was newly in love, declined an offer to accompany him, referring to his 'heavenly mademoiselle', Charlotte Benecke, and the generally uncertain situation in France:

> But do you dare travel after this latest spectacle and are you not afraid of 'the red Republic'? It would be the devil were you to end up residing in one of the suspect quarters and Monsieur Cavaignac were pleased to have you perform gymnastics over the blade!

Felix was referring to General Louis-Eugène Cavaignac, who had suppressed a workers' revolt in Paris in June with bloody cruelty, to practically operate as a dictator for some months thereafter.

No letters from Albert are preserved from his time in Paris in 1848, but in the words of his son Karl Otto 'one could take it as read' that he enjoyed himself.

But time was passing. Albert's thirtieth birthday was approaching and he was established as a book publisher. Both of his brothers had settled down. His friends started to joke about the happy fellow's bachelor life. When the news of the oldest Bonnier brother's engagement to Sophie Hirsch reached Oscar Patric Sturzen-Becker, he wrote to Albert:

> Send Adolf many greetings from me! They say that he is an engaged gentleman, bravissimo! I congratulate him a thousandfold. But as to Sir himself?

CHAPTER 4

A CHANGE IN CIRCUMSTANCES

**A bachelor settles down – at last. Betty.
Contact across the Bothnian Sea. Albert buys a printworks.
Problems at the bookshop. Financial crisis.
Albert takes command.**

———

The early 1850s were a trying period for at least two of the Bonnier brothers. In competition with Östlund & Berling in Norrköping, Adolf published an imposing edition of the Bible, but because his book had been printed in Leipzig it was subject to customs duty at 20 per cent. On top of that, a fairly ludicrous objection was made about Adolf's project in the press; that as an adherent of the Mosaic faith, he should not be allowed to publish the Bible. However, he was able to note one important success for the future. In 1853 Adolf was able to obtain exclusive rights to the writings of Carl Michael Bellman via his friend and fellow publisher Philipp Meyer. The following year he also gained the rights to the music.

In Gothenburg, Felix Bonnier continued with the publication of *Sverige, framstäldt i taflor*, but business at the bookshop was more sluggish. He was newly married, a state which brought with it a more serious manner, demonstrated in his letters, which sounded less like they had been written by a spirited youth than they had previously. Felix was the keenest correspondent of the trio of brothers by a wide margin. Albert teased him for this shift in temperament, whereupon Felix complained to Adolf:

> Albert thinks I have reined myself in somewhat compared with before – I should think so too! When you have a wife and a home you need to be prudent. As a young man you can take on the whole world and if you go under – *adieu la compagnie!*

Albert was leading a busy life too, but in a different way. He had first moved with Adolf and Sophie to their new flat on Drottninggatan, but in autumn 1850 he finally found a place of his own on Brunkebergstorg, near De la Croix salonger. One of the most popular restaurants in Stockholm, this establishment opened in 1843 as an elegant subsidiary branch of the *schweizeri* on Norrbro. Professionally, Albert worked hard at his duties in the bookshop and editing *Svea* and his novel library, but once he had locked the door of the shop he made his way out into the Stockholm night.

In the late 1840s, Albert mainly spent time with a couple of friends he had got to know in Uppsala, where he sometimes travelled on Adolf's behalf. These were Alfred von Betzen and Victor Enblom, the former a physician, the latter a humanist. Together with the young wholesaler Adolf Schück, they formed a quartet that as Karl Otto Bonnier laconically put it, 'enjoyed themselves heroically'. They were parted in about

1850 when von Betzen gained a job as a doctor in Gothenburg and Enblom became a lecturer in Västerås, but continued to keep in touch.

In Stockholm Albert now joined a group of radical men about town, whose stamping ground covered not only De la Croix, but also Brunkebergs Casino, the Artists' Association and various theatres. They included Karl Anders af Kullberg, Frans Hedberg, then an actor, the painter Josef Wilhelm Wallander, Talis Qualis, Theodor Sack – a violinist in the Royal Court Orchestra – and Rudolf Wall, publisher of the radical weekly paper *Friskytten* (*The Marksman*) and later the founder of *Dagens Nyheter*. Sometimes they were joined by Sven Adolf Hedlund, later a leading liberal newspaperman, editor of *Göteborgs Handels- och Sjöfarts-Tidning* and a mentor to Viktor Rydberg.

A series of articles in *Friskytten* in 1851, under the headline 'Swiss Promenades' depicted the motley environment at the De la Croix *schweizeri* in Norrbro Bazaar, a place that, it was said, offered 'liberty, equality and especially fraternity'. According to Rudolf Wall's biographer Gudmar Hasselberg, the phrase's originator must have been Wall himself:

There, unless the view is blocked by clouds of cigar smoke, you will see a multitude of the capital's luminaries of all kinds (...) Ministers and generals, civil servants and sub-lieutenants, who intend to become the former or the latter – sometimes professors and students (...) Like the newspapers on the table, here gather editors of all colours (...) A young man calls for Punch and receives a glass instead of the paper, which, to be fair, is not dry either; some members of Parliament come in and a farmer raises a motion on port wine.

The central figure in the circle in which Albert Bonnier fraternised was August Theodor Blanche, nine years older than Albert, who had caused a sensation in the 1840s with popular plays such as *Positivhataren* (*The Hurdy-Gurdy Hater*) and *Ett resande teatersällskap* (*A Travelling Theatre Troupe*). Blanche had trained as a lawyer at Uppsala University and was much talked about in Stockholm's radical circles, an outstanding speaker and showman who captivated his audience, whether on stage or at the dinner table. Albert looked up to him with boundless admiration.

In the late 1850s, August Blanche gained a seat in the Riksdag as a representative of the burghers, where he pursued women's rights, the abolition of the death penalty and representational reform. Blanche, who died in 1868, is also associated with the Swedish Shooting Movement, a voluntary, popular defence movement that emerged in the 1860s. When Albert installed himself in a private suite of rooms overlooking Berzelii Park, he gave a bust of Blanche pride of place.

* * *

Politically, the start of the 1850s was a time of relative calm, characterised by a conservative reaction to the turmoil of 1848–9. This by no means dampened Albert's liberal sympathies. When the expelled Hungarian freedom fighter Lajos Kossuth, well-known to Albert from his time in Pest, visited Stockholm in 1851, a public party was held in his honour. The tickets cost two riksdaler each and were sold – naturally – at the Bonnier bookshop on Norrbro.

The popular unrest that was bubbling under the surface was not manifested in massive riots as in 1838 or 1848 but in *gåsmarscher*, literally 'goose marches': public gatherings usually from the lower social classes, moving slowly through towns such as Uppsala and Stockholm in strict and eerie silence.

In March 1851, the Riksdag of the Estates rejected a proposal to extend the rights of adherents of the Mosaic faith.

The liberal revolution was on the back burner for the time being, but for Albert Bonnier, major upheavals of a private and a professional nature were on the horizon.

It was time for him to find a life partner and build a family. He had established contact with an author who was to become the publishing firm's biggest commercial asset. And soon Albert was to put in train his biggest and potentially riskiest deal so far: a printworks of his own.

* * *

Letters from friends, many of whom had settled down by this point, bear witness to a mounting lack of tolerance regarding Albert's unwillingness, or inability, to find a wife. August Blanche wrote to him from Paris in 1851:

> I hope you are well and flourishing, and that on my arrival I will have a new, pleasant house to spend time in and that I will be able to stand godfather to your first child, provided the synagogue has nothing against it.

Blanche and Albert, both bachelors, had something in common. In the late 1840s they were both attracted to the same woman, the beautiful Swedish soprano Mathilda Ebeling, alongside Jenny Lind the great opera star of the day. Mathilda was not interested in either of them. She prioritised her singing career and moved to Berlin to develop as an artist. She died of tuberculosis there in 1851.

One woman who Albert does seem to have considered actually proposing to was called Fanny Behrens, but he could not make up his mind and Felix sighed at his brother's indecision:

> What on earth are you hesitating over? Is it to be or is it not to be? 'The girl is pretty, and money she has, tra-la-la-la, etc'. and if the former isn't guaranteed to last, the latter is much more so, so take your match and *que ça finisse!*

In the end Fanny Behrens married one of Albert's good friends, the doctor Axel Lamm. On Lamm's stag night in 1851 Albert gave a speech in verse that hinted at a self-deprecating awareness that this state of affairs could not go on much longer:

> Our circle of bachelors has nearly expired
> soon pretty much all will have wives.
> It looks as though we're growing tired
> of being bachelors all our lives.

The following year Albert received a letter from another friend, bookseller Reinhold Frenckell in Helsinki. Frenckell did not mince his words:

> As an old friend of yours I would like to employ this occasion to seriously remind you that it is time for you to stop shilly-shallying, in other words cease your

flattery and your falling on your knees before all the beauties of Stockholm, and become a respectable man once and for all.

Albert was simply fussy. From Gothenburg, his friend Alfred von Betzen wrote, consolingly, that it undoubtedly was high time that Albert 'sacrificed the delights of the bachelor life' but that 'it doesn't do to take the first, the best'. That being the case, von Betzen pointed out, 'it is better to do without'.

At last, in 1853, Albert started an association that was to culminate in marriage.

Betty Rubenson, eight years younger than Albert, belonged to one of the oldest and more prominent Jewish families in Sweden. Their roots lay in Poland and they had come to Sweden in the 1790s with the surname Wolff. The first member of the family to settle in Sweden, Ruben Wolff, became the rabbi of the Mosaic congregation in Stockholm and his children then changed their surname to Rubenson. His son Wolff Rubenson, Betty's father, established a business in Stockholm as a wholesaler of manufactured goods. It was therefore quite natural for Betty and Albert to sometimes meet socially in the Jewish community. What first seems to have been a superficial acquaintance developed into friendship and eventually love. They became engaged in January 1854. But there was a fly in the ointment.

Betty suffered from what in the nineteenth century was called nervous melancholia, a vague condition that today would probably be termed recurring depression. The symptoms were so serious that, despite his strong feelings, Albert started to have doubts. He pondered this vital decision for several months and seems to have isolated himself even from his brothers. When Felix finally received a sign of life from his brother in May he expressed his relief that Albert had 'reawakened from illusory death'.

The invitations to the wedding were held back until the last minute – for so long that Felix felt himself forced to decline his as he had already agreed to attend another wedding in Gothenburg. But on 27 June 1854 Albert Bonnier married Betty Rubenson, who had recovered from her plunge into depression.

And so began a marriage that was to swing between effervescent joy and deep despair. However, there is no doubt that the union was founded on true love.

In one of the first letters to her 'dear, beloved old man', written in bed while Albert was away, Betty lamented 'the terrible emptiness beside me' and concluded with 'many kisses into the air, adieu, adieu to you, my beloved'. An added PS shows a touch of gallows humour and self-awareness that probably contributed to Albert's conviction that they would be able to weather any trials to come: 'Otherwise I feel so-so, la-hitt la-ha, but that's just how it is and it will pass, said the old woman.'

On 7 June 1855 the couple's first child was born, a daughter Jenny, named after Betty's mother who had died of cholera eight months earlier.

* * *

If the 1850s were something of a lost decade politically, the same was true of Swedish literature. Few novelists made their breakthrough in the fifties. One exception was Marie Sophie Schwartz, one of Sweden's most read and translated authors in the second half of the nineteenth century, and a woman with a social conscience. She lived with Gustaf Magnus Schwartz, who was more than forty years older than she was, previously Head of the Institute of Technology and one of Gerhard and Adolf's old benefactors. Marie Sophie Schwartz is best known in Sweden for *Mannen af börd och qvinnan af folket* (*A Man of Birth and a Woman of the People*) from 1858, but Albert had started to publish her books six years earlier. He also published her in *Svea*.

Adolf too became the publisher of a committed female author, albeit already properly established: Fredrika Bremer. He published her epoch-making feminist novel *Hertha, eller en själs historia* (*Hertha*) in 1856.

In the absence of new literary works in Swedish, Albert focused on the latest non-fiction, often foreign in origin. The Crimean War between Great Britain, France and the Ottoman Empire on the one side and Russia on the other was raging in 1853–6 and attracted great interest in Sweden, where King Oscar I harboured plans to exploit the situation to make gains in terms of Sweden's positions in the Baltic at Russia's expense. Albert published maps and brochures depicting and commenting on the course of the war and these were hugely popular. Another success was *Scandinavian Adventures, during a Residence of upwards of Twenty Years*, Llewellyn Lloyd's follow-up to *Field Sports of the North of Europe* from 1830.

* * *

The most important literary connection that Albert Bonnier made at this time was with a Swedish-speaking newspaperman two years older than he was, an author and PhD from Finland, as yet unknown in Sweden but well-known on the other side of the Bothnian Sea where he published poems, humorous articles and serials in the Helsinki newspaper *Helsingfors Tidningar*. His name was Zacharias (or Zachris) Topelius, a man of unusually varied talents.

When Topelius' play *Efter 50 år* (*After 50 Years*) was a success at Djurgårdsteatern in Stockholm in the summer of 1851, Albert secured the Swedish publication rights. This was the start of a relationship that was not only to be highly profitable for Albert Bonniers Förlag; it was also to grow into a close friendship between author and publisher.

Starting in 1854, Albert began publishing Topelius' historical suite *Fältskärns berättelser* (*The Surgeon's Stories*) in his novel library, and over the next three decades these tales formed the basis of a commercial success unparalleled in Albert's publishing career.

Otherwise, Albert's actions in these years were characterised by great caution, even greater than before. Several publishing plans were put on hold because he saw them as being too risky, including a conversation lexicon and an illustrated history of Sweden. One reason, besides the shadows cast by his father Gerhard's excesses, was that he had started a family. He was also gearing up for an investment that in a way meant a step into the unknown.

On 4 July 1856 he wrote to Adolf:

> May it have happened at a fortunate hour. I am in any case considerably anxious at the extravagance I am embarking on thereby.

A few days earlier, Albert Bonnier had bought a printworks.

* * *

In 1838, book printer Carl Fredrik Björklund had taken over a printworks that had previously been owned by Johan Hörberg and therefore bore the name Hörbergska boktryckeriet. Albert had often used Björklund's services and it was consequently natural for Björklund to turn to Albert when he had decided to move on. The negotiations were concluded without any difficulties and Albert gained access to the works on 1 October 1856. The printworks was located on Riddarholmen and adjoined Geijerska huset.

Björklund had expanded capacity with a high-speed cylinder press, but there was still a certain need for modernisation. True to his habit, the cautious Albert chose to delay: 'I do not intend to fling myself into extravagance in the first year but will let everything run in its old condition for the time being.' It was not until 1864 that he purchased two new presses from a manufacturer in Copenhagen.

As part of the deal, Albert gained an extremely competent printer, C. V. J. Psilander, who kept him carefully informed about the business. An equally important factor was that Albert was able to retain Björklund's client list, which included a long line of prestigious institutions, such as the Royal Swedish War Academy, the office of the Estate of the Clergy in the Riksdag, the Ministry of Civil Affairs, the Institute of Technology and the Swedish Land Survey Office.

Albert's purchase of the printworks became a minor irritant in his relationship with Felix, who opened a printworks of his own almost simultaneously in Gothenburg, where he had started thinking about publishing a newspaper.

Clearly Albert had not informed his brother of his plans in advance. In early October, Felix wrote Albert a letter whose tone was justifiably a little put out. 'In fact I had been counting on commissions from you and Adolf but nothing will come of that, will it, if (unbeknownst to me) you have really bought Björklund's printworks.'

Albert's new position as the director of a printworks – he was addressed as 'Patron' by Psilander, a form of address that soon stuck – meant that his interest in the bookshop on Norrbro waned even more.

This process had been going on for a while and had accelerated as Albert expanded his publishing business, but there was another problem that curbed his enthusiasm too; the bookshop was in disarray and revenues were slowly drying up. Already in failing health, the fifty-year-old Adolf was in no fit state to deal with all the shortcomings. Instead the burden on Albert increased. In summer 1855 he complained in a letter to Felix that several assistants 'were suffering from *laziness*' and at his own situation:

> Although in general I am up 1 to 2 hours earlier than before – and no single evening leave the shop before half past nine – when Betty has usually been sitting down there waiting a while – I still have not managed to see to either the Danish or the French business – yes, even Letters with Orders, which should have been sent long ago, have had to lie there waiting.

A further complication in relations between the two brothers was that Albert found Adolf's new wife Sophie hard to abide, perhaps because he missed Esther, who had been almost as close as a mother to him. As was so often the case though, Albert's loyalty to Adolf had the upper hand.

Even after the purchase of the printworks, Albert continued

to do what he could to help his older brother. And he was furious when Ludvig Josephson, who owed Adolf so much, left his position to start a competing business.

Even Felix, who had financial problems of his own to deal with, felt a growing despair at the state of affairs in Stockholm and sometimes found himself arguing with Adolf when deliveries to Gothenburg failed to appear. He was also weighed down by another family burden.

In 1855 Felix had taken on their nephew Adolf, one of their sister Hanne's sons, the result of an unhappy marriage in Copenhagen. Young Adolf was sent to school in Gothenburg, but Felix and his wife Charlotte grew tired of the boy, who, in their opinion, was good for nothing. Finally, on Christmas Eve 1857, they sent him by stagecoach to Stockholm for Felix's older brother Adolf to take over the responsibility. Adolf ignored this proposal, clearly afraid of how Sophie would react. Instead Albert and Betty had to step in, as Albert wrote to Felix, 'to take the lad in hand'.

This long letter, sent between Christmas and New Year, is one of few preserved documents in which Albert went into any detail on Betty's mental state. With a choice of words that reflects the patriarchal attitudes of the day, he set their tolerant, open relationship in contrast to Adolf and Sophie's fearful one:

I who barely comprehend whining, and thank God do not suffer from delicate nerves, have succeeded, despite my wife out of all the sisters-in-law probably by nature having the most hereditary tendency for suchlike, regarding which, for example could be cited her nervous illness during the period of our engagement, of which you have probably heard – have, thank God, succeeded in re-moulding her after the course of four years into a brisk and capable Character, whom I can inform of every piece of information, the sorrowful and the pleasant alike, without beating about the bush, and so ought a Companion, a wife, a fellow traveller through life, to be, and it is, as I see it, precisely the delight of marriage to have a creature to whom one can confide one's sadness, one's troubles and sorrows, and who shares them with us. Behaviour à la Adolf of going about for several days burdened by something unpleasant without telling my wife would be an impossibility for me in another respect too, as, with a strangely fine capacity for observation, as soon as something less pleasant has happened she reads it on my face, and it would thus be impossible to attempt to fool her.

In the meanwhile, a financial crisis hit Sweden.

* * *

The Crimean War, which ended with a painful Russian defeat, fuelled a speculative economic boom. This rapidly collapsed after the Treaty of Paris in 1856. In late August of the following year, large parts of Stockholm's Söder district were ominously destroyed by a raging fire.

In the wake of industrialisation, increased trade, improved communications and a modernised credit system, the international economy had become more interwoven than ever before.

Far away in New York, a financial crisis started that spread to London and then reached Hamburg and large German banks with Swedish connections. In the autumn it hit Sweden, where a wave of bankruptcies swept the nation. Panic broke out. People flocked to the banks to exchange notes for more secure coins of the realm.

In December 1857 one of the largest Swedish private banks, Skånes Enskilda Bank in Ystad, was on the verge of collapse. The situation was saved by Johan August Gripenstedt, who had become Minister for Finance in 1856. Practically single-handedly, Gripenstedt succeeded in averting a total collapse. With the help of financier André Oscar Wallenberg and a foreign loan the bank was saved and with it Sweden's financial system; the otherwise ultra-liberal Gripenstedt simply allowed the State to intervene. It was, one could say, the first 'banking crisis' – and a defining moment for Sweden's pragmatic political culture.

The crisis came extremely close to bankrupting one of the Bonnier brothers. This was not Adolf but Felix, whose printing investment had not produced the rapid results he had hoped for. Unlike Albert, he had no established customer base to fall back on. In December 1857 he appealed to Albert:

> It is with a heavy heart I write these lines, to tell you that I am *ruined*! Yes, *ruined*, unless I receive help – and it is to you I turn with prayers that you for God's sake will rescue me.

One could say it was at this moment that Albert Bonnier's perhaps sometimes excessive caution paid off. He was not yet an impressively rich man, but he had very consistently made sure to manage his own capital to serve every eventuality and had not even allowed the purchase of the printworks to disrupt this principle. Felix immediately gained access to the funds he needed. Once more, Albert's family loyalty took top priority.

Having worked in Adolf's shadow, Albert now emerged as the brother who would lay the foundation for the success that was to be associated with the Bonnier name. The fact that the investment in a printworks was a kind of declaration of independence on Albert's part is shown by the letter to Felix in which he accepted looking after Hanne's son:

I have bought the printworks, *merely* to be able to reserve for my own boy – if he may live – some anchor in an emergency – there at least I am my own master and able to do what I please.

On 20 June 1856, just a couple of weeks before Albert signed the contract on the printworks, Betty had given birth to a son. Betty loved double names and she and Albert first considered the ultra-Swedish-sounding name Sven Erik. Adolf ridiculed this with slightly sarcastic good humour, indicating that the friction between the brothers had not had any far-reaching consequences:

Sven Erik! Why not add Jöns, Nils, Måns, Pärsson – though the name itself makes no difference and can be changed in the future. God grant you and him all earthly happiness and success in this life.

The boy was finally given the name Karl Otto.

CHAPTER 5

WINDS OF CHANGE

**Felix launches *Göteborgs-Posten*.
Literature for the masses. A royal rejection.
The trade directory. Albert falls ill.
'Mussa' and Gustaf Banck. Railways and freedom of trade.
Rudolf Wall and *Dagens Nyheter*.
The printworks moves.
Albert's release. Adolf's death.**

_____

One of Sweden's largest and most historic daily newspapers, Gothenburg's *Göteborgs-Posten*, is usually associated with the surname Hjörne. It is less well known that the paper was founded by a Bonnier.

In October 1856, as the new owner of a printworks, Felix Bonnier wrote to his brother Albert:

> Numerous among our finer businessmen here want a new newspaper and are willing to fund it in lots between them – and I would be allowed to print it. This will be a brilliant enterprise for my printworks and a superb foundation for its existence.

The newspaper, which according to Felix was to be *'liberal* but reasonably sensible', needed an editor and Felix wondered if Albert could suggest someone suitable. Albert could. In early 1858, when Felix's newspaper plans had solidified, Albert recommended his good friend Rudolf Wall, who had recently been forced to shut down *Friskytten*. He wrote to Felix:

> By coincidence, Wall (who invited me the other day to the truly elegant wake for Friskytten he was holding at Hotel de Suède) came into the shop yesterday afternoon quite as if he had been sent for (...) It is true that the man lacks what they term academic studies (...) However he has a good (*almost brilliant*) head and above all *knows the business*.

Via Albert, Felix offered Rudolf Wall a generous salary. Wall turned it down. He did not want to move to Gothenburg and become a competitor to his and Albert's friend Sven Adolf Hedlund, editor-in-chief of *Göteborgs Handels- och Sjöfarts-Tidning, GHT*, usually known simply as *Handelstidningen*. But the most important reason for Wall's refusal was that he was harbouring newspaper plans of his own in Stockholm. Six years later, in 1864, he started *Dagens Nyheter*, with Albert's assistance.

This makes for a strange circumstance in the history of the Swedish press – *Dagens Nyheter*, today Sweden's largest morning newspaper, might perhaps never have come about had its founder instead followed Albert Bonnier's advice and become editor-in-chief of the second largest. *Göteborgs-Posten* started to come out regularly in January 1859.

One of the first high-profile employees of the new

newspaper was Adolf, Albert and Felix's good friend Oscar Patric Sturzen-Becker, a cutting and witty character who wrote under the pseudonym Orvar Odd. Like the proposal to Rudolf Wall this was proof as good as any that the Bonnier brothers had built up a network of sharp pens.

* * *

In Sweden, the years around 1860 were relatively uneventful in a purely literary sense, with individual exceptions such as Viktor Rydberg's *Den siste athenaren* (*The Last Athenian*) from 1859, which was first published as a serial in *Handelstidningen*. Rydberg was later to become one of the foremost names in Albert Bonnier's stable of authors.

For Albert, this was still a formative period, filled with hard work. The printworks needed attending to, as did the publishing company and the bookshop, where Adolf needed all the help he could get. Moreover, Albert's family was growing. On 17 November 1857, Betty gave birth to a daughter, Eva Fredrika. Her middle name was a clear nod, in Swedish, to Albert's deeply missed older sister Frederikke.

The publishing company's position in the market for literature was boosted a couple of years later when Albert started to publish cheap pamphlets aimed at the general population. Called *Öreskrifter för folket*, emphasising their low price (in öre), one of their most popular authors was Pehr Thomasson, a self-taught farmer's son from Blekinge, whose depictions of popular life such as *Kung Oskar och Skogvaktaren* (*King Oskar and the Forester*) and *En fyndig bonde* (*An Ingenious Farmer*) attracted a large readership. Thomasson had come to Albert's attention thanks to his novel *En arbetares lefnadsöden eller Slaflifvet i Sverige* (*The Life of a Worker or Slavery in Sweden*), an early predecessor of the proletarian novels of the twentieth century.

Öreskrifter became a major commercial success.

Once more, Albert was the right man at the right time. From the mid-nineteenth century onwards, as literacy increased and the middle class grew, demand for printed matter soared. Some 167 issues of *Öreskrifter* came out before the series was shut down in 1900, the year of Albert's death.

However, a publisher's duties not only involve publishing, they also involve turning manuscripts down. In early 1858 Albert was offered a poetry collection written by the Duke of Östergötland, Prince Oscar, later Oscar II, a member of the royal family with literary ambitions. These unintentionally comic paeans to the fatherland, *Ur svenska flottans minnen* (*Memories of the Swedish Navy*), had first been submitted anonymously to a competition announced by the Swedish Academy, which had awarded them a prize. Bernhard von Beskow, the permanent secretary, was particularly impressed: 'It is as if a fresh sea breeze runs through his song, and there is often something touching about the piety with which he paints the old naval heroes.'

Now the prince was looking for a publisher.

Albert Bonnier received an enquiry to purchase the manuscript for 1,250 riksdaler and then print 2,500 copies. Here he was faced with a dilemma. On the one hand, he instantly recognised that the poems were substandard, but on the other, they had been written by a prince well-connected with the arbiters of taste of the Swedish Academy. To be on the safe side, he asked Felix for advice, who answered with his customary acerbity: 'In these dismal times the public will send him and his poetry to the devil and I would most strongly advise against the purchase.'

Albert said no.

The book was instead printed by Norstedts. The poems are virtually unreadable today, but they are at least free from some of Oscar's worst excesses.

In the poem 'Psilander', about a Swedish naval officer who refused to strike the flag for the English navy in 1704, the prince had written the following:

> One ship alone he had – and small it was –
> but – men it bore, not easy to force,
> and iron from our ancient Swedish hills so narrow,
> and a captain with steel itself in his marrow.

In the margin of the manuscript, someone from the Academy had written 'May be omitted'. In his entertaining depiction of Oscar's literary tribulations, *Skaldernas konung* (*King of Poets*), literary scholar Germund Michanek gives a blunt verdict on the Academy's recommendation, pointing out that in following it and cutting the whole strophe, Oscar failed to be the man who introduced the Man of Steel to world literature.

* * *

Albert Bonnier remained in the shadow of competitors such as Lars Johan Hierta, but it was in these years that Albert started an anything but literary project that over time was to provide much of the financial foundation for Sweden's leading publishing company in the field of quality literature.

It all really began with a failed attempt by Albert and Adolf's publisher friend Philipp Meyer to launch a Mercantile Directory, a kind of catalogue of addresses and other information about businesses across the country in 1855. Meyer's directory failed due to poor-quality production with numerous errors, but Albert nevertheless felt that the idea itself, which had been taken from Denmark and Germany, was an excellent one: a new marketing channel for the entrepreneurial zeal that was starting to gain pace after the abolition of the guild system and the expansion of transport and communications.

The railway had come to Sweden, eagerly cheered on by Albert, not least in articles in *Svea*. The first electric telegraph lines had been taken into use in 1853, while the introduction of stamps made postage easier.

All Albert needed to do was to carry out the directory project with greater accuracy than Meyer – and find a suitable editor.

Albert turned to his friend Rudolf Wall, who lacked permanent commitments after shutting down *Friskytten* and was now earning a living from sporadic articles in *Aftonbladet* and *Handelstidningen*. Wall said yes to Albert's offer.

Rudolf Wall, who had started his career as a messenger boy for Lars Johan Hierta, was not only a competent journalist; he was also interested in business and engaged in speculation, albeit with limited success. 'I am amassing capital in spirits and grain,' he wrote, boasting slightly, to S. A. Hedlund at *Handelstidningen*. As far as amassing capital went, it was a bit hit and miss. Wall did not enjoy any major success as a wholesaler in either of these products, but the combination of journalistic talent and an interest in commerce – and possibly also their friendship – meant Albert saw Rudolf Wall as being made for the trade directory job.

Sveriges Handels-Kalender came out for the first time in May 1859, edited by Wall, and this investment soon produced real dividends. To begin with the directory was issued every two years, becoming an annual publication in 1895. Wall, though, left the editor's post after a few years as he had decided to start the daily paper *Dagens Nyheter*.

It is hard to imagine the success of Albert Bonniers Förlag in the decades that followed without the significant income generated by the trade directory. In his history of the publishing company and the family, Albert's son and successor Karl Otto wrote: 'Without any exaggeration, it can be said that Sveriges Handelskalender has become one of the most solid foundations of the Bonnier publishing business.'

The directory reflected the dynamic expansion of Swedish trade. The first edition had 95 pages in one small volume; barely a hundred years later the directory was divided into three volumes with 3,500 pages in total.

The directory format was not new to Albert, who, after all, had made his name with the literary annual *Svea*, his 'baby', in the 1840s. And a few years before the launch of the trade directory, he had taken over the publication of *Sveriges Ridderskaps och Adels kalender*, the directory of the Swedish peerage. This had been founded by Gabriel Anrep, an early genealogy enthusiast, who Albert sensibly kept on as editor.

Anrep, who edited the directory until 1903, was not only skilled and precise; he was also fearless and therefore controversial in noble circles, because he had no compunction about publishing less than flattering information, in which Albert backed him up.

A few years after Albert's death, Anrep confided in a letter to Karl Otto:

I have never been on a good footing with the nobility, particularly women, who could not forgive me for revealing their ages. In some dubious verses in Allehanda a couple of years after the directory was published, it was proposed that I be both hanged and burned for that damned black book – this opus was inspired by Countess Gyllenhaal, née d'Orozco, born in 1796, who swore that I had made her ten years older, thereby forgetting that she had a son, born in 1820, and had been married for several years prior to his birth.

On the literary front, the first half of the 1860s also brought some commercial strokes of luck for Albert. He started publishing Elias Sehlstedt's collected works. Forgotten now but highly popular in his day, Sehlstedt worked as a customs inspector in Sandhamn, but alongside this employment had published minor works of poetry with different publishers, including Adolf Bonnier. They were well received and Albert decided to buy the rights to everything Sehlstedt had written. *Samlade sånger och visor* (*Collected Songs*) was published in five parts in 1861–76 and became one of the publishing firm's top-selling works. To posterity Sehlstedt is best known for the song 'Litet bo jag sätta vill', in praise of simple country life.

Another success was *Bilder ur Werkligheten* (*Pictures from Reality*) by Albert's idol August Blanche, a collected series of previously published short stories which sold in large editions. Albert also published popular plays, including Frans Hodell's *Andersson, Pettersson och Lundström*, which were welcomed by a wide audience.

But the most important element was his continued

relationship with Zacharias Topelius, who achieved great success with *The Surgeon's Stories*. This was followed, starting in 1865, by yet another top-selling suite from Topelius' pen, *Läsning för barn* (*Reading for Children*).

* * *

In practice, Albert Bonnier had three jobs, one at the printworks, one at the publishing house and one in the bookshop. In 1861 the high demands these made of him and the workload involved caused an otherwise hale and hearty Albert to largely ignore the fact that he had contracted jaundice, or hepatitis. His condition worsened and his doctor prescribed a trip to a German spa. Naturally, he took Betty with him, writing to Felix:

> I would not have been able to make up my mind to go, had I had to travel alone, as if I had, I might have been bored to death, but as my dear Betty is coming with me, it ought to be bearable.
>
> And after having been a nurse for several weeks at least, she highly deserves to enjoy herself a little.

This was the first of many long trips abroad that Albert and Betty made together. They left in May and were not home again until October. After a couple of months in Germany, they moved on to destinations including Geneva, Marseilles and Nice. After having returned to Germany – Albert found Nice 'cold and unpleasant' – he concluded by fulfilling a promise to Betty; they travelled to Paris and stayed there for at least a month. On his return, Albert was largely recovered.

In his demanding roles as a publisher, bookseller and director of a printworks, Albert Bonnier had never been absent for such a long time and therefore felt a nagging worry over how all his undertakings at home in Sweden would manage without him. The printworks was run by the reliable Psilander and in the bookshop his brother-in-law Joseph Rubenson stepped in to manage the till, as Adolf could not be counted on as he had in the past. And at home, since 1859 a two-storey building that Albert had had built on a corner plot on Norrmalmstorg, he and Betty were able to rely on a person who came to play an extremely important role in the family's life, Marie Banck, known as 'Mussa'.

Here quite a touching element in the more personal story of Albert Bonnier is revealed, confirmation that the sometimes hard-headed businessman had what was for his time a highly unprejudiced approach to social conventions and class barriers.

Marie Banck, from a simple soldier's croft in Östergötland, had been employed as a servant girl by Albert and Betty in 1855. As the family grew with the birth of Jenny, Karl Otto and Eva, she became their beloved nursery maid, then housekeeper, and after Betty's death she ran the home. She remained faithful to the Bonnier household until her death in 1906 and her portrait was lovingly painted several times by Eva.

But there is more to the story of the Bancks and the Bonniers than that.

'Mussa' had a younger brother, Nils Gustaf, usually known only as Gustaf, whom she recommended in 1858 when Albert was looking for a new servant lad after several less than successful recruitment attempts. Gustaf Banck was employed despite his credentials stating only that he 'understood how to care for horses'.

Albert soon realised that the young man was unusually gifted: intelligent, energetic and with a head for detail. He made sure that Gustaf, who had had no schooling, was taught Swedish, writing, arithmetic and bookkeeping, and allowed him to advance in the publishing business and then move into a flat in the new printworks property on Ålandsgatan, where he lived almost up to his death in 1912.

In the words of Karl Otto Bonnier, Gustaf Banck was 'invaluable' as Albert's closest and for a long time only employee in the publishing office, and was responsible for bookkeeping and the cash book. In later years Gustaf was able to title himself 'accountant' and was called, with respectful teasing, 'Bonnier's bank'.

The Bonnier archive contains numerous letters from Banck in neat handwriting in which he informs a travelling Albert about details of the business. The letters are always addressed to 'Herr Patron' and Banck seems to have seen it as one of his foremost duties to soothe a boss who was easily worried, sometimes unnecessarily. It will suffice to reproduce a condensed quote from one of these many letters, dated February 1870:

> The cashbox has lasted very well so far for wages and other things (...) Everything is good here at home.
> Humbly
> Gustaf Banck.

Gustaf Banck was without doubt one of the most important contributors to the publishing business in the second half of the nineteenth century – and Albert's generous opinion of him appears fully justified:

Banck is and remains the cornerstone of the business
– mainly through the seriousness, conscientiousness,
industry and interest he constantly devotes to its
affairs.

* * *

Towards the end of the 1850s Sweden embarked on an
unparalleled period of social reform. It was driven by two
members of the government, Minister of Justice Louis De
Geer and Minister for Finance Johan August Gripenstedt, both
caught up in the winds of liberalism of the era. The pace of
change was dizzying.

In 1858 unmarried women were granted the opportunity
to apply for their legal majority, a first miniscule step on
the way towards greater gender equality. Five years later, all
unmarried women over the age of twenty-five gained their
majority automatically. New career paths opened for women;
in 1861, for example, women were allowed to train as dentists.

Interest rates on loans were unrestricted. Compulsory
passports were abolished. The old parishes and their meetings
were replaced by the *kommun* as the administrative body, a
reform from 1862 that reduced the local power of the church
and the priests. A ban was imposed on distilling spirits for
household use.

In June 1864 an ordinance introduced freedom of trade.
In the text one can almost hear the last chains of the guild
system and mercantilism bursting loose:

A Swedish man or woman is entitled (...) in a town or
in the country to engage in trade or manufacturing,

crafts or other work; to export goods to a foreign location or import therefrom and to transport goods between domestic locations.

After long drawn-out debate and a hard battle, in 1865–6 a representational reform was implemented which replaced the Riksdag of the Estates with a bicameral system. Sweden joined the European free trade system that had grown up by entering into a treaty with France.

Albert's sympathies naturally lay with the liberal reform camp, which he indirectly supported through his publishing firm. In the wake of the representational reform, he published the militant newspaper editor Adolf Hedin's manifesto for a newly formed liberal party, Nyliberalerna, entitled *What the people expect of the new representation*. It set out demands for an expansion of the franchise, parliamentarism and female emancipation. Nyliberalerna did not achieve any major success but the party is considered to have been the first Swedish experiment in modern party politics.

One can definitely talk of a new Swedish self-confidence, particularly economically, a hope in the famous words of Esaias Tegnér, 'to reconquer Finland within Sweden's borders'. This was manifested among other things in Sweden's first international industrial exhibition, inspired by London's Great Exhibition of 1851.

The General Industrial Exposition of Stockholm was opened by Queen Lovisa in June 1866 and ran until October. It was held in Karl XIII's torg, the square that is now Kungsträdgården. Here Sweden-Norway, Denmark and the Russian Grand Duchy of Finland displayed the best of what they had to offer in the industrial and cultural spheres. The opening ceremony opened up hitherto unseen mass media opportunities. The picture of Queen Lovisa on the podium of honour, taken by Court photographer Johannes Jaeger, is considered to be the first Swedish reportage photo.

All this naturally delighted Albert Bonnier, who to judge from letters from the 1860s was in at least fleeting contact with J. A. Gripenstedt, the foremost proponent of reform in the Government.

Like the entrepreneur he was, Albert made sure to derive commercial advantage from the accelerating developments. The same year as the Stockholm Exposition, with the mainline rail network expanding at a rapid pace and travel growing easier, he was the first in Sweden to produce an illustrated travel guide, *Illustreradt Sverige*. His trusted employee Gustaf Thomée was the editor. Success was assured. The guide was printed in several new editions in the decades that followed. Seizing the moment, Albert published a small guide to Stockholm at the same time.

What must have pleased Albert most of all in this wave of reform, however, was that he and his companions in faith were able to take further strides on the road towards emancipation. The provision whereby Jews were prohibited from settling freely in towns other than Stockholm, Gothenburg, Norrköping and Karlskrona had largely been abolished in 1854. Six years later, Jews also gained the right to settle in rural areas and own real estate there. In 1863 the ban on marriage with people of other faiths was abolished and in conjunction with the representational reform of 1865–6, Jews were given the right to vote in Riksdag elections. Resistance to reforms of this type slowly tailed off but antisemitic attitudes lived stubbornly on in some places, fanned by less scrupulous newspapers like the scandal sheet *Fäderneslandet*, in which Jews and Jewish interests were incessantly attacked, often accompanied by drawings of stereotypes that lingered on far into the twentieth century: Jews as swarthy individuals with big, hooked noses and brandishing a coin purse.

However, the reforms and the economic upturn, which initially benefitted well-off urbanites, could not hide the fact that Sweden was still an underdeveloped nation, where the majority of the population lived in rural areas with widespread poverty. This became tragically obvious in 1867–9 when the harvests failed and Norrland especially, but also Småland were hit by famine. Emigration to America had already begun on a small scale, but now it soared, reaching its peak towards the end of the century.

* * *

In terms of technology, the most tangible change that began in the mid-nineteenth century was the expansion of the railways. The first two links in what was to be a State-financed mainline network, from Malmö to Lund and from Gothenburg to Jonsered, were opened in 1856. In barely ten years, 1856–65, the length of Sweden's railways grew from 66 to 1,305 kilometres. This was to have direct consequences for Albert Bonnier's engagement in a newspaper project that is now almost synonymous with the name of Bonnier.

Railway enthusiast Albert realised that a new and faster means of transport favoured an idea, the seeds of which had come from Rudolf Wall. In spring 1864 Albert wrote to Felix, who was also privy to Rudolf Wall's plans:

A Morning paper here I think would certainly have many Chances of success (...) Not merely for Stockholm – but for Rural areas, which, by the Morning trains, could naturally obtain such a newspaper *at the same time as* the Evening papers for the previous day – but this could always include all their news and more news that had come in since too.

He told Felix that Rudolf Wall had urged him to publish and print such a daily paper a year earlier, but that he had refused 'for fear of night work' – 'That requires a double crew of energetic young people – and being young oneself.'

These lines, expressing interest but also Albert's typical caution, are the start of the story of Bonniers and *Dagens Nyheter*.

In 1864 Rudolf Wall was seeking support from several potential stakeholders, including Albert and Felix Bonnier and Lars Johan Hierta, Wall's old benefactor. Stockholm only had one morning paper, *Stockholms Dagblad*, which was mostly an organ for advertising. Other newspapers in the capital came out in the afternoon. Wall's idea was to follow French, British and Danish role models, including *Le Petit Journal* in Paris, and publish a newspaper capable of competing both on lower price and on getting the news out more quickly.

'Albert Bonnier was enthusiastic about the idea,' wrote grandson Åke Bonnier in his family chronicle.

That is the edited version of the truth.

Wall's intention was to form a limited company but Albert and other potential investors dropped out and the company did not come into being. Albert had originally signed up for a modest stake, ten shares, but withdrew the offer. Felix did not sign up for any shares either.

In Albert's case there were several different explanations for his doubts. He was more than keen to be involved in publishing a liberal morning paper in Stockholm, but was sceptical about Rudolf Wall's business sense and the idea of printing the newspaper at night.

Another factor that contributed to Albert's disquiet was that at about the end of March or early April of 1864, potentially calamitous news had reached him.

A major railway line was to be constructed across Riddarholmen. This meant that Geijerska huset, a building on the verge of falling down which housed the Hörbergska tryckeriet printworks, would have to be demolished. In April Albert wrote to Felix that this would lead to 'much confusion and higher costs'. In December, barely two weeks before the first issue of *Dagens Nyheter* came out, he cited the impending demolition as a reason for his not having bought shares, once more in a letter to Felix:

> Wall's enterprise seems hardly likely to come off; he has not managed to get enough shares (...) I had signed up for ten shares but only provided that I would get to print the paper until my shares were repaid or until I had earned out their value. It seems unlikely that this will be possible, partly since I will be leaving Riddarholmen next autumn and it is uncertain whether I will find premises in the city.

Albert also had a tendency to worry about what he himself considered to be his financially straitened circumstances. Earlier that year he had complained to Felix using phrases that were hardly founded in reality: 'I am terribly short of money here – to the extent that soon I won't know how to go on.'

There was also another reason for Albert's doubts. This did not involve finances but politics.

Rudolf Wall and Albert Bonnier were both liberals and their political sympathies seem to have been one of the cornerstones of their friendship, but on one point they differed. Wall disliked Scandinavianism while Albert, born in Denmark, was a passionate advocate.

In 1864 the situation had come to a head in the Schleswig-Holstein War between Denmark and the great German powers of Prussia and Austria, who attacked Denmark to regain control of the disputed duchies. The war ended in a crushing defeat for Denmark, and in the Treaty of Vienna in October the same year, Denmark lost the duchies of Schleswig, Holstein and Lauenburg. Sympathy for Denmark was strong in Sweden and more than four hundred Swedes joined the Danish army as volunteers.

The conflict made its way into Albert's publishing through *Taflor och skildringar från Slesvigska kriget* (*Pictures and Descriptions of the Schleswig War*), the result of a collab-oration with a Danish publisher. However, it did not enjoy the same success as his similar work on the Crimean War ten years earlier.

In the same letter to Felix in which he set out the practical reasons why he had refrained from buying shares in *Dagens Nyheter*, Albert added a couple of lines on an additional point on which he distrusted Wall: 'Since I fairly certainly believe that he wants to counteract Scandinavianism, I cannot deny that I would preferably avoid having any rag in that bundle of washing.'

Despite these doubts, Albert finally undertook to print

Dagens Nyheter, whose first edition was published on 23 December 1864. The price per single copy was five öre, less than for *Stockholms Dagblad*, *Aftonbladet*, *Nya Dagligt Allehanda* and *Posttidningen*. In his 'Announcement', Rudolf Wall wrote that the intention of the newspaper was 'to seriously address the major questions of the day and of the country':

> In all these questions *liberty* is our watchword and our aim. The road to achieving it is long and beset by many obstacles. We cannot hope to eradicate many in the comparatively short lifetime of a newspaper, but it would please us were we able to contribute to the fall of one or two.

One of the 'obstacles' to be eradicated was the Riksdag of the Estates. And almost exactly a year after the arrival of *Dagens Nyheter*, that decision was finally taken. It was such aims, quite radical for their time, that later led August Strindberg to give *Dagens Nyheter* the name 'Red Cap' in *The Red Room*.

To begin with, *Dagens Nyheter*'s small editorial team and office were housed three floors up in the Hörbergska tryckeriet building on Riddarholmen where the paper was printed for its first nine months, albeit with certain technical problems; the press was not big enough for the job. Operations subsequently moved to Stora Nygatan, where Wall gained a printworks of his own.

The new morning paper was a success. Circulation rapidly increased, hitting its initial target of 5,000 copies in just a few years and reaching 10,000 in 1870. After ten years, in 1874, *Dagens Nyheter* finally became a limited company.

Albert Bonnier's printworks problem was also solved.

In May 1865 he bought a large property at numbers 15 and 17 Ålandsgatan, now Mäster Samuelsgatan. It cost him 150,000 riksdaler. He had some smaller adjoining buildings demolished and replaced them with a printing house on two floors plus an attic. He also set up an office for himself, relatively modest, but somewhat more impressive than the cubbyhole he had presided over on Riddarholmen. It was to be his focal point and that of the publishing business for many years to come.

It could be said that Albert Bonnier was one of the 'godfathers' of *Dagens Nyheter* in the sense that he provided the initial printing capacity, but when it came to ownership, he continued to be wary of proposals from Rudolf Wall. Albert remained unconvinced that the newspaper would prove a profitable business in the long term. He made some supportive purchases of shares and out of loyalty he took over a holding from his nephew Isidor when the latter found himself in financial difficulties. At his death Albert Bonnier only owned 129 shares in *Dagens Nyheter*.

It was not until 1909 that a Bonnier became the chairman of the board and holder of the single largest shareholding. This was Karl Otto, Albert's son, who made an oft-quoted promise to never exploit his ownership to exercise 'unwarranted intervention in the newspaper's editorial management and independence'.

* * *

The move from the centrally located Riddarholmen to Ålandsgatan in the more remote district of Norrmalm launched a new phase for the book publisher Albert Bonnier. He could not count on retaining as clients the Government authorities, parliamentary committees and other public institutions that had used Högbergska tryckeriet due to it being located on their doorstep. To keep the presses on Ålandsgatan rolling, he needed to prioritise publishing books to a much greater extent, mainly literature, but also textbooks.

Albert had published his first textbook back in 1846. It was a French grammar one – and not that odd a choice considering the Bonnier family's oft-cited French roots. In the 1860s textbook publishing took off further, especially after the move, with titles such as *Matematiska och fysikaliska problemer* (*Problems in Mathematics and Physics*), a German Grammar and a history textbook.

Finally, Albert Bonnier had gained an opportunity to dedicate himself entirely to his own publishing and printing business. At the end of 1865 he left the bookshop in Norrbro Bazaar with Adolf's agreement. This was no easy decision considering the strong bond between the brothers but at the same time it was a relief; for several years Albert had been weighed down by the burden of helping his older brother in a bookshop that was in a state of increasing collapse.

* * *

Adolf had been in poor health for some time, exacerbated by many years of hard work and now also worry over the state of the business. Several trips to German spas had failed to improve matters. He developed a hernia and when he fell down the stairs at home, it became so painful that surgery was necessary. Something went wrong and gangrene set in. After a few days' fighting for his life, Adolf Bonnier died on

31 March 1867.

Albert informed Felix of his death:

Peace be with him. Any better or more good-hearted person would be hard to find, and his truly gentle childlike mind and tender heart will remain in the memory of all those who knew him well.

In his chronicle of the Bonnier family of booksellers and publishers, Åke Bonnier quoted bookshop historian August Hånell, who described Adolf's efforts as 'almost epoch-making' in mainly two areas: through his international connections he had given Sweden a 'proper foreign bookshop' and simultaneously created 'a staff of expert assistants, who then took the good ideas they had obtained under Adolf Bonnier's management further in their own independent operations'.

Now all that remained was for Albert and Adolf's brother-in-law Abraham Hirsch to fulfil their duty to Adolf as executors of his estate.

Albert was horrified by what he found: 'Unfortunately all is in chaos and disorder.'

One of the steps that Albert and Abraham saw themselves forced into was to take Adolf and Sophie's son Isidor out of school, where he only had a few months left until matriculation. At the school, Stockholms Lyceum, Isidor happened to be a classmate of August Strindberg, a coincidence whose import no-one had any reason to think anything of in 1867. Strindberg would not write his first work, the drama *Master Olof*, until five years later.

Isidor was instead put to work in the bookshop, something Adolf had refused to do. When Albert explained the step to

Felix, he revealed a certain lack of respect for formal education. He himself was a self-made man and he clearly felt that other Bonniers ought to follow the same path:

> Many times I have urged Adolf to place Isidor in a bookshop here at home and then do a course abroad – but Heavens, as the boy has a good head he absolutely had to have his white cap and Academic credentials.

Much later, Karl Otto Bonnier described his father's reaction to the figures he was confronted with when going through Albert's estate:

> He, who in his own affairs had always had the principle of no loans! No business that requires placing oneself in debt! became more and more despairing over the position of the estate and the lack of liquidity.

Albert even considered entering into an agreement with the creditors to reduce the debts, well aware that this would be a stain on Adolf's reputation as a bookseller and publisher. The situation turned out not to be quite as desperate as he had feared. The creditors accepted a four-year payment plan for which Albert and Abraham Hirsch stood surety. Under the plan, the debts were paid off, to Albert's great relief. Isidor Bonnier took over running his father's book publishing business but handed the whole business over to his cousin Karl Otto Bonnier and Albert Bonniers Förlag in 1904.

Adolf Bonnier is often overlooked in the history of Bonniers, a surname that has also become a brand. The spotlight has been focused on Albert and Karl Otto. In a way, this is fair enough. It was Albert and then Karl Otto who expanded the publishing firm and forged the most important and long-lasting literary contacts. They were undoubtedly more highly skilled businessmen than Adolf. Still, it is impossible to understand the triumphs of Albert, Karl Otto and their successors without taking into account the role of Adolf Bonnier as a trailblazer, inspiration and – in Albert's case – a kind of father figure.

* * *

When the 1860s drew to a close – a decade that Albert Bonnier found challenging and turbulent with *Dagens Nyheter*, the move of the printworks and Adolf's demise – he was in great need of recovery and relaxation. And he was to have it. On 12 December 1869 Albert and Betty left for Rome. They planned to be away for six months. It was the start of one of the happiest episodes in a marriage that was at times weighed down by problems.

CHAPTER 6

WRITING FRIENDS
AND OTHERS

**Happy days in Rome. Emancipation at last!
Viktor Rydberg and Zacharias Topelius.
Pseudonymous women. Good times. Family and friends.
Betty's darkness.**

————

The choice of Rome as the main destination for the Bonniers'
long journey was primarily because Betty wanted to visit 'the
eternal city' for the sun, the warm weather and the culture. As
far as Albert was concerned, the destination would have been
interesting for another reason too. Italy, formerly politically
split into smaller states, was in the final phase of the unification
process, *Il Risorgimento*, an offshoot of the ideas of national
liberalism of 1848 that had so left their mark on him.

As far as warm weather went, the trip was less successful;
Rome in the winter of 1870 was chilly and damp. However,
that did not prevent Betty Bonnier from enjoying every bit of
all the sights and the light-hearted, relaxed social life in the
small Scandinavian artists' colony that received her and Albert
with open arms. Her many letters home to the children and
her sister Rosalie Rubenson bear witness to that.

A hundred years after Betty's birth, in 1928, her son Karl Otto had these letters from Betty printed in a collection that he entitled *Minnen från Rom* (*Memories from Rome*) and dedicated to his own children. The purpose, he wrote in the foreword, was to 'bring her memory to life and give you, her descendants, an idea of how enthusiastic, interested and loved by all Betty Bonnier was'.

After a few weeks in Germany, taking in Dresden, Albert and Betty travelled on to Italy via Munich and Switzerland. Following a few days in Rome, their first long stop was in Naples, where they joined up with a couple of friends from Stockholm, the Norwegian art historian Lorentz Dietrichson and his wife Mathilde, a painter. Together they explored Pompei and Salerno before returning to Rome for a stay that was to last six weeks.

In Rome they made the acquaintance of new and exciting people including the composer Edvard Grieg and his wife Nina, professor of aesthetics Gustaf Ljunggren from Lund, the Danish painter Vilhelm Rosenstand and sculptor John Börjeson, later professor at the Royal Swedish Academy of Fine Arts and the sculptor of the famous mounted statue of the conqueror of Skåne, Karl X Gustav, in Stortorget in Malmö. They visited museums, churches and exhibitions, enjoyed food and wine and generally spent their time in a far more carefree way than at home in Stockholm. Betty's happiness knew no bounds:

> It is impossible for me to describe how I am enjoying myself here and what I feel here – as here one enjoys things not in one way but in hundreds, and one passes whole days utterly exhilarated, spiritually in the mornings and physically in the evenings.

John Börjeson in particular was quite taken with Betty, who in one of the letters recounted what seems to have been a fairly typical dinner in those happy weeks in Rome:

> At about half past ten, all the women left and some of the men, but as Alb. then lit a cigar I was allowed to stay, so then I was the only woman and they sang a Danish quartet and then when I said that must be for me because I was the only woman left, Börjeson said they would sing a song just for me.

A little later during the stay in Rome, Betty and John Börjeson began to use the familiar 'du' when addressing each other, unusual on such short acquaintance, but entirely in line with the informal atmosphere that prevailed.

The contact with Börjeson led to Albert and Betty commissioning him to make busts of them and the sittings became part of their routine in Rome. Betty wrote:

> Yes, this new life we lead here, in all its simplicity, amusement and strangeness, is a special pleasure for me. My days run like this: between 7 and 10 I go and sit for Börjeson, such fun; I usually stay there until he goes to eat breakfast, and then we make an excursion or visit some collections, rest a little at home, at 6 we go to eat, and it is cheerful I must say as we gather together in dribs and drabs, first one and then the next, sometimes 2 full tables.

The extent to which Albert, with his interest in politics, gained an opportunity to demonstrate his sympathies for the formation of the young Italian state up close is not shown by his correspondence; he was mainly in touch with Gustaf Banck, who kept him informed of the publishing house's affairs. But in late March Albert made a detour to Naples to attend a ball in honour of King Victor Emanuel, regent of the free Italy declared in Turin in 1861.

Albert and Betty Bonnier left Rome on 21 April. Their departure was preceded by a farewell dinner at the taverna *Piccolo Colosseo*, where Lorentz Dietrichson performed a song he had written in honour of his friends. It ended:

> But as you now leave us and our merry life,
> The room echoes with cheers for Bonnier and Wife!
> 'That was nice,' said ye,
> 'Hurrah for you two!' said we.

The day before they left, Betty wrote a final letter from Rome:

> Farewell Rome, farewell all friends there, some of whom one may perhaps see again, others probably not, some certainly not – as everything here is a dream, but what a pleasant dream it has been; it will probably be quite difficult to accustom oneself once more to conventional manners, but it must be done – No, farewell now, else I grow melancholy.

What no-one could have known at the time was that those happy days in Rome were only to bring brief respite. Three years after their return, Betty Bonnier sank into her deepest darkness yet.

* * *

Adjoining the family home on the corner of Hamngatan and what is now Kungsträdgårdsgatan, Albert Bonnier had established a private flat of his own. In autumn 1869, when he and Betty were preparing for their Italian journey, he offered it to a friend to stay in when visiting Stockholm:

> I have a very nice little bachelor flat of a few rooms with a hallway (yes even with a small kitchen) and a quite separate entrance, on the third floor with views over Berzelii park (...) The rent will not be dear – as I want none at all (...) There is only one person in the rooms, but he will definitely not disturb you – as he is unfortunately dead. It is a bust of August Blanche (modelled by Kjellberg). However, I shall hope that his spirit inspires you.

His friend replied by return of post:

> I was just sitting debating where I will stay in Stockholm with a couple of female acquaintances when your letter arrived and resolved the question in the most pleasant way. A nice flat, views over Berzelii park! What more could one want? Communing in solitary moments with the shade of friend Blanche will remind me of an upright soul and friendly brother in Apollo!
>
> But the terms of the lease are perhaps quite strict, as a service of friendship such as you have offered me is very difficult to repay (...) When you come home I hope to have something in the literary way to offer you.

The friend was Viktor Rydberg, recently elected to the second chamber of the Riksdag as a representative for Gothenburg. Rydberg wrote to Albert that thereby the city 'has gained a member of the Riksdag who does not consider himself up to the task but who, nevertheless, will come up to Stockholm, to do his job to the best of his abilities'.

Born in 1828, today Rydberg is best known for poems such as the Christmas verse 'Tomten' (translated into English as 'The Christmas Tomten'), 'Betlehems stjärna' ('Star of Bethlehem') which was set to music by Alice Tegnér, and possibly 'Den nya Grottesången' ('The New Song of Grotti'), his attack on the factory system. In the nineteenth century he was not only one of Sweden's most renowned authors but also a central cultural figure, who was to be awarded an honorary doctorate by Uppsala University, and become a member of the Swedish Academy and a professor of cultural history and then art history at Stockholms Högskola (the forerunner of Stockholm University).

Rydberg reached this celebrated position despite a miserable background. His mother died of cholera when he was six years old, his father descended into alcoholism and he was boarded with foster parents. After this unhappy childhood, he went in for a career in journalism and, via the local paper *Jönköpingsbladet*, made his way to a post at *Handelstidningen* in Gothenburg, where S. A. Hedlund became his friend, mentor and adviser. It was in Gothenburg that he first became acquainted with Albert, through Hedlund and Felix Bonnier, in about 1860.

At that time Rydberg had written three novels, the pirate story *Fribytaren på Östersjön* (*The Freebooter of the Baltic*), the medieval love story *Singoalla*, and *The Last Athenian*, set in fourth-century Athens, in which the culture of the ancient world collides with Christianity. But it was not until 1862 that he gained fame, not with a literary work but with *Bibelns lära om Kristus* (*The Teaching of the Bible Concerning Christ*), a study in the field of theology, which was increasingly absorbing his interest. The book, which questions the divinity of Christ, reflected Rydberg's critical attitude to religious dogma and sparked powerful counter-reactions, but also appreciation in radical circles for its quite challenging language for the time, such as this:

> To believe in liberty in science is to believe in human common sense; to believe in liberty in the political and social sphere is to believe in a moral world order; to believe in liberty in religion is to believe in God.

Albert decided to invest in Rydberg's writing and, with Hedlund as an intermediary, in 1865 he wrote a contract for a new edition of *The Teaching of the Bible Concerning Christ*. It took three years to produce but sold out.

During these years Albert Bonnier and Viktor Rydberg developed a respect for each other which was to evolve into true friendship. Apart from purely commercial considerations, this was the background to Albert's offer of the flat in autumn 1869. However, he may also have had other motives for smoothing the way for Rydberg's presence in Stockholm.

* * *

After a long, drawn-out process of alternating setbacks and progress, the question of Jewish emancipation was nearing a definitive resolution – and the new Member of the Riksdag Viktor Rydberg was a keen supporter of the issue. It involved nothing less than granting the Mosaic minority, then barely 2,000 people, rights as citizens. The Riksdag had adopted a constitutional proposal with this content in 1867 but it was awaiting a further decision following a new election.

Albert Bonnier was unable to experience this important moment in the history of Swedish Jews with his own eyes and ears because he and Betty were in Italy at the time, but when the news from home reached him, he must have been delighted.

On Wednesday 16 February 1870 the galleries of the Riksdag were full. Public demand was so great that some of the audience had to be let into the plenary chambers.

In the second chamber, the debate was begun by Rydberg, whose first name was spelled Victor in the records; Rydberg changed it to Viktor slightly later in the battle over linguistic purism in which he railed against the influence of German.

The speech was Rydberg's maiden speech in the Riksdag.

The introduction was magnificent:

The question that is now to be decided is ultimately this: which fundamental principle is Sweden's Constitution to apply hereafter? The principle of forced confession or of freedom of confession? Vacillating between the two is a weakness and will soon be an impossibility. We must courageously and properly decide in favour of one or the other. Vacillating is a weakness, as he who does not wish to abandon forced confession acts weakly and dishonestly when, considering this to be good and charitable, he does not call for its application in its strictest sense and advocates the reintroduction of *hard* pressure, imprisonment and fleeing the country and, why not, the axe and the stake.

Perhaps Rydberg had immigrant Jews such as the Bonnier brothers in his thoughts when he continued:

> Vacillating between the two fundamental principles will also become a physical and political impossibility as constantly increasing communications between peoples facilitate not only the exchange of ideas but also mutual influences and thus wipe out the old confessional boundaries. These boundaries, previously geographical, are becoming more and more what they should be: spiritual boundaries.

After a reminder of how Christians over the centuries had made Jews the victims of 'nefarious persecutions, with plundering and murder committed in the name of religion' Rydberg concluded with a mighty cadence:

> For that reason I hope to God that we shall come through the trial that we today have to undergo and that this day will be inscribed in our annals as a day of victory, not defeat, for Christian freedom and civilised society.

Other speakers in favour of emancipation included Adolf Hedin and the former Minister for Finance Johan August Gripenstedt. The latter, severely marked by illness but still a first-rate orator, dwelt on 'respect for what is the most uniquely human, that can never be taken away, yes, what above all makes a person a person – I mean their thoughts, beliefs and convictions or the entire inner life of the soul'.

By this point the tide in favour of reform had grown so strong that the outcome of the process in the Riksdag was more or less a foregone conclusion, but a certain amount of resistance lingered on, mainly among members with posts in the church. They were particularly opposed to the proposal that Jews be able to be appointed as judges and Justices of the Supreme Court and that no exception was made for teaching posts. Their argument derived from the assumption that the State was a cultural institution and that adherents of a foreign faith should not therefore be allowed to influence the exercising of public power whose duty was normative.

The emancipation cause won by an overwhelming majority – 93 votes to 18 in the first chamber and 116 to 58 in the second chamber. Jews were given access to all non-clerical posts, with a couple of exceptions: Ministers of State and teachers of religion. Jews were also able to be elected to the Riksdag. The decision was signed by the King on 8 April.

Later that same year, on 16 September, an impressive new synagogue was opened on Wahrendorffsgatan, very near Albert's home, as the Jewish congregation had grown out of its more modest place of worship on Tyska Brunnsplan, where it had been located since 1795. Stockholm's large synagogue was designed in oriental style by architect Fredrik Willhelm Scholander. Several of the city's prominent Jewish businessmen, including Albert Bonnier, were involved in making the synagogue a reality.

Antisemitism lived on, as Albert Bonnier in particular was to find out, but the emancipation decision was still a milestone. The crushing majority in the Riksdag and a welcoming reception in the press and among the general public strengthened the position of Jews in society. In his standard work on the history of Jews in Sweden, Hugo Valentin pointed out that the wave of pogroms and other antisemitic attacks that started to roll across Central and Eastern Europe just a few years later never directly touched Sweden's small Jewish minority.

* * *

Viktor Rydberg enjoyed staying in Albert's flat but was not a demanding presence. According to Karl Otto, aged thirteen at the time, the children and the servants viewed Rydberg as 'a strange gentleman who left early and came home late and whom we saw very little of'. His claims on their hospitality were extremely modest, although his favourite dish, crispy bacon, was sometimes served. Betty had told the children to be nice and polite to 'the Genius' which thus became the name by which Rydberg was known in the Bonnier household. Oldest daughter Jenny, who was in charge of the domestic accounts in their parents' absence, noted in her cashbook: 'soap for the Genius – 50 öre'.

When Albert and Betty had returned home, Rydberg sent a letter of thanks in which he repeated his earlier offer to repay Albert's generosity by writing 'a good book'.

The result was not quite what Albert had been expecting.

Albert harboured hopes that Rydberg would return to the historical novel, the genre at which he had excelled, mainly with *The Last Athenian*, but Rydberg was set on theology. After a trip to Rome, he wrote a series of observations, *Romerska sägner om apostlarna Paulus och Petrus* (*Roman Legends of the Apostles Paul and Peter*), for *Handelstidningen*, which Albert published in book form for Christmas 1874.

The next major project, with S. A. Hedlund as intermediary as was so often the case, was Rydberg's translation of Johann Wolfgang von Goethe's *Faust* in 1876. Albert won the bid for the rights – the fee was 5,000 kronor, a huge sum at the time – and had the richly illustrated work printed in a first edition of 3,000. It sold out in a year despite a high price of 18 kronor in paperback and 27 kronor in hardback, and received effusive reviews.

Karl Warburg, Rydberg's biographer, explained the success thus: 'the interpreter internalised the poem, made its thoughts his own and gave them a new existence in the new language'.

For almost a hundred years, until Britt G. Hallqvist's translation in the late 1960s, Viktor Rydberg's Swedish version of *Faust* held a dominant and unique position.

While completing the *Faust* translation in 1875, Rydberg also emerged as a poet in his own name for the first time. His poems were published in the literary monthly magazine *Nu* and, of course, in *Svea*.

It was not until 1882 that Albert Bonnier published a major original work from the pen of Viktor Rydberg. This was *Dikter* (*Poems*), the second collection of which in 1891 contained 'Den nya Grottesången' ('The New Song of Grotti'), ominously doom-laden in its metaphorical depiction of greedy ruthless human exploitation and with clear influences from *Faust*:

Chancellor-Priest of Mammon enters,
Makes an ornate bow,
Says more labour must be found

Workers more to Grotti bound,
Even more
Than before,
To haul the grindstone round.
All your slaves have not the power,
Though a hundred thousand men.
The holy mill, hour upon hour,
Demands more thralls to toil again.

The same year, 1891, Viktor Rydberg came full circle in a literary sense by returning to the historical novel with *Vapensmeden* (*The Weaponsmith*), naturally published by Albert Bonniers Förlag.

* * *

The relationship between Albert Bonnier and Viktor Rydberg was not entirely friction-free, however. Albert could be irritated by Hedlund's interventions to extract the highest possible fee. Another niggle was that one of Albert's competitors, Joseph Seligmann, published Rydberg's *Romerska dagar* (*Roman Days*) at the same time as the *Faust* translation came out. Moreover, Albert disagreed with both Rydberg and Hedlund on one political point.

The major foreign policy issue in the early 1870s was the war between France and Germany, which, following France's defeat, led to the declaration of a German empire in 1871. In tune with Swedish public opinion, Albert supported France, while Rydberg and Hedlund leaned towards Germany. This is one of few occasions when Albert Bonnier, albeit worded with caution, urged an author close to him to mute his political sympathies. In 1870 when they discussed the potential publication of texts Rydberg had written in *Handelstidningen*, Albert asked him 'not to add too many essays that are distinctly *anti*-French and only elevate "Das Deutschtum".'

Albert Bonnier's distrust of Germany's ambitions as a great power was deep-seated, which had to do with his family's experiences in antisemitic Dresden and the German attack on the land of his birth, Denmark, in 1864.

Later, during the *Getting Married* trial against August Strindberg, the relationship between Albert Bonnier and Viktor Rydberg would be further put to the test. On top of this can be added the fact that Rydberg, originally a radical, gravitated more and more in a conservative direction, while Albert held firm to his liberal principles, though these were slightly tempered compared with the unabashed radicalism of his youth. For example, Rydberg was on the freedom of the press jury that in 1888 condemned the future leader of the Social Democratic party Hjalmar Branting for 'denial of God and of an afterlife and of pure evangelical doctrine'. Branting, who had previously admired Rydberg's defence of religious freedom, was imprisoned in Långholmen prison and commented on the great author's role in the court case with magnificent acerbity: 'His liberalism went no further than the drawing-room door.'

However, differences of opinion could not disrupt the friendship between author and publisher, even though it never quite took on the same familiarity as the relationship between Albert and Zacharias Topelius.

Especially from the 1870s onwards, their correspondence overflowed with declarations of honour and friendship. 'How deeply fond I am of you I cannot say,' Rydberg wrote to Albert in April 1878. A few months later in a letter to S. A. Hedlund, Albert corroborated how much he appreciated the contact with Rydberg, 'a noble and exalted person whom I admire and value to such a high degree'.

One might say that in purely symbolic terms the closeness between Viktor Rydberg and Albert Bonnier was at its height in 1894, a year before Rydberg's death, when Albert published a new edition of *Singoalla* illustrated by Carl Larsson. Rydberg insisted on a printed dedication that a slightly abashed Albert accepted with gratitude:

To Albert Bonnier.
As my 'Singoalla' now for the first time appears, in a garb with which your care and Carl Larsson's genius has dressed her, it is my wish to have the public answer the question of whether between a publisher and author there can be a better relationship than that of many years between you and me with a resounding no.
Thank you.
Viktor Rydberg.

Rydberg's importance for Albert Bonniers Förlag did not cease with his death. Soon after Rydberg passed away, the firm launched a plan to publish his collected works, edited by Karl Warburg. 'It came to be a major sales success and was one of the foremost reasons why the publishing company was able to significantly increase its turnover in the last years of the century,' states the economic historian Staffan Sundin, who has studied the growth of the Bonniers media house.

* * *

Alongside Viktor Rydberg, there was another top-selling writer with whom Albert Bonnier became close friends, Zacharias Topelius. This was a more long-distance relationship because Topelius worked in Finland. Their first contact came about in 1851 in conjunction with the Swedish performance of Topelius' play *Efter 50 år* (*After 50 Years*) in Stockholm.

Albert saw potential in this son of a provincial doctor, an academic and journalist from Nykarleby on Finland's Swedish-speaking west coast, two years older than he was, and when Topelius began a series of historical short stories set in Sweden's Age of Greatness in the Helsinki paper *Helsingfors Tidningar*, where he was editor, Albert grabbed them.

The book was *The Surgeon's Stories*, whose first part, or cycle, reached an audience in Sweden in 1854 via serial publication in *Europeiska följetongen*, one of his most important projects at that time. The stories, which revolved around the fictional noble family of Bertelsköld, and Sweden and Finland's shared history in the seventeenth and eighteenth centuries, became hugely popular and were published in book form. The last part, part five, was published in 1867. Despite urging from Albert, Topelius did not write a part six. However, in 1883–4 a decorative edition of the work was published with illustrations by Carl Larsson, another of Albert's creative friends. An impressive 30,000 copies were printed.

What attracted Albert to Topelius is unclear; their early correspondence has not been preserved. Perhaps Albert appreciated the way that Topelius' writings, with their tinge of national-romanticism, incorporated certain progressive features, at least to begin with. Topelius advocated social reform and expanding the rights of women. This tendency was sometimes marked in *The Surgeon's Stories*, where conflicts between the people and the nobility, between subjects and those in power, were a recurring theme, described in the verbose style typical of the period. It could be seen in the very first story. Cavalryman Gustaf Bertila, the son of a peasant from remote Ostrobothnia, reminds himself of his simple background, during the Thirty Years War in 1631, just before he flings himself into the battle of Breitenfeld and impresses Gustav II Adolf with his bravery:

> All these memories crossed the young warrior's brow in a moment, for now, now it was come, the moment when he, a youth from the masses, would fight his way to equal rank with this proud nobility that had hitherto looked down on him and his like with contempt.

***

After the success of *The Surgeon's Stories*, Albert published all of Topelius' literary works: poetry, drama and prose. Topelius' illustrated collections of tales, songs and verses, *Reading for Children*, in particular proved a major and lasting success. *Reading for Children* came out in eight parts, the first in 1865 and the last in 1896, two years before Topelius' death; a special selection for use in schools was launched in 1890–1. Topelius also submitted, in due order, recurring contributions to *Svea*.

Albert Bonnier and Zacharias Topelius were unable to meet very often for obvious reasons – the first time they met was in 1856 – and initially their contact mainly concerned fees, publishing questions and other practical details. The tone of their correspondence was amicably respectful, despite the odd difference of opinion.

As Topelius made a name for himself in the Swedish book market, he increased his financial demands, but without complaining. 'Despite the fact that Herr Bonnier received my earlier works almost too cheaply, I have no reason to regret our business,' Topelius wrote in early 1867. A couple of years later, he emphasised that their collaboration was to the advantage of both parties:

> I am not impractical enough, if not to say unreasonable, to deny a publisher any proceeds from his publishing. On the contrary, it pleases me, in the interests of literature and in our common interest, when such occurs, since it is clear, after all, that sales are often sluggish, and the better business the publisher does, the better he can support the authors (...) I wish that Herr Bonnier may do good business both off me and off others. The knack lies in arriving at a common benefit so that the interests of both are met.

Zacharias Topelius was one of the very greatest commercial assets of Albert Bonniers Förlag and Albert was keen to preserve the relationship, to ensure a steady flow of material from the other side of the Bothnian Sea for that reason at the very least. If it proved necessary, he could metaphorically almost fall to his knees. In 1873, when Topelius reacted against Albert having voiced the objection that a number of short stories were rather 'old fashioned', the otherwise hard-hearted publisher and businessman grew deeply regretful:

I have undoubtedly overstepped the mark and judged hastily and would probably in general do best to never dare to render any judgment on the works of a known master. I deserved a scolding and a reprimand and am truly thankful for the noble and dignified manner in which it was given.

Topelius replied that their 'connections should not be disrupted by honesty, but rather gain thereby'. The matter was soon forgotten.

Through this correspondence one can follow how the relationship gradually turned into one of genuine friendship, especially after Topelius visited Stockholm with his wife Emelie and his children in 1875. At that point, Topelius and Albert dropped use of their titles.

The Topelius family were passing through the Swedish capital on their way to Cannes and Albert immediately offered an advance so that the trip could be extended to Italy, a country of which he himself was especially fond after his and Betty's stay there a few years earlier.

The letters grew more frequent and the title 'Herr' was replaced with 'My dear brother'. In February 1880 Albert wrote to Topelius:

> It is a great joy to receive a letter from you every week or so (...) It brings us closer in a way (...) and for me your letters always bring this and that extra entertainment – I mean beyond the purely business-related.

Private contacts between the two families were eased by the fact that Topelius' daughters Toini and Eva were of an age with Jenny, Karl Otto and Eva Bonnier. They used to visit the Bonnier home when they were in Stockholm and could always count on being well looked after. When Toini and Eva were in Copenhagen in 1882 and were to pass through Stockholm on the way home, their father, to be on the safe side, made a proposal to his friend Albert: 'They are provided with travelling funds by me this time, but should they find themselves in unforeseen difficulties, I know well that they may rely on your always open bank.'

Half a century later, in a look back at the past in the weekly magazine *Idun* in 1927, Topelius' daughter Eva described her and her sister's first visit to Stockholm:

> Uncle Albert Bonnier was 'our very kind protector' all winter (...) When we left in the spring, he gave us gold watches as a souvenir from Stockholm, which were naturally great fun to come home with.
>
> The young Bonnier children made a huge impression on us unsophisticated children, thanks to their evident superiority in all areas, reinforced with self-confident judgments. We felt inferior, but not crushed, and got on well with them. But the boy Karl Otto I viewed as one of the most spoilt creatures I could imagine. Since then a whole long life of unflagging friendship has invalidated that harsh verdict.

Eva Topelius married the Swedish artist Johan Axel Gustaf Acke, better known as J. A. G. Acke. The couple became close friends of Karl Otto Bonnier and his wife Lisen.

The early 1880s was a period characterised by particularly high productivity on Topelius' part, despite the fact that he had other demanding duties besides his writing; he was appointed professor of history at Helsinki University in 1863. With Albert Bonniers Förlag, he published the collection of short stories *Vinterqvällar* (*Winter Evenings*), a title that Albert disliked but finally accepted, *Dramatiska dikter* (*Dramatic Poems*), and volume five of *Reading for Children*, all in parallel with working on editing *The Surgeon's Stories*.

One contributory factor behind this frantic activity was that Topelius had to finance the purchase of Koivuniemi (Björkudden in Swedish), a property outside Helsinki.

* * *

To an even greater extent than was the case with Viktor Rydberg, the conflicts around August Strindberg in the 1880s were to strain contacts between Zacharias Topelius and Albert Bonnier almost to breaking point. Their friendship and their mutual respect survived, however, professionally as well as personally, despite a factor that one might have thought would have complicated their relationship.

Topelius' liberal instincts waned over the years and he moved more and more towards what could best be described as a romantic and religiously influenced national conservatism with some reactionary elements. In the second half of his life – and under the protection of the Russian Tsar – he emerged as the Grand Duchy of Finland's kindly but strict educator of the people, fighting against modernism and materialist decadence. But above all, Zacharias Topelius was an antisemite. And the raging attacks that Albert Bonnier was subjected to in the debate on Strindberg and 'filthy literature' were impregnated with such prejudices.

Now antisemitism was not uncommon in so-called educated circles in the nineteenth century, but in Topelius' case it hardly involved thoughtlessly adapting to some spirit of the age but was a consistently held opinion, partly from religious motives, Jews bearing the guilt for the death of Jesus, and partly from a political, economic and social worldview that is still rife today; the Jews as a greedy, power-hungry, rootless people secretly exercising destructive power over society and humanity. Here Topelius, like many other European cultural personalities at that time, was under a certain amount of influence from opera master Richard Wagner's essay *Das Judenthum in der Musik* (*Judaism in Music*).

Such notions in fact ran throughout Topelius' writings. In *Helsingfors Tidningar* in 1845, in the short story 'Lindanserskan' (*The Tight-rope Walker*), he wrote: 'Jews and gypsies have taught humanity how low one can sink when one does not possess a fatherland'. Half a century later, Topelius' last great novel *Planeternas skyddslingar* (*Protégés of the Planets*), later retitled *Stjärnornas kungabarn*, featured one of the most ingrained mocking stereotypes of Jews, greed for money. The novel is set in the seventeenth century, and one of the main characters, a rich Jew, is described as follows:

Ruben Zevi was a cosmopolitan, like the gold he controlled. Who asks where it has come from or who it previously served? It is enough that one owns it: *non olet*, it does not stink.

These antisemitic attitudes do not seem to have affected his relationship with the Jewish publisher Albert Bonnier, possibly because Zacharias Topelius had some Jewish ancestry himself and was also convinced that over time the Jews would be converted to Christianity. He called his world view 'providential', in other words a reflection of historical events planned by God from the outset for specific purposes. The correspondence between them confirms that Topelius never let his antipathies towards Jews and Jewishness tip over into questioning Albert's personal or professional qualities.

The deep trust on which their association was based was perhaps expressed most clearly in a letter from Topelius to Albert dated 21 March 1876:

> Yes it is true that our 24 year-long business relationship has been *bona fide*, as agreed from the beginning. I am pleased that you have found it so, and for my part I owe you the same admission. The circumstance that the first honorariums were small came about because I did not request more at a time when my works were as yet barely known nor circulated. The fact that the circulation, and consequently the honorariums, have since increased, is obviously partly due to the manner in which an enterprising publisher with wide-ranging relationships has benefitted my interests at the same time as benefitting his own. The advantage has been mutual, as is only fair.
>
> Still, I believe that it is fortunate and advantageous if both the contracting parties, author and publisher, view their mutual relationship from a standpoint that is more to do with friendship than merely contractual. I believe they are able to serve each other, like the composer and orchestral conductor, like the writer of a play and the theatre's director.

* * *

In January 1898, when he was occupied with a 'book of thoughts', Zacharias Topelius received floods of praise on his eightieth birthday in Helsinki. A few days later he travelled home to Koivuniemi in severe cold. He fell ill a couple of weeks later and died on 12 March. His *Blad ur min tänkebok* (*Leaves From my Book of Thoughts*) was published posthumously. The women of Finland raised a memorial to him at Hietaniemi cemetery in Helsinki.

With one natural exception, his literary opposite, and opposite in character too, August Strindberg, there was no single author who played as important a role for Albert Bonniers Förlag in its first hundred years as Zacharias Topelius. Few, if any, have had as close a link with its family of owners.

In his memoir *Längesen* (*Long Ago*) one of Karl Otto's sons, Tor Bonnier, repeated a touching episode from one of Topelius' very last meetings with his publisher. It says a great deal about Topelius' apparent rigidity and social restraint but possibly even more about the easy relationship that existed between him and the Bonnier publishing family.

It was 1897 and Topelius was in Stockholm, where on setting foot ashore he had been cheered by the schoolchildren of the city:

> My grandfather invited the Topelius family to dinner at Hotel Rydberg and my brother Åke and I were allowed to come too – he was a children's author after all. At dessert, my mother proudly announced: 'My son Tor knows "The Raspberry Worm" off by heart. Recite it!' I was prepared and stood up to declaim but

Above right: Albert Bonnier.

Top left: Albert's father, Gerhard Bonnier.

Albert's brothers, Adolf Bonnier (*centre*) and
David Felix Bonnier (*bottom left*).

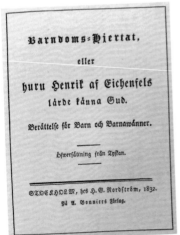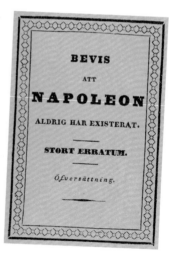

Above: The first books published by Albert Bonnier.

Below: Illustration taken from *Stockholms Mode-Journal*.

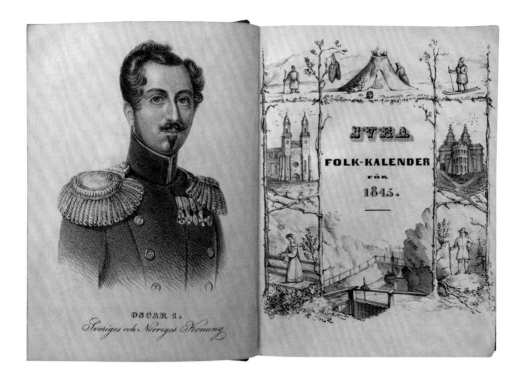

OSCAR 1.
Sveriges och Norriges Konung

Above: From *Svea*'s first issue.

Svea was an annual publication that Albert Bonnier edited up until his death in 1900, and was a base from which he published literary talents such as August Strindberg.

Jenny. Betty och KarlOtto och Albert Bonnier
Eva

Above: Albert Bonnier with his young family.

Right: While Albert Bonnier's satirical humorous magazine *Stockholm Figaro* was short-lived, it was where he published some of the sharpest wits of the time.

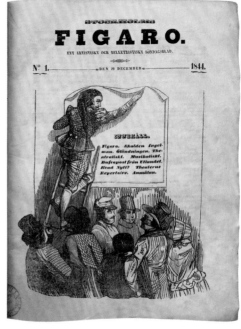

Bonnier office and printing room interior.

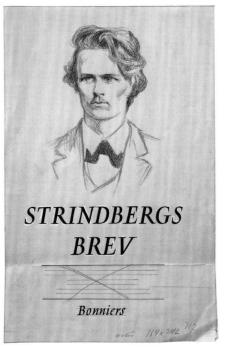

Above: August Strindberg.

Below: August Strindberg's provocative book *Giftas* or *Getting Married* was accused of blasphemy and an order was issued for the books to be seized. When Strindberg was found not guilty, the books were returned to the publisher, as the cartoon below shows.

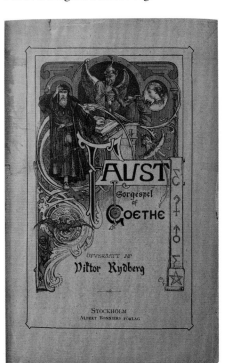

Above: Victor Rydberg's translation of *Faust*, which Albert Bonnier published in 1876, was considered definitive until the 1960s.

Below: Josefina Wettergrund, who wrote under the nom de plume Lea, was one of Albert Bonnier's favourite authors.

Gustaf Fröding.

Above: Friends, Gustaf Fröding and Verner von Heidenstam, both important Bonnier authors.

Verner von Heidenstam.

Below: A typical, anti-Semitic caricature of the time, from the proceedings against Fröding in 1896. 'Old Man Moses', Albert Bonnier (right), is depicted as a pamphleteer with skullcap.

Above: A happy Albert Bonnier with good friends, probably at one of the summer places the family rented in the Stockholm area.

Below: Eva Bonnier in the studio with her portrait of the geologist and industrialist Hjalmar Lundbohm. In the background, Per Hasselberg's sculpture *The Frog*.

Above right: Eva was a celebrated painter. This portrait is of the Bonnier's beloved housekeeper, Mussa.

Left: Albert Bonnier on the balcony of Harbour Street in June 1900.

Right: Albert Bonnier 1820–1900.

Topelius patted me on the head and said: 'I know "The Raspberry Worm" too. Sit down.'

* * *

Alongside Viktor Rydberg and Zacharias Topelius, the publishing firm's literary figureheads, Albert Bonnier also cultivated close contact with a whole host of other authors, although not with the same private warmth. This was Albert's signature as a book publisher from the very start; it was not entirely easy for an upwardly mobile author to force their way through the eye of his needle, but any who succeeded were received with a degree of professional and personal recognition that still set Albert apart in the Swedish publishing sector.

One of Albert's favourites was Josefina Wettergrund, better known under the pseudonym Lea, whose short stories and poems became very popular. She was a frequent contributor to *Svea* and Albert published her *Selected Tales* in book form. Their frequent correspondence reveals a mutual appreciation that says a great deal about Albert's capacity to forge bonds of friendship with his authors.

'I never remember Herr Bonnier other than in conjunction with some generous or kind act, which is very pleasant or perhaps not quite so common between author and publisher,' wrote Lea to Albert in 1879.

Less successful was Albert's connection with the pseudonym 'Mattis'. When he first received a manuscript from Mattis, in 1866, he returned it under the assumption that its author was a man. But behind Mattis was Mathilda Tengbom, who replied with a round rejoinder:

You may not be any friend of women (a very serious fault in you) and thus there may be little hope that this letter awakens any feeling of contentment or goodwill in you. – It is namely written by a lady (...) I wonder whether you truly believe that in our pretty heads we women have smaller brains than the ugly men; or whether you might possibly think we are dull. Ah, Sir, what would the world be without us?

The answer clearly made an impression. Albert published several books by Mattis in the years that followed. After a few years she disappeared from the literary scene, which, according to Karl Otto Bonnier 'hardly suffered any major loss thereby'.

On occasion Albert intervened as a kind of protector of authors on whom he personally placed particular value. One such author was the now forgotten Nils Lilja, an intellectual jack-of-all-trades who had studied several different subjects at Lund. He mainly made his name as a botanist depicting the flora of Skåne. Lilja also wrote books of popular science with quite radical social messages, the most important of which was published by Albert in 1858. *Menniskan. Hennes uppkomst, hennes lif och hennes bestämmelse* (*Mankind – Origin, Life and Destiny*).

In 1870, when Albert discovered that a text extremely critical of Lilja was to be included in poet Daniel Klockhoff's *Efterlämnade skrifter* (*Posthumous Writings*), he wrote to editor Pelle Ödman asking him to reconsider. Albert agreed that Lilja was no great author but emphasised that he had 'benefitted the cause of freedom from prejudice and done quite a deal of good for the spreading of enlightenment'. Albert therefore wished to 'spare an old man, with whom I have been on good terms through a long working life, the indignity of this attack against him being once more brought to light and through me into the bargain'.

The matter ended, however, with Albert accepting the criticism of Lilja, because 'true liberality lies in not supressing any opinion'. Possibly the fact that Viktor Rydberg was Pelle Ödman's co-editor had a part to play.

Teacher and writer Nils Petrus Ödman belonged to the circle surrounding the literary Nameless Society in Uppsala, founded in 1860 by Albert's friend Lorentz Dietrichson, and acted as a link between Albert and the poetry associated with the society known as '*signaturpoesi*'. These poets included Carl Snoilsky, later a member of the Swedish Academy, and Daniel Klockhoff and Ernst Björck, both of whom were subsequently published posthumously by Albert.

* * *

It was not uncommon in the patriarchal nineteenth century for female authors to hide behind male pseudonyms. The best-known example is Victoria Benedictsson, who used the name Ernst Ahlgren. Benedictsson's books started to be published by Albert Bonniers Förlag in the early 1890s, a few years after her death when Bonniers took over the rights.

Another female author with a pseudonym, who is less known today, was Aurora Lovisa Ljungstedt, who wrote under the name of Claude Gérard. Her Collected Works became one of the publishing company's major successes in the 1870s.

Albert Bonnier's greatest undertaking in this decade, however, was in publishing new editions of August Blanche and Carl Jonas Love Almqvist. The former venture proved to have been a successful move in the years that followed, more than compensating the publisher for the high price that Blanche's estate demanded and received – 12,000 riksdaler. A special illustrated edition was printed in 1890 with a print run of 30,000.

The latter investment, the Almqvist edition of 1874–8, on the other hand, was a miscalculation. Almqvist had died in 1866 and if a wider Swedish audience had heard of him at all, it was as a highly controversial figure. This was not solely down to his challenging novels like *Sara Videbeck and the Chapel*, but also to the fact that he had fled Sweden in 1851 after having been accused of the attempted murder of a loan shark.

'Albert's Almqvist edition had one fault; it came out too early. The time was not yet ripe to understand and appreciate Almqvist', stated Karl Otto Bonnier, an assessment in which he was entirely correct. Interest in Almqvist did not blossom until 1897, after Ellen Key's study *Sveriges modernaste författare* (*Sweden's Most Modern Author*). Today he is seen as one of the greatest authors in the Swedish language.

In the field of non-fiction, Albert prioritised travel literature, where the translation of Henry Stanley's *How I Found Livingstone* and *Through the Dark Continent* caused a sensation. Another translation from English was Charles Darwin's *The Descent of Man, and Selection in Relation to Sex*.

* * *

As the 1870s drew to a close, Albert Bonnier was thoroughly established as one of Sweden's leading publishers, a position confirmed by the fact that in September 1877 he was elected as chair of the Swedish Publishers' Association.

The Swedish economy was doing well in the first seven years of the decade. Down on the continent, the bubble of speculation that had formed after the Franco-German war burst, but it took time for the ripples to reach Sweden. The population grew, from 2.8 million inhabitants in 1840 to 3.9 million in 1880, at the same time as the Elementary School Act started to make a greater impact on general literacy, hastening the spread of printed written material. Industrialisation and urbanisation started to gradually gather pace, a trend stimulated by Ministers De Geer and Gripenstedt's reform offensives. On the book market, Norstedts was still the biggest player in the country with its concentration on textbooks and non-fiction, but Albert Bonnier's more literary-focused publishing business was growing and now employed more than fifty people.

However, there was no longer a bookshop under the Bonnier name. Adolf's son Isidor had taken over the shop in Norrbro Bazaar, but was never happy in the role. He sold the shop and the name of Bonnier disappeared from above the door in 1875.

By this point, Albert had very cautiously started preparing his son Karl Otto for a future in the publishing industry. As early as 1873, the seventeen-year-old Karl Otto had been allowed to accompany Albert to a meeting of Scandinavian booksellers in Christiania, today's Oslo. There Karl Otto was particularly impressed by Frederik Hegel from the Danish firm Gyldendal, publisher of Henrik Ibsen and Bjørnstjerne Bjørnson. It was a formative moment for the young Karl Otto: 'I knew what I wanted to be. I wanted to be Sweden's Hegel.'

Albert published some works by Bjørnson in Sweden, with varying success, although he was sceptical on one political point; Bjørnson's adulation of Germany. But it was Ibsen in particular who exercised a huge influence on his times. When *A Doll's House* created a sensation on stage with its message of female liberation in 1879, Ibsen received an offer from Albert for a Swedish edition of this drama plus four more. Nothing came of it, possibly due to disagreement over the fee. In other words, Albert Bonnier's contact with the two Norwegian giants was highly limited.

* * *

Albert's life was not only about literature and business. He worked long hours, but, for his time and social class, seems to have been a present, open-minded and supportive husband and father.

The Bonniers were a close family, despite strains in the form of Betty's depression and Karl Otto's battle with tuberculosis, one of the most feared contagions of the age. He contracted the disease in 1877 and spent the next three years at spas abroad, in countries including Italy and Switzerland, often under Betty's tender care. At Christmas 1877 the whole family gathered around Karl Otto in San Remo and a year later in Davos.

The relationship between children and parents seems to have been relatively easy-going, although it was made clear to Karl Otto what was expected of him as the only son and predestined heir to the printing and publishing business. He left school at the age of sixteen, as Albert, who cared little for formal educational qualifications, thought it was time he started helping out in the publishing firm.

Oldest daughter Jenny, an early sports enthusiast, took on

the responsibility that went with the role of eldest sister as a matter of course, especially when Albert and Betty were away. When she had grown a little older, Jenny was often hired as a literary consultant, translator and extra proofreader. In his extensive correspondence with Albert, from time to time August Strindberg would send a thank you for her help to 'Miss' Bonnier.

When Eva Bonnier showed evidence of an artistic bent at an early age, she was encouraged by Albert, and nor did he object when she later joined the radical Artists' Association, in stubborn opposition to the stuffed shirts that in her view ran the Royal Swedish Academy of Fine Arts.

Much later, Karl Otto's son Åke wrote of his aunts Jenny and Eva:

> One can hardly imagine two sisters less like each other, perhaps not so striking in terms of appearance but so much more in terms of character and personality. Both were highly intelligent; they had inherited much of the clear intellect and open free-thinking that characterised their parents. But while Jenny was meditative by nature and generally calm and matter-of-fact, Eva – three years younger – was emotional, passionate, and, one might say, emotionally volatile.

Both were unlucky in love. When she was young, Jenny was courted by August Bondeson, author of works including *Skollärare John Chronschoughs memoarer* (John Chronschough's memoirs), but turned him down when she suspected that his motives were pecuniary rather than emotional. Instead she was interested in Arthur Thiel, brother of financier and patron Ernest Thiel. She was advised against the connection by Lisen Bonnier, who married Karl Otto in 1882.

Jenny Bonnier remained unmarried, as did her younger sister Eva, who harboured strong but unrequited feelings for the sculptor Per Hasselberg. He was in love with another woman and a planned marriage between him and Eva never took place. The break-up threw Eva into a severe depression from which she never recovered. She was hospitalised for a period and almost entirely gave up painting.

When Hasselberg died in 1894, at the age of only forty-five, Eva took on his baby daughter Julia and looked after her with great warmth. Probably suffering from the same depressive inclination as her mother Betty, Eva Bonnier died in Copenhagen in 1909. Elder sister Jenny lived a long and relatively undramatic life, over the years overshadowed by rheumatism. Visits to Wimbledon for the tennis were recurring highlights, however. She died in 1927.

* * *

Alongside family life, Albert and Betty had a lively social life. They enjoyed holding dinners and large parties, especially during the slightly calmer summer months when the family rented summer homes in the Stockholm area, including in Tollare and Gustavsvik and on the islands of Lidingö and Dalarö.

Their closest circle of friends included Lorentz and Mathilde Dietrichson, travelling companions from their trip to Italy in 1870, the liberal newspaperman and editor-in-chief of *Aftonbladet* August Sohlman and his wife Hulda, and summer neighbours Gustaf and Sigrid Hegardt. It also included Betty's cousin Semmy Rubenson and his wife Jeanette. Trained as a lawyer, Semmy Rubenson made what was for Jews an unusual career as a police officer and was appointed Stockholm's Chief of Police in 1885.

From among the authors, the Bonnier home sometimes received Viktor Rydberg and Zacharias Topelius as guests, but none were as close to Albert as playwright Frans Hedberg, married to Amanda. They had a large family and Albert was constantly prepared to pass on new commissions and thus additional income to his friend Hedberg, whose best-known play was *Bröllopet på Ulfåsa* (*The Wedding at Ulfåsa*). Hedberg remembered their first contact in the 1850s:

> It was as a newly begun playwright I found myself before him with my first piece for theatre, *Hin ondes gåfva* (*The Devil's Gift*). We easily agreed the deal, the fee was not particularly great, but it was paid immediately and the friendly reception was that much greater. The best of it all, however, was that this latter relationship between publisher and author was never disrupted over the many years that have passed since then.

The connection would be passed down the generations. Frans' son Tor Hedberg, author and later member of the Swedish Academy, became a close friend of Karl Otto Bonnier.

Another central figure among Albert's friends was August Malmström, artist and professor at the Royal Swedish Academy of Fine Arts, best known for the painting *Grindslanten* from 1885. Malmström, known as 'Kulan', was Eva Bonnier's teacher for a period and produced illustrations for Topelius' *Reading for Children*.

Albert, 'Kulan' and their friends were often seen enjoying

food and drink together in the restaurant of Hotel du Nord, one of their two favourite haunts. The other was Berns Salonger.

Tor Bonnier later remembered hearing Frans Hedberg give a speech about these nights on the town at Albert's seventy-fifth birthday celebration:

> Hedberg described the daily, cheerful get-togethers in a group over an after-dinner toddy at Berns Salonger. To my great surprise (I was a twelve-year-old boy) Hedberg talked about my grandfather, this strict, serious man, weighed down by work, as a jolly fellow amid a circle of happy writers and artists. I remember Hedberg mentioning, besides himself, painter August Malmström, sculptor John Börjeson and other celebrities of the day among their companions.

Despite all these joys – the success of the publishing business, the children, friends – a heavy darkness loomed over the Bonnier family: Betty's mental health.

* * *

At New Year in 1873 Albert and Betty returned to Italy. In Rome they met several old acquaintances from their previous trip, but something was not quite right. Betty did not seem to feel any real enjoyment. Some months after their return home, at the end of the year, the situation grew critical. Betty's depression turned into mental illness and the previously happy home was transformed, in the words of Karl Otto Bonnier, into 'an abode of sorrow'.

Betty was in the grip of uncontrollable despair and, Karl

Otto wrote, 'a total incapacity to overcome her sick mind'. For a period she was placed in a 'hospital' in Vadstena, the Swedish word used at the time for a mental institution, and Jenny had to take over much of the responsibility for the home, while Albert buried himself in even more work in an attempt to repress what was going on. The marriage – and the family – were close to breakdown.

No psychiatric care in the more modern sense existed and the treatments were as meaningless as they were unpleasant. Betty was prescribed large amounts of potassium bromide, a substance that was then used as a sedative and which is now mainly found in veterinary medicine. This was combined with hot baths. Her doctor kept Albert informed: 'Herr Bonnier must not be concerned if for a while now the Pat. starts to grow more silent and appear lazy and indifferent.'

Albert did what he could to make Betty's stay at Vadstena easier. She was served meals in her room, she was kept separate from other patients and a lady companion was employed. But Betty only wanted to escape. In a long and moving letter from 1874, reproduced in Per I. Gedin's *Litteraturens örtagårdsmästare*, she begged in despair and confusion for Albert to release her:

> I know that the doctors would say that you must pay no attention to this but I beg you in God's mercy take me from here unless it is merely to get rid of me, as for all you hold dear this seems and cannot seem other than distressing, and if I am not to become like the other madmen that I hear crying and then dancing and jumping and swaying around me every minute night and day and I am so afraid of them.

Then, in autumn 1876, a sudden and almost miraculous change occurred in Betty's condition. On a stay on the island of Dalarö, as usual in the company of the loyal Marie 'Mussa' Banck, she regained her joie de vivre. The darkness had lifted.

A radiantly happy Albert wrote to Karl Otto, who was in Vienna.

> You can believe that we feel glad and happy at the state that now prevails at home compared with the almost three heavy years that now, God willing, lie behind us. Mamma is as much like herself as she was in her happiest moments – she enjoys everything – the air and sunshine, rain and bad weather, her home, her rooms, her girls, her food – yes everything.

Albert also informed the family's friends that Betty had now recovered. Viktor Rydberg was one and he replied:

> Brother Albert, Your letter, which I have just received, has given me great joy. So family happiness has moved back into your home where she once was secure! May she now stay throughout your lives (...) Let me now hope that I may sit in your company at some time or other and see your wife's beautiful, soulful eyes as clear and trusting as in days past. God bless you both!

Hardly had Betty regained her peace of mind and new energy before the next trial occurred: Karl Otto's tuberculosis. He did not conquer the disease until 1880.

Meanwhile a trial of a different kind was on its way into Albert Bonnier's publishing life. His name was August Strindberg.

CHAPTER 7

FIRE!

A new age and new literature.
August Strindberg introduces himself. Felix dies.
The Red Room, *The New Kingdom* and antisemitism.
In 'Abraham's bosom'. Strindberg's poems.
The *Getting Married* trial. Two friendships tested.
Close to breaking point.
Awaiting the next battle.

———

Financially, the years around 1880 were characterised by a long-drawn-out crisis in the wake of the financial optimism fuelled by the expansion of trade and industry. After rapid, speculation-driven booms, especially following the Franco-German war, prices and stock exchanges collapsed in Europe and the USA. Called 'the Long Depression', the crisis had begun in 1873 with a burst bubble in Vienna, and in countries such as Austria and Germany, the downturn was blamed on Jewish financial interests.

The ripples spread, reaching remote Sweden in late 1878, where the slump lasted for ten years, although the book industry coped better than many others, thanks to an ever-increasing interest in printed stories.

Emigration to America soared, peaking in 1887, when approximately 50,000 Swedes left the country.

Under the surface, forces unleashed by social, technological and political revolutions – urbanisation, electricity, the Paris commune and the growing labour movement – bubbled and simmered. Their impact was felt in Sweden too, with a slight time lag. In the 1880s Stockholm's population grew by almost 50 percent, new industries emerged such as ASEA, the General Swedish Electrical Limited Company, and in Malmö in 1881, tailor August Palm gave a speech that introduced the ideas of social democracy from the continent.

The changes also affected the arts. Artists like Paul Cézanne were developing a new style of painting and Late Romantic composers such as Franz Liszt and Camille Saint-Saëns were stretching the bounds of musical form.

In the field of literature, France was something of an epicentre in the footsteps of Honoré de Balzac, where Gustave Flaubert and Émile Zola had blazed the way for a new, more realistic school, usually termed naturalism.

In Sweden and Scandinavia, this literary epoch is referred to as 'the Modern Breakthrough', a term coined by the influential Danish literary scholar and critic Georg Brandes. From Jewish stock, he was the brother of journalist and politician Edvard Brandes and his lectures *Hovedstrømninger i det nittende Aarhundredes Litteratur* (*Main Currents in Nineteenth-Century Literature*), published in 1871–90, made him a central but also controversial figure in the debate on the potential of literature to change society, asserting that social problems needed to be highlighted and debated. The Nordic figureheads of the breakthrough were Norwegians Henrik Ibsen and Bjørnstjerne Bjørnson.

Partly inspired by Georg Brandes, a younger generation of Swedish writers – Gustaf af Geijerstam, Axel Lundegård, Ola Hansson, Oscar Levertin – broke with courtly idealism and were nicknamed '*åttiotalisterna*' (writers of the eighties) and 'Young Sweden'.

A significant number of writers were women. Anne Charlotte Leffler, sometimes known by her married name of Edgren, with the consciously feminist novel *En sommarsaga* (*A Summer Tale*) and above all Victoria Benedictsson, unhappily and fatally in love with Georg Brandes, are numbered among this group. One can even talk of a female awakening in Swedish public life, symbolised by the paper *Framåt* (*Forward*), edited by teacher Alma Åkermark. *Framåt* became an arena for discussions on everything from labour issues to sexual morality. It came to a tragic end when Åkermark was forced to flee to the USA after having been accused of causing a moral decline. The Swedish climate was oppressive.

However, his creative obstinacy and huge productivity placed the most famous innovator in Swedish literature in a class of his own.

* * *

August Strindberg exploded onto the literary scene in 1879 with his debut novel *Röda Rummet* (*The Red Room*), his satirically critical depiction of a stagnant, bureau-cratically stuffy society. Strindberg became one of the very biggest names among the authors linked to Albert Bonniers Förlag, but the original edition of *The Red Room* was not published by Albert Bonnier, but by Joseph Seligmann, one of his competitors, publisher of the then renowned Carl

Snoilsky, a count, diplomat and poet who was a member of the Swedish Academy.

The Red Room contains a familiar, inaccurate, antisemitic caricature of a publisher named Moses Smith, who conceals unsympathetic contempt behind an ingratiating façade. Joseph Seligmann was also a Jew, dismissed by Strindberg as a 'thieving Jew', but Smith cannot possibly have been anyone other than Albert Bonnier. Albert read it that way too. When his son Karl Otto expressed his disappointment at Strindberg having chosen another publishing house, Albert wrote in reply: 'Read the chapter "At the Publisher's" and you will see why he did not come to me.'

The Red Room does indeed contain details that point towards Albert, including the existence of a magazine, 'Our Land', inescapably recalling his literary annual *Svea*.

Arvid Falk, Strindberg's alter ego, seeks out Smith in the hope of having a manuscript accepted and published:

> Being well aware of Smith's great power, the young man climbed the dark stairs of the publisher's house close to the Great Church, not without misgivings. He had to wait for a long time in an outer office, a prey to the most unpleasant mediations, until suddenly the door was burst open and a young man rushed out of an inner office, despair on his face and a roll of paper under his arm. Shaking in every limb, Falk entered the sanctum, where the despot received his visitors, seated on a low sofa, calm and serene as a god; he kindly nodded his grey head, covered by a blue cap, and went on smoking, peacefully, as if he had never shattered a man's hopes or turned an unhappy wretch from his door.

Not particularly flattering to Albert, the picture of Smith in *The Red Room* illuminates the relationship between Strindberg and Bonniers, as complicated as it was symbiotic.

Personally, Albert Bonnier found August Strindberg hard to stand and much of the new literature, alien, but at the same time he recognised that Strindberg was an exceptional talent with exceptional potential. The provocative attitude – and the antisemitism – were part of the package.

* * *

It was through his wife and son that Albert came into closer contact with the new literary trends on the continent. Towards the end of the 1870s, when Betty and Karl Otto were in San Remo in Italy where Karl Otto was recovering from tuberculosis, they read Flaubert's *Madame Bovary* and Zola's *L'Assommoir* and urged Albert to translate them for publication in Sweden. He immediately took their advice on Zola and published *L'Assommoir* under the Swedish title *Fällan* (which means 'the trap'), but Flaubert had to wait a few more years.

Karl Otto, in particular, was interested in more modern literature, but Albert, who had the last word, preferred more traditional storytelling, as personified in Sweden by Viktor Rydberg and Zacharias Topelius. Many of the authors of 'Young Sweden' consequently sought other publishers, with more of an eye for new talent. In his memoirs, Karl Otto listed them: Leffler, Geijerstam, Levertin, and more. Bonniers also lost two authors, Georg Nordensvan and August Bondeson.

Karl Otto did not hide his disappointment:

I had hoped and believed in my mission of nurturing and publishing young Swedish literature – and now it was starting to pop up here, there and everywhere other than with Albert Bonnier. But I was still too young and unsure of myself to seriously seek to make connections with my contemporaries against my father's will.

Despite his conservative literary preferences, in this period Albert Bonnier nevertheless was savvy enough to establish contact as a publisher with August Strindberg. Born in 1849, Strindberg had been brought up in a well-off family in Stockholm, where his father was a shipping agent. The lower-class origins that Strindberg later sought to highlight, chiefly in the autobiographical *The Son of a Servant*, had very little basis in reality.

After leaving Uppsala University without graduating, Strindberg led an insecure existence as a freelance writer and journalist, and was a contributor to *Dagens Nyheter* and other publications, before gaining a post as an assistant librarian at the National Library of Sweden in 1874, which made his situation more stable.

Albert knew of Strindberg through Adolf's son Isidor, who in 1871 had helped his former schoolfellow by publishing *Hermione*, one of Strindberg's earliest plays. Albert must also have known of Strindberg through his good friend Axel Lamm, a Jewish doctor in Stockholm who took the young and slightly lost student under his wing in the late 1860s. Strindberg lodged with Lamm in exchange for helping the family's sons with their homework.

It was here, in a lonely room on Trädgårdsgatan, that

the twenty-year-old bookworm Strindberg discovered that he himself possessed literary talent, paradoxically enough inspired by Zacharias Topelius' *The Surgeon's Stories*, almost the antithesis of his own creative work in the future.

Another link between Albert and Strindberg was Frans Hedberg, Albert's closest friend, who besides being a writer, was also an actor and head of the drama school attached to the Royal Dramatic Theatre, Dramaten, where Strindberg had sometimes worked as an extra. However, this relationship was complicated, because Strindberg considered that Hedberg was complicit in Dramaten's refusal of his play *Master Olof*.

In all events, Albert tried to give Strindberg a helping hand from time to time in the form of translation commissions and contributions to *Svea*. One of Strindberg's translations from English was a set of nursery rhymes, published in Swedish as *Daddas visor*, which he took on in parallel with work on the reformation drama *Master Olof* in the summer of 1872, in one of his first stays on the island of Kymmendö, an archipelago paradise that was to inspire him to write *The People of Hemsö*.

Daddas visor included the nursery rhyme 'Baa, baa, black sheep', which, however, only gained its Swedish breakthrough with Alice Tegnér's version twenty years later. Unlike Strindberg's version, she changed the colour of the sheep from black to white.

So, on an October day in 1877, August Strindberg turned up at Albert Bonnier's office with an original manuscript of his own. This was *Från Fjerdingen och Svartbäcken* (*Town and Gown*), a collection of short stories set in Uppsala. Albert showed the texts to his daughters Jenny and Eva and then wrote to Betty and Karl Otto in San Remo that he had received 'some Uppsala sketches' from Strindberg: 'None of them are complete masterpieces but there are good bits among them. The girls think them very funny so perhaps I shall take them.'

The book did not attract any great attention, but this was the tentative beginning of an association that was to be fiery at times and was to define Albert Bonniers Förlag as much as it did August Strindberg's authorship. As Strindberg wrote to his first wife, Siri von Essen:

'My fire is the greatest in Sweden.'

* * *

In the years immediately following *Från Fjerdingen och Svartbäcken* nothing happened in the relationship between August Strindberg and Albert Bonnier apart from a minor set of essays in cultural history and a short story, 'Solrök' ('Sunsmoke'), which was included in *Svea* for 1881. For Albert, the experience that hit him hardest in the early 1880s was the death of his brother Felix. Felix had long been suffering from poor sight, probably caused by a tumour. He died on 1 May 1881.

Felix's death was not as hard or as deep a blow as Adolf's. Contact between the two brothers had waned over the years. One sign of this was that only about six months earlier, Felix had apologised for having forgotten his brother's sixtieth birthday. But there must have been a kind of existential dimension to Felix's death for the otherwise unsentimental Albert; he was now the only one left of the three brothers – four if we count poor Sally – who had left Denmark to seek success in Sweden.

Felix's son Knut Bonnier continued to run his father's business in Gothenburg for a time, but sold the publishing company to Albert Bonnier in 1893. Apart from Knut, Felix and his wife Charlotte had five daughters: Elise, Hilda, Anna, Helene and Alida. Hilda and Anna did not reach adulthood.

About six months after Felix's death, at New Year 1882, Strindberg resumed contact with Albert to present a project that he intended to launch in partnership with Knut Wicksell, later one of Sweden's foremost economists:

> Knut Wicksell and I have felt ourselves called to publish a magazine in the newest colours, absolutely radical and differing from other papers in that it would be intended to be read.

For this purpose they would need a publisher and so Strindberg now turned to Albert Bonnier, because he 'was once in a similar movement to ours', a blatant reference to Albert's previous involvement in radical circles.

Albert did not turn them down flat. 'That doesn't sound at all a bad idea,' he wrote to Karl Otto, who was on his honeymoon, which included stays in Naples and Capri. Albert and Strindberg met a few days later. The meeting was long-winded, probably due to the volubility of the enthusiastic Strindberg, and a rather exhausted Albert wrote to Karl Otto 'that the first benefit of the new magazine was that I arrived home at half past four instead of half past three and was castigated as I deserved'.

From Albert's conversation with Strindberg it became clear that the magazine was to have a number of younger contributors, several of whom would make a name for themselves in the years that followed. These included the brothers Pehr and Karl Staaff, the former a journalist, the latter twice a liberal Prime Minister of Sweden in the early twentieth century. There was the progressive teacher Anna Whitlock, and Hjalmar Branting, later to become leader of the Social Democratic Party and Swedish Prime Minister. Like Wicksell and the Staaff brothers, he was one of Strindberg's comrades from coteries of radicals in Uppsala and Stockholm.

Between Strindberg, Pehr Staaff and the slightly younger Branting there was a special bond. They called themselves nihilists, a term associated with the battle against Tsarist despotism in Russia. All conceivable means were acceptable in opposing authoritarian systems, a view glimpsed in Fyodor Dostoyevsky's *Brothers Karamazov*: 'If God does not exist, everything is permitted.' Consequently, they welcomed the assassination of Tsar Alexander II in 1881, and Staaff and Branting's shared sailing boat was named *Peroffska* after the Russian revolutionary Sophia Perovskaya, who was executed for participating in the murder plot. When Strindberg was awaiting the arrival of both friends at Kymmendö in early summer 1883 he wrote impatiently to Staaff: 'Isn't Peroffska on the water?'

Branting came from a wealthy family and had apparently promised financial support for the project. On this point Albert wrote to Karl Otto:

> S—g says that Branting wants to donate money to the company – but, he added naively – 'I felt sorry for the boy' – and so he is coming to me, who he does not feel sorry for. I have not given a definite promise – as they wanted to get 1 to 2 issues out before the summer – and that is almost impossible of course – unless other things are dropped.

Nothing came of the idea for a radical magazine published by Bonniers on August Strindberg's initiative. However, later the same year, Strindberg did publish a book, though not with Albert Bonniers Förlag.

In autumn 1882 *Det Nya Riket* (*The New Kingdom*) came out, a cuttingly satirical depiction of Sweden after representational reform. The original was published by Claes Looström, who happened to be one of the buyers of the Bonnier bookshop in Norrbro Bazaar. Later the book was to be a permanent feature of the Bonnier publishing house's Strindberg catalogue.

Probably the most quoted section of *The New Kingdom*, a masterly illustration of political cynicism and self-interest, is Strindberg's depiction of the deciding debate at Riddarhuset, the chamber of the nobility in the Riksdag of the Estates, which preceded the representation decision in December 1865. Speaker after speaker 'asserted their passionate love for their fatherland like elk in the rutting season':

> Anyone hearing all this might in truth ask themselves the unanswered question: do they believe what they are saying? Or are they possessed! They were likely possessed, as people become so when the interests they hold most holy – their own – are at stake.

However, as far as Strindberg's relationship with Albert Bonnier was concerned, there was another element in *The New Kingdom* that was to create a certain amount of friction and played a part in Albert handing over much of the business's contact with Strindberg to his more patient son and heir. After recovering from tuberculosis, Karl Otto Bonnier took an increasingly active part in the publishing business before becoming a partner in the firm on his thirtieth birthday in 1886.

The distaste that Albert felt following the portrait of the publisher Smith in *The Red Room* was hardly lessened by reading the chapter 'Moses' in *The New Kingdom*.

In scornfully ironic phrases, unassailable in their ostensibly respectful tone, Strindberg attacked the striving for assimilation that had characterised Albert and his brothers ever since their arrival in Sweden:

> There is not one of the peoples of the Old World that has embraced the Swedish nation with such whole-hearted and persistent goodwill, one might say love, as the Jews, or Moses, as they with their usual humour love to call themselves. – 'I like that Thwede so terribly much,' said a hairdresser once while being whipped by the man engaged to the girl whose hair he had cut. 'The man beath me because I cut the girlth hair but I think tho terribly highly of that Thwede nevertheleth.' Prettier evidence of Moses' steadfast devotion would be hard to find (...) Love of the new country is beautifully expressed in adoration for the royal family and respect for the country's old nobility, laws and institutions.

Albert Bonnier was not mentioned by name, but he featured indirectly when Strindberg wrote that no Swede has 'dedicated himself to Swedish literature as much as Moses', whereupon he listed various publications, including *Svea*, Albert's literary annual.

Strindberg cannot be blamed for the way the conclusion

reads now, as he knew nothing of the terrors of the twentieth century to come, but it had an unpleasant air of blood and soil about it:

> Moses must behave nicely to the meek aboriginals as they behaved nicely to him when he arrived impoverished and muttering in Yiddish and was granted permission to scythe the fields that they had broken and sown.

* * *

It was not as if the 'Moses' chapter in *The New Kingdom* had sprung out of nowhere. Starting in 1881, Fritzes had been publishing Strindberg's history, *Svenska Folket* (*The Swedish People*), in a series of small pamphlets. This included an essay, 'Judarne' ('The Jews'), whose message tied in with the sentiments in *The New Kingdom*: 'A wandering people who wanted to be given land that had been farmed for a thousand years.'

August Strindberg was quite simply an out and out antisemite.

This naturally provoked reactions from Jewish critics and literary figures, among them Edvard Brandes, who broke off contact with Strindberg for a time, and Karl Warburg, who took issue with Strindberg's 'love of nationality':

> For him (...) the immigration of foreigners to Sweden is hateful, the culture they have brought, the contributions they have made to the development of the life of society, to education, to literature likewise; if their families have been here for a century, they remain foreigners to him nevertheless.

Strindberg could be particularly capricious in the values he espoused. He catapulted between nihilism, socialism and occultism. His fundamental disposition was radical and in some respects that of a social revolutionary, but this was combined with prejudiced and backward-looking elements. The latter came out in his view of women and female liberation and in the often overlooked fact that he preferred the creation story of the Bible to Charles Darwin's theory of evolution. Such paradoxes and lack of clarity were also found in Strindberg's antisemitism, at least superficially.

In December 1884, a couple of years after the publication of *The New Kingdom*, Strindberg attempted to modify his view of Jews in public in the magazine *Tiden*. In an article entitled 'Mitt judehat' ('My hatred of Jews') he admitted 'some guilt' for the repugnance directed towards the Jews and described them, apparently regretfully, as 'an intelligent people, perhaps the most intelligent in Europe'.

Strindberg denied that he was perpetuating racial hatred and instead sought to clad his antisemitism in class terms. In his opinion, some Jews constituted a kind of self-appointed upper class, but in the next moment he could resort to traditional antisemitic notions, such as that of Jews being to blame for their own misfortune. In January 1885 he wrote to Pehr Staaff:

Aristocratic followers of Satan! But hate them as reactionaries not as Jews! But if you slap them down, then it is *naturally* the Jew that is persecuted. That tactic has got them a long way.

Strindberg avoided directly confronting Albert Bonnier with antisemitic outbursts, but such attacks were frequent in his other correspondence. When Albert had decided to pay off Strindberg's debts to Claes Looström, Strindberg wrote to Looström from Kymmendö on 23 August 1883:

> You don't seem to be that inclined to keep me as you're not complaining. And you are quite right! We shall see how long Moses and I pull together! A more demonstrative illustration of the omnipotence of the Jews I can't provide, yet I cast myself into Abraham's bosom to save my life and my future!

The tone of his letters to 'Herr Albert Bonnier' was entirely different. The reason, one might say, was pecuniary. A few months later, when Strindberg was in Paris, he wrote to Albert:

> I do not know the state of our affairs but I assume I still have something remaining, provided that paying off the loan is postponed to the second half of the year, by which time my position will be slightly improved as making ready for the journey and the journey itself made a terrible hole in my funds. I therefore ask Herr Bonnier to be good enough to *immediately* send me 500 francs.

And a couple of months later:

> If I might now ask Herr Bonnier to silence some creditors by the end of the year, I would be grateful, as

sending French money here to send it back to Sweden
is a long way round that could be avoided by the
benevolent intervention of your kind assistance.

In these early years of his relationship with the Jewish
publisher Albert Bonnier it is plain and clear that Strindberg
was ingrained with an antisemitism that he could unleash
in his private contacts one day while politely grovelling to
Bonnier for financial support the next.

With hindsight one can attempt to explain, or even excuse,
Strindberg's antisemitism with references to it being 'of its time',
in an era when prejudice against Jews and Jewishness was rife,
but he went even further than that. Author and arts journalist
Nina Solomin sums it up in her study *Strindbergs judefientlighet
fram till 1882* (Strindberg's antisemitism up to 1882):

Was this kind of view widespread and accepted in
Strindberg's day? No, it appears that Strindberg's
hatred of Jews was exceptional even for its time.

* * *

August Strindberg is best known as a highly productive
dramatist and novelist, but it was his poetry, more modest in
its extent, that opened the doors to Bonniers.

In early summer 1883, when Albert and Betty were on one
of their trips abroad, Karl Otto was holding the reins in the
publisher's office. One day he was sitting flicking through
Ur dagens krönika (*Today's Chronicle*), an arts magazine and
important organ for 'Young Sweden' that had been launched a
couple of years earlier by author and journalist Arvid Ahnfelt.

In it Karl Otto's attention was grabbed by a number of poems by Strindberg and he wrote immediately to Albert saying that he would permit neither Looström nor Fritzes to publish them. If Strindberg was offered 'a really decent fee' he might perhaps be persuaded to choose Bonniers. Albert's answer was positive, but wary, bearing in mind previous experiences: 'And it would also be best to check whether I am to be excessively abused in the book.'

Once Albert had received a copy of *Ur dagens krönika* in the post, he gave the go-ahead for Karl Otto to contact Strindberg on the matter, even though a poetry collection would not sell as well as *The New Kingdom*, 'as insults in prose are more easily understood by absolutely anyone'.

By that point Karl Otto had already taken matters into his own hands and written to Strindberg on Kymmendö asking him to consider Bonniers as a publisher. The initiative indicated that Karl Otto felt increasingly secure in the role of the publishing business's representative, but who ultimately made the decisions was shown by the concluding lines:

> With the greatest respect, Albert Bonnier via Karl Otto Bonnier.
> P. S. My father is on a long journey abroad, which is why this enquiry is being made through me.

Strindberg answered that he was open to an offer, which he received: 4,000 kronor for an edition of 5,000, and 4,500 kronor for 6,000 copies. When Strindberg did not reply, Karl Otto went out to Kymmendö, where he was well received. Strindberg explained that he first had to offer Looström the poems, but if they failed to agree, Bonniers would have them.

A couple of weeks later, on 8 August, Strindberg specified his demands in a letter to Karl Otto:

> Having several publishers at once is not at all amusing. The most important thing a writer looks for in a publisher is capital and freedom from censorship. Looström is a very decent and pleasant chap to deal with, but he lacks capital. If you will release me from Looström, to whom I owe some 7,000 kronor, you can be my publisher for life.

The sum was to be paid off over six years. Strindberg also stated that he was planning a new prose book 'Portraits of Women' and offered Bonniers the opportunity to publish his Collected Works. Then he added re. his shifting publisher contacts: 'I am not the trouble-maker people think I am (...) Now I'm tired of running around.'

After a further visit from Karl Otto to Kymmendö and Albert's return, a draft contract was drawn up, which Strindberg finally accepted, once Albert had bowed to his wishes regarding format and fee:

> Otherwise I am neither stubborn nor unreasonable, and as my son Karl Otto – who following the order of nature will soon enough perhaps become the sole owner of the firm – as he wishes it and you have both planned this contract together, a minor divergence such as the one in question will not cause any breach.

It was thus Karl Otto who pushed for the company to deepen its connection with August Strindberg. Albert, on the other hand, was sceptical. 'My father did not love Strindberg as a person – more the opposite', remembered Karl Otto, adding, however, that Albert 'could not deny me anything'. For Karl Otto, Strindberg, for whom he had boundless admiration, meant a long-awaited opening towards the younger authors that the Bonnier publishing house was finding it difficult to attract.

The result became *Dikter i vers och prosa* (*Poems in Verse and Prose*), followed by *Sömngångarnätter på vakna dagar* (*Sleepwalking Nights in Broad Daylight*).

It is easy to understand Karl Otto Bonnier's blazing delight in Strindberg's poems, which he wanted to publish 'whatever the cost'. The direct, clear approach blew like a breath of fresh air through the festering atmosphere of much of Swedish poetry at the time. Here are lines that have become classics, like the concentrated, powerful anger in 'Loki's curses':

Our time's Gods, I who have cursed you
Come to curse you yet again!
Our time's Gods, who I have blasphemed,
Hear me blaspheme in a song!

You have power, I have language,
I have language in my power;
Thirteen you are at the table;
Signifying, as they say,
Death, destruction, great misfortune:
Gods, I want you to beware.
For the time is fast approaching;
Gods I warn you, watch your backs!

Albert Bonnier found the content of 'Loki's curses' in particular pleasingly 'devilish', although he could not resist commenting to Karl Otto with gallows humour. Should it not, he wondered, instead be addressed to 'Our time's Jews'?

Another often quoted passage is from *The Esplanade system*:

'Demolition everywhere
But reconstruction? – Dreadful stuff!'
'We're laying waste for light and air
Isn't that enough?'

However, contemporary Sweden failed to appreciate Strindberg's poems when they were published in 1883. They were condemned in several major papers and sales were slow. *Aftonbladet* warned against 'unhealthy reading' that risked 'besmirching young minds'. One probably contributory factor here was that Strindberg was attacking the most powerful literary heavyweight of the era, Oscar II's swaggering court poet, Carl David af Wirsén. As reactionary as he was prone to backstabbing, he was a member of the Swedish Academy, and from 1884 its permanent secretary.

Albert and the publishing company were attacked too, partly with hints that they must have bribed Strindberg not to write negative things about Jews this time.

Strindberg, who had had an inkling of what the reception would be like, had gone to France, from where he wrote asking 'Herr Bonnier' to 'leave me in as complete ignorance of all the complaints and insults as possible'.

The follow-up, *Sleepwalking Nights in Broad Daylight* received a considerably better reception in early 1884, but Albert's scepticism regarding the arrangement with Strindberg had hardly grown any less. Possibly Strindberg feared a breach, because he reminded Albert, in a slightly challenging tone, of why he had chosen him as a publisher: 'I took you because you were the most fearless.'

The possibility of dropping Strindberg had hardly crossed Albert's mind, as he had been aware that publishing him was a high-risk project from the start. And if the storm of criticism over the poems made him doubt Strindberg's talent, he was thoroughly set right by an author he admired – Bjørnstjerne Bjørnson. They met in Paris in May 1884, where Albert, Betty and Jenny had stopped off on the way home from Spain to see Eva, who was studying art in the French capital. In a long letter to Karl Otto, Albert repeated what Bjørnson had said about Strindberg:

> I rate him highly; he is not merely Number One in Sweden – he is your one and only – as the others are nothing [he was clearly forgetting Rydberg].

Karl Otto Bonnier was to be the central publishing figure in Strindberg's writing life, but the poems and the contract that went with them also started a relationship that was to place Albert Bonnier under severe strain, so severe that a change in his personality can be seen towards the end of the 1880s. The cheerful openness that so often shone through his business-like manner more and more gave way to a tired and slightly grumpy tone.

When Strindberg informed Claes Looström that he intended to switch to Bonniers in a letter of 19 August 1883, one of the reasons he gave was precisely that aspect of himself that Albert found so hard to stomach:

B is more fearless than you and a little freer from prejudice! He had nothing against an anti-Semitic poem, for example.

It was not a new outbreak of antisemitism on Strindberg's part that would ultimately test Albert Bonnier's apparent loyalty. It was a collection of short stories that Strindberg had given the working title 'Pictures of Women', but which on publication had been given the title *Giftas* (*Getting Married*) and the sub-title 'Twelve tales of marriage, with interview and foreword', a reckoning with institutionalised family life in which radical social criticism was blended with patriarchal constructs. Strindberg accused the modern 'cultural woman', with her demands for emancipation, of undermining the ideal division of responsibility between men and women of peasant society. One of his targets was Henrik Ibsen's *A Doll's House*. Several of Strindberg's friends and sympathisers, from Georg Brandes to Hjalmar Branting, criticised him for being a reactionary on women's issues.

The first Riksdag motion on female suffrage was submitted the same year, written by newspaperman Fredrik Teodor Borg, member of the second chamber for Helsingborg.

* * *

In the spring of 1884 August Strindberg was in Switzerland. After a pause in his literary production, instead devoting himself to cultural and social criticism in the series of pamphlets *Likt och olikt* (*Alike and Unlike*), he started to long to 'envelop himself in poetry', as he put it. He intended now, he told Albert and Karl Otto, to 'write the most remarkable book ever written'.

This was *Getting Married*, which was written at breakneck speed.

Twelve short stories were completed in less than a month and after another week or so, the introduction was written. The book would, Strindberg explained in a letter to his brother Axel, 'tear up heaven and earth'.

His hopes were to be proved right. *Getting Married* was a highly deliberate and carefully calibrated provocative polemic against the closed society of Oscarian Sweden and its double moral standards.

Strindberg sent copies of the manuscript to Albert and Karl Otto. Albert, who was in Marienbad, was not wholeheartedly positive:

> There are powerful and impressive things in these pieces – but I only regret that he splits himself in composing these smaller tales instead of creating one great, coherent novel.

Albert feared 'Lamentations at his impropriety' and urged Karl Otto to tone down the language: 'The coarseness must absolutely be crossed out'. Strindberg made some minor edits and removed words such as 'whore' and 'harlot', but most was allowed to remain.

Both the author and the publishing firm seem to have been well aware that the book might become the subject of a prosecution case. Albert, and to some extent Karl Otto, were mostly concerned about immoral elements of a sexual nature, but even at an early stage, Strindberg seems to have identified another section in *Getting Married* that could lead to prosecution based on an antiquated crime heading in the third chapter of the Freedom of the Press Act, 'blasphemy against God or mockery of God's word or sacrament'.

On 13 September, a couple of weeks before publication, he wrote to Albert:

'Do you think they'll prosecute me for that Piccadon?'

Albert hardly thought it likely; he did not even answer Strindberg's question. But prosecute they did.

Getting Married was printed in a first edition of 4,000 and went on sale on 27 September. There was a great deal of interest and Strindberg himself was immeasurably proud of a book he called 'the most beautiful, cleverest, rudest I have written'.

Less than a week later, on 3 October, everything took a different turn. On the initiative of Minister of Justice Nils Vult von Steyern, an order was issued for the book to be seized, i.e. confiscated. A few days later a prosecution was brought for 'blasphemy', a crime that could mean a two-year prison sentence for the author.

The passage that gave rise to the prosecution was in the first short story in *Getting Married*, 'The Reward of Virtue', an ironic, finely worded play on the sacrament, more precisely on the confirmation process and the eucharist:

He was confirmed in the spring. The shocking performance in which the upper classes exert an oath from the lower classes on the body and word of Christ that the latter never concern themselves with the doings of the former stayed with him a long time. The shameless fraud played out with Högstedt's Piccadon wine at 65 öre for half a gallon, and Lettström's maize wafers at 1 krona a pound, which the priest passed off as the flesh and blood of the rabble-rouser Jesus of Nazareth, executed more than eighteen hundred years ago, was not something he thought much about as in those days one didn't think, one had 'moods'.

Under the ironic surface an aspect reverberated that was particularly sensitive for Albert Bonnier, as pointed out by Olof Lagercrantz in his biography of Strindberg, otherwise quite frosty in its assessment of Albert's actions; what could be seen as an attack on Jesus might be able to be linked to the book's Jewish publisher, based on the ancient notion of the Jews as the murderers of Jesus.

When the bailiff and his minions arrived at the publishing house on the afternoon of 3 October, there were only 320 copies in the place, plus 141 copies in Stockholm's bookshops. The rest had been sold or spread across the country. The prosecution, which caused a major stir in the press, made Strindberg's book extremely desirable. Private individuals took the opportunity to 'hire out' their copies and there was a run on the bookshops and lending libraries.

The same day that the police carried out their raid on the publishing firm, Albert wrote to Strindberg down in Switzerland:

Looking at the next few days, the mood is naturally against me. The worst is that I myself am by no means capable of making any plea before a court, and it is equally unfortunate that — at least as yet — I do not know who I am to hire as legal counsel.

Albert's letter reflected the fact that printers of books could be prosecuted for a crime under the Freedom of the Press Act unless the author took on responsibility themselves by issuing an affidavit, a witnessed and sealed document showing the author's name and place of residence. What Albert needed to do now was to obtain such a document, endorsed by Sweden's Consul General in Geneva. The next day he wrote to Strindberg: 'I take it absolutely for granted that you will come home yourself and defend the case.'

As yet no trace of nerves can be discerned in Albert, who seems to have felt convinced that the prosecution was unsustainable, if not to say ridiculous, and that a freedom of the press jury could hardly do anything other than acquit. To Strindberg he wrote: 'However, an immediate journey back ought not to be necessary. Doubtless presenting an affidavit should be enough to separate me from the case.'

The tone in the press became increasingly heated while waiting for the case to be brought before Stockholm City Court on 21 October.

The liberal paper *Dagens Nyheter* defended Strindberg as 'the greatest genius among Sweden's writers now living' and considered that the Minister of Justice had made Sweden a laughing stock, while the conservative *Nya Dagligt Allehanda* regretted that the police had not managed to sequester more copies of *Getting Married*. The right-wing organ *Smålandsposten* called Strindberg 'a stinking muck-spreader'. The officious *Posttidningen* blamed the author and publisher for having ridiculed 'what every person of true religious mind holds most dear and holy'. Once more, claims circulated that Albert Bonnier had bribed Strindberg, now to make him come home and take responsibility.

Albert denied this in public and 'under oath', perhaps a somewhat risky tactic considering that he had offered Strindberg 1,000 francs to enable him to travel home from Switzerland.

The criticism that upset Albert the most came from old friends who now turned their backs on him. Some terminated their acquaintance and returned gifts, others hoped he was looking at a long time in Långholmen prison.

Both Albert and Karl Otto received anonymous threats: 'Beaten up on a dark street might be the language you understand.'

At one point they were visited by a well-known Stockholm doctor who said he represented a number of people who, in the event of a jury acquittal, were prepared to buy up the entire stock of Getting Married in order to burn it. In this way they would be able to prevent the spread of this terrible book while the publisher would still be able to make a profit. He was shown the door.

Nothing else was to be expected, of course, but Albert was able to console himself with the fact that the whole family were behind him. From Paris, Eva wrote to her older sister Jenny: 'I would like to be in S[tockholm] just to be plucky and bold.'

Albert now began to worry that the court might not accept an affidavit and that Strindberg might refuse to come home. The signals from Switzerland were not that easy to interpret. In a first reply to Albert after the books were seized, Strindberg wrote: 'Will come home if you are to go to prison, certainly. Otherwise not.' He blamed illness in the family.

The following day, 8 October: 'Am sending the affidavit tomorrow. Too late to see the Consul today. If the case against you is dropped, I can be charged abroad (from what I understand of the copy of the law which I have here).'

Strindberg initially had 'no thought of returning home', said literary scholar and Strindberg expert Ulf Boëthius in his detailed commentary on the national edition of *Getting Married*: 'It looked as though the publisher, Albert Bonnier, would be prosecuted if Strindberg did not appear.'

Albert asked Hjalmar Branting and Pehr Staaff to urge Strindberg to make his way homewards, which they did, as did Bjørnstjerne Bjørnson. The latter's advice made Strindberg so angry that he broke off the friendship.

The letters from Albert to Strindberg took on a more pleading tone, especially once Albert had been called before the City Court where a judge confidentially informed him that 'if Strindberg does not come home and appear, Herr Bonnier will be going to gaol!' An affidavit was not enough. Strindberg had to appear in person. On 9 October Albert wrote to Strindberg:

> No, there is no time left for compromises – it is time
> for a courageous decision – it will also do you the
> greatest honour. And nor is there any more thinking
> time left either (...) Let the call of honour work on you.
> Trust to Providence and come.

That night Albert and Karl Otto consulted Betty's cousin, the lawyer and chief of police Semmy Rubenson, who shared the opinion that had left Albert shaken on his visit to court. Rubenson proposed that Karl Otto should travel down to Geneva and fetch Strindberg back. Karl Otto left the very next day.

How afraid Albert Bonnier was of going to prison is shown

by a memory from one of his acquaintances, the anatomist Gustaf Retzius, now most associated with discredited theories of racial biology. For a period Retzius was editor-in-chief of *Aftonbladet*, which he owned with his wife. In his autobiography Retzius recounted an incident during the *Getting Married* court case:

> August Strindberg himself remained absent for as long as possible and poor old Albert Bonnier, the book's publisher, was about to be held responsible and go to prison for it. One fine day he came up to me in the newspaper office, totally terrified, shaking like an aspen leaf. He asked me in a quavering voice what in the world he was to do, to which I answered that in the first instance he needed to get the author, Herr Strindberg, back to Sweden to defend his case himself, but that otherwise he could probably take the matter calmly for the time being, as – however incautiously he had proceeded – Strindberg largely had opinion and a sense of justice on his side among experts and right-thinking people.

Karl Otto Bonnier arrived in Geneva on 14 October via Copenhagen, Cologne and Bern. This was the start of an episode with a number of strange elements that Strindberg himself would depict in a series of prose pieces, *Qvarstadsresan (Sequestration Journey)*.

Karl Otto immediately sought out Strindberg, who was staying in a guest house in Plainpalais, outside Geneva. They ate a good dinner together and drank wine, although Strindberg had said he was temporarily teetotal. In these relaxed conditions, Karl Otto attempted to convince Strindberg of the necessity of coming home. He was turned down flat. Karl Otto gave up hope but next morning when he woke in his hotel, Strindberg appeared, now in a completely different mood, declaring:

'Now I shall travel!'

Strindberg had slept on the matter and friends' hints that he was not attending the trial because he was scared, had had an effect. He was filled with a lust for battle. Well aware of expectations in Sweden, he telegraphed *Aftonbladet*: 'I am coming home.'

Strindberg's mood shifted this way and that during the journey, however. On the station platform in Hamburg, he suddenly burst into tears and said, according to Karl Otto: 'Excuse me, but it is my nerves that I cannot control.' On the way from Hamburg to Kiel, Strindberg was nervous and worried.

Then the train stopped at the steamer quay in Kiel beside the ship that was to transport him and Karl Otto on to Copenhagen. Strindberg noted the name of the ship, *Auguste Victoria*, and was as if transformed. 'Omen accipio! Auguste Victoria. Victory!'

Strindberg and Karl Otto arrived in Stockholm via Malmö on the morning of 20 October. A large crowd had gathered to meet them at Stockholm's Central Station. It included Hjalmar Branting, Knut Wicksell – and Albert Bonnier.

On the station platform Strindberg gave a speech to an admiring audience, which was reproduced in sympathetic newspapers. In it he said he was pleased that 'we could now start to get air in our lungs' after the suffocating oppressiveness that had prevailed in Sweden, whereupon he promised to 'do my duty'. It was a clear indication that Strindberg saw the prosecution as something bigger than himself and one single book; it was about freedom of expression and freedom of the press.

The reception at the station was followed by a dinner at the Grand Hôtel and a special performance by Ludvig Josephson at the New Theatre of Strindberg's drama *Lycko-Pers resa* (*Lucky Peter's Travels*).

The court case itself began the very next day, on the morning of 21 October.

As Strindberg had made an appearance and taken responsibility, the case against Albert Bonnier was dropped. It was now Strindberg's task to defend himself and *Getting Married*, which he did by consistently claiming that he had not at all intended to 'ridicule', but to 'educate'. The contested passage about Jesus as a 'rabble-rouser' was, he claimed, based on the Gospel of Saint Matthew.

A jury was appointed and Strindberg exercised his right to propose his own jury members, including the liberal journalist and politician Adolf Hedin, despite having previously declared that there would be no point. The day after the raid on the publisher, Strindberg had written to Albert:

> If there's a jury, I shan't appoint any jurors. What would be the good? I'll be condemned in any case! This time I'll probably also stand quite alone against the judges, papers + hermaphrodites and pederasts + Ibsenites = the radicals (my friends!). When I worked at the R. Library, it was said quite openly that half the Supreme Court was made up of pederasts. Is it they who will judge me now?

The jury met on 17 November and acquitted Strindberg after over four hours. Celebrations broke out among thousands of people who had gathered in Riddarhustorget outside the court. In the midst of the chaos, Strindberg managed to get as far as the Grand Hôtel, with the help of police, where he gave a brief speech of thanks 'for the victory that free thought and free speech have won'.

The very next day he made his way south, towards Switzerland, once more cheered by crowds. *Budkaflen*, one of Strindberg's supporters among the voices of the press, described his departure:

> And the cheers echoed for ten minutes under the glass ceiling of the railway hall.
>
> And then the train whistle blew. A last thundering hurrah:
>
> 'Long live August Strindberg! Long live freedom of belief, freedom of thought, freedom of the press and freedom of speech! Send greetings to Switzerland! Come back soon!'

The ruling finding Strindberg not guilty was confirmed by Svea Court of Appeal on 8 December 1884.

* * *

Albert Bonnier was relieved, but also exhausted after the ordeal he had been forced to undergo. He was as yet unaware of the consequences the debate on *Getting Married* and 'filthy literature' were to have for him in a personal and a professional sense, but there were signs that the campaign was far from over and that the guardians of public morality were merely biding their time. *Nya Dagligt Allehanda* bewailed the outcome of the case and urged booksellers to boycott *Getting Married*, 'this immoral product'.

Albert also needed to manage relations with his two most important authors. Viktor Rydberg and Zacharias Topelius had both been affected by the storm surrounding Strindberg. The former case was easier to resolve than the latter.

In the first worrying weeks after the book was confiscated, when he feared that he would have to bear the responsibility, Albert had thought of suitable jury members. One name seemed an obvious choice – Viktor Rydberg, defender of freedom of religion. Albert went to Stockholms Högskola to see Professor Rydberg, who was not in his office. Evidence for this is a small piece of paper in the Bonnier family archive, written in haste and sent by messenger. Albert's tone was nervously humble, which is anything but typical of him:

> Brother Rydberg! I took the liberty of seeking you out but see on your door that you only receive visitors on Mondays.
>
> However, you would do me a particular service if you would make an exception for once and grant me a brief conversation on what is a particularly urgent matter for me which cannot wait until next Monday.

It seems obvious that Albert wanted to discuss the possibility of placing Rydberg on the freedom of the press jury.

Had the prosecution ultimately been brought against Albert and not Strindberg, it is likely that Rydberg would have stood up for his friend, but he did not want to be linked with Strindberg, particularly not since Strindberg, a touch ironically, had cited Rydberg's *The Teaching of the Bible Concerning Christ* in his defence. Rydberg chose to distance himself from both author and publisher.

On 27 October Albert invited Rydberg to dinner at his house, with guests including Strindberg. Albert's invitation made it clear that Strindberg had already decided on his jury members and that Rydberg therefore did not need to worry about being troubled by the matter. Nevertheless, Rydberg refused the invitation, as if for safety's sake:

> The more I have thought about your friendly invitation, the more determined my conviction has become, that my presence today at your table can only be to the displeasure of other guests.

He concluded with a quite sharp addition: 'NB. This is my last word on the matter.'

Karl Otto Bonnier, who was one of the decimated company at dinner, wrote afterwards: 'As far as I can remember, the atmosphere was quite subdued.'

In Rydberg's actions one can trace a terrified unwillingness to risk his place on Parnassus, but it never developed into anything more than a minor jolt in their friendship, according to Per I. Gedin. The relationship between Albert and Viktor Rydberg was strong and deep enough to survive the strain, as was confirmed ten years later by Rydberg's charming dedication in *Singoalla*.

* * *

Zacharias Topelius' dislike of August Strindberg came as no surprise to Albert Bonnier. When *Poems in Verse and Prose* came out, Topelius wrote to Albert: 'I have read numerous works by A. Strindberg with enjoyment but his most recent poetry is a cartload of dung.'

The *Getting Married* affair saw Topelius' tone towards Albert grow sharper regarding his role as publisher. The same day the trial started in Stockholm, he sent a letter to Albert that contained a challenge: 'Were I the biggest publisher in Sweden, I would use my mighty influence for *good* literature.'

Albert's response, sent only once Strindberg had been acquitted, was an honest and courteously worded declaration of his principles:

I can assure you that I do what I can to achieve good literature – but it is not so good for us older ones to constantly work against the younger and newer directions in taste, which of course may also have their merits. I think that a publisher must not be too exclusive and does not have the right to exercise excessively strict censorship.

Topelius did not give in. In a letter in December he complained that 'the unfortunate connection with Strindberg damaged the firm both in Sweden and in Finland', whereupon he rejected Strindberg as 'a literary docker' in whose company no serious author would want to be seen. Topelius was hinting that he was considering leaving Bonniers due to Strindberg, which terrified Albert. Matters did not go as far as that, but Topelius continued in letter after letter to attack Strindberg and what he considered to be the publishing house's inaction. When the first part of *Tjänstekvinnans son* (*The Son of a Servant*) came out in 1886, Topelius wrote to Albert:

> I have heard too much about *The Son of a Servant* – also from impartial readers – to want to soil my hands by touching this book. If it is true that it finds the majority of its readers amongst school pupils, who it teaches to despise everything that people consider holy, I deplore the publisher and the authors who stand in such serried company on the shelf.

Albert avoided mounting a defence and the previously lively correspondence across the Bothnian Sea became increasingly sporadic. However, Albert took note. Criticism from his 'friend and ally' Topelius was one of the factors behind Albert's decision not to publish a sequel to *Getting Married* unless Strindberg allowed the story 'The Reward of Virtue' to be cut and toned down some of his language. Strindberg refused: 'I will not change the way I write or my opinions because I have been vilified.' In strong language he accused Albert of attempting to force him 'into silence by the might of capital'. In his reply, an offended Albert pointed out that 'during the late troublesome events' he had 'deserved a fairer judgement on your part', whereupon he told Strindberg he was entirely free to publish the book elsewhere.

Then Albert gave what was the single most important reason for his caution.

In his business contacts, it was extremely rare for Albert Bonnier to bring in his Jewish origins, but now he referred to his 'faith' and that the 'huge reactionary mood' made his position 'more sensitive than it would be for anyone else'.

The worst outbreaks of antisemitism in the wake of the *Getting Married* trial were yet to come, but the undertones of the debate on and surrounding the prosecution were clear enough, with persistent blaming of 'commerce' and greed for money. To Strindberg he wrote: 'You yourself can have no idea of the unrelenting mass of foul abusive language with which I and Karl Otto have been shouted down.'

Another factor that undoubtedly also played a part was that Albert had been visited by representatives of the Jewish congregation in Stockholm who had begged him not to reprint. One of them was Semmy Rubenson, who according to a footnote in Karl Otto's memoirs said to Albert: 'There are two kinds of people who more than others may never allow themselves to do anything that can be criticised: policemen and Jews.'

Rubenson did not know how right he was to be proved in purely personal terms. The following year, 1885, in his capacity as Stockholm's Chief of Police he was subjected to harsh criticism over the police's actions in conjunction with a performance by opera singer Christina Nilsson. A mass panic broke out in the sea of people outside the Grand Hôtel and about twenty people were crushed to death. Rubenson was prosecuted, but released. The campaign against him had antisemitic elements.

Getting Married II, angrier than its predecessor, came out in 1886. The publisher was anonymous. It was not until later that Karl Otto found out it had been published by his cousin, Isidor Bonnier, Strindberg's old schoolfellow.

* * *

The relationship between Strindberg and Albert Bonnier was stormy in the years that followed the *Getting Married* trial. Strindberg, still abroad and under tough pressure in terms of his private finances, lurched between serious accusations and regretful retreats. 'When the children cry for food and medicine the "male" becomes a tiger,' he excused himself in a letter to Albert after having threatened to shoot himself a few days earlier.

Albert was getting tired of this and in early 1886 prepared for what in practice could have been a break with Strindberg.

The trigger was an article in the weekly magazine *Stockholm* in which Strindberg, under the headline 'Capital and literature', dismissed 'the publisher' as an 'unnecessary middle-man'.

In February Albert wrote a letter to Strindberg about their 'mutual relationship', an arrangement that meant that Albert had right of first refusal to Strindberg's works:

> This condition, which forms the main basis of our
> agreement and was therefore important to me from
> a business point of view, you may perhaps find
> oppressive, since you seem to see it as involving some
> kind of censorship of your work.

Albert offered to terminate the contract and simultaneously write off Strindberg's debts to him; these amounted to more than 8,000 kronor, which would be about half a million kronor or £44,000 today. The aim seems to have been to clear the table. He had had enough.

The letter was never sent. Albert showed it to Karl Otto, who asked him to delay. After a few weeks of discussion between them, a reworded letter was sent that did not mention the possibility of terminating the contract but which did include the offer to write off the debt.

Strindberg's reaction to this generous offer says everything about his inconsistency at this period. To his brother Axel he wrote:

Great Shylock!
Can you imagine he gave me the 8,000 kronor I owe him.
There's something going on under that!
Something devilish about it.

The same day, Strindberg asked *Stockholm* to include a letter to the editor thanking 'the one of my publishers who has so generously written off my accumulated debts to him'. The letter must have been incomprehensible to the readers of the paper as it was unsigned.

The relationship between Strindberg and the publishing house soon stabilised, at least for the moment. It had to do with Strindberg asking Albert what he would think 'if I wrote my life'? After several weeks of thought, Albert decided to give Strindberg a chance. When the manuscript was delivered, Albert was delighted: 'There are splendid sections and few really tedious bits at most. I am prepared to take the book.' After that he added, almost as a small pin prick: 'It is pleasing that you refrained from peppering the book with "coarse words".'

This was *The Son of a Servant*.

Albert's enthusiasm was not shared by Strindberg's conservative critics. Carl David af Wirsén of the Swedish Academy thought the book was 'brazen and raw' and attacked Albert, 'the publisher who pays for and has printed a work distinguished by so much impudence'. More tolerant critics, on the other hand, like Karl Warburg in *Handelstidningen*, praised Strindberg's latest work.

It was as if *Getting Married* had split Swedish cultural circles into two antagonistic camps, for or against Strindberg – and thus for or against Albert Bonnier.

Then, at Christmas 1887, there followed a magnificent archipelago novel, originally titled *På landet* (*In the Country*), but then renamed *Hemsöborna* (*The People of Hemsö*), the book that today, perhaps in competition with *The Red Room*, is synonymous with Strindberg to a wider Swedish audience.

However, *The People of Hemsö* too caused convulsions between publisher and author. Strindberg offered the manuscript to other publishers, who were reluctant to publish him. And he continued his attacks on Bonniers. Their relationship was reaching freezing point.

At Whitsun 1887 Strindberg wrote to Karl Otto – 'because my natural bashfulness forbids me from writing an insulting letter to your father' – accusing the 'reptilian' publishing firm of upholding a 'system of boycotts' against him. At the same time, he asked for money. Karl Otto was furious and on 2 June wrote a sharp answer:

> You can hardly seriously imagine that we want to print any of your works at all after a letter like your last one.
>
> The bond that I made with you four years ago, due to my then naive admiration of your authorship, and that you now find 'too painful', has caused *us* even greater agonies and therefore it will be no loss to us to break it!

He put 500 kronor in the envelope 'from my private account as I have not yet dared to show your letter to my father, who would certainly be angered even more by it'.

Strindberg was in the process of becoming isolated from the world of Swedish publishing and reacted with furious explosions against 'Alb. B and his red reptile spawn'. His brother Axel, who often acted as Strindberg's intermediary, intervened and was of the firm opinion that despite everything it would have to be Bonniers again. Reluctantly, Strindberg agreed, with the condition that 'Alb. B is as hateful to me as a slimy reptile and so I will have no correspondence with him if the purchase comes off'. Even this argument petered out once Strindberg – equally reluctantly – agreed to allow the publishers to make cuts in the text. *The People of Hemsö* became a great success, like its successor *Skärkarlslif* (*The Men of the Skerries*).

The phantom pains from *Getting Married* lingered on, however, and contributed towards the publishing house in 1888 turning down Strindberg's *Miss Julie*, a drama steaming with lust and class consciousness. *Miss Julie* was instead published by Joseph Seligmann, despite his reservations considering Strindberg personally: '[A] snake, a rattlesnake.'

Albert and Karl Otto Bonnier had had enough of Strindbergian conflagrations. Karl Otto would later dub the refusal of *Miss Julie* 'the greatest publishing mistake (...) that I and my father were ever guilty of'.

The connection with Strindberg brought numerous problems for Albert, Karl Otto and the publishing house and was likely a contributing factor to the nervous breakdown that Karl Otto suffered in 1886, while Strindberg drowned a completely exhausted Albert in constant ideas for new books. But it also had a fortunate consequence for the future.

'Young Sweden' viewed Strindberg with distrust not least due to his views on women, but Bonniers' publicly standing behind their controversial author increased interest in the publisher among Strindberg's younger colleagues. The year after the *Getting Married* trial, three of them – Tor Hedberg, Georg Nordensvan and Oscar Levertin – published books with Bonniers. This was the start of the modernisation of Bonniers' literary catalogue that Karl Otto sought, though he did have to put a great deal of time and effort into convincing his father, who was heartily tired of controversy. Karl Otto recalled later how Albert said about Hedberg, Nordensvan and Levertin that 'they probably won't come to anything anyway'.

In 1892, after his divorce from Siri von Essen, Strindberg went to Germany to try to heal his spiritual wounds and start again. Contact with Albert Bonniers Förlag tailed off, to cease entirely in the 'Inferno years' when Strindberg was in crisis. Only after Albert's death in 1900 was close contact resumed, now with Karl Otto Bonnier.

It was a complicated and explosive relationship but until his death in 1912 Strindberg always returned to Bonniers – and Bonniers always to Strindberg. The one became, for better or worse, mutually bound to the other. And despite all his troublesome dealings with Albert Bonnier, Strindberg was, in between, careful to express his respect. To his cousin Gotthard Strindberg he wrote in 1891:

Teach my children to always mention Albert Bonnier's name with respect and gratitude, to always – whatever they may hear others say – speak well of members of his family. For Bonnier once saved these children's father from ruin.

* * *

Albert Bonnier's relationship with Zacharias Topelius was repaired after a few years. Topelius took the initiative when around New Year 1888 he asked Albert's forgiveness for having in an interview spoken 'inconsiderately' about 'publishers with no conscience'. A pleased and relieved Albert replied accommodatingly but once more enclosed a kind of manifesto:

> A publisher – particularly of the branch of literature that is denoted by the word quality literature – can and should however not be afforded the unconditional right to always set himself up as judge and exercise censorship – as who can give us absolute certainty that some of the things we complain about, dislike or condemn today will not be judged differently by the future.

In his next letter to Topelius, however, Albert protested that he had now 'become *more cautious*' and that in the future he intended to be even more so, 'as I in no way wish to risk such an old and valued friendship as yours'.

In his memoir, Karl Otto was critical of his father's 'submissive' attitude. In *Litteraturens örtagårdsmästare* Per I. Gedin is more understanding and points out that Topelius was 'the very symbol of Albert's success as a publisher'. Hence the humble language that was to be used a few years later during the court case against Gustaf Fröding.

Nevertheless the experiences from the *Getting Married* trial and its aftershocks affected Albert Bonnier, heart and soul. He was, he wrote to Strindberg, 'tired and sometimes exhausted'.

And he did become more cautious. The radical fearlessness that he had carried with him since his youth was increasingly having to give way to his ambition to safeguard the position his courage had built up. The immigrant boy from Copenhagen had, in the words of Zacharias Topelius, become 'a great power in Scandinavian literature'.

Now that position was threatened.

When *The People of Hemsö* achieved its success, Albert Bonnier had just survived the toughest battle of his life. In the autumn of his years – his seventieth birthday was approaching – he was hung out to dry as a personification of all that was wrong, unethical and immoral.

CHAPTER 8

ENEMY OF PUBLIC MORALITY

**A hate brochure. Albert at the centre of a storm.
Moral panic. A formidable opponent.
The Publishers' Association implodes. Verdandi.
Betty dies. A stylish visitor.**

———

The book and newspaper sector continued to expand towards the end of the 1880s in parallel with developments in Swedish society in general, the advent of new technology, rising industrialisation and the breakthrough of more liberal ideas. There was greater diversification in publishing, while interest in printed matter increased even more, in pace with growing widespread literacy across all social classes. Larger editions were printed, and the 'popular press' grew, with *Svenska Familj-Journalen* (*Swedish Family Journal*) and the Dane Carl Aller's *Illustrerad Familj-Journal* as trailblazers.

According to surveys of young recruits called up for military service, a majority, about six out of ten Swedes, were judged to have 'good skills' in reading by the middle of the decade. And four out of ten were classified as 'reasonably practised'. The Elementary School Act of 1842, plus the emergence of education-oriented popular movements such as nonconformism and the temperance movement, were starting to produce results. Being able to read was no longer the preserve of the upper classes.

This dynamic unavoidably led to clashes between old and new, between established social morality and its challengers, and between the elite and the people. Given the strict Lutheran order that prevailed in Sweden, the collisions were particularly pronounced where religion was involved. Growing religious apathy, or actual denial, provoked a counter-reaction in the defenders of the Christian faith, or, more precisely, in the guardians of double morality of Oscarian Sweden.

A Swedish subsidiary of the British, Continental and General Federation for the Abolition of Prostitution was formed as early as 1878. That same year the Federation started to publish a journal, *Sedlighetsvännen* (*Friend of Morality*). Its target was the book industry. In late 1879 the Federation published an appeal urging booksellers and publishers to jointly 'work to prevent the publication and spread of such literature that must clearly lead to moral decay and thus to the downfall of society'.

The *Getting Married* trial in 1884 and the fury invoked against August Strindberg and Albert Bonnier reflected these attitudes. Barely three years later it was time for another moral panic. And Albert was once more in the eye of the storm.

* * *

In autumn 1886 some 'immoral' incidents took place among senior school students in Stockholm who, it was claimed, had fraternised with 'loose women'. Many were horrified and in February 1887 the indignation was channelled through a pamphlet written by John Personne, a priest, a lecturer in Christianity and Swedish at the Norra Latinläroverket school in Stockholm, and later Bishop of Linköping. Personne had been a somewhat furtive participant in the outcry against *Getting Married* through letters in the press, but now he came out into the open, on the warpath.

The pamphlet was entitled *Strindbergs-litteraturen och osedligheten bland skolungdomen* (*Strindbergian Literature and Immorality among Schoolchildren*) and was addressed in a sub-title 'to parents and guardians and those in power'. In it Personne attacked not only Strindberg as a poisoner of youth, but practically the entire young generation of authors who, in his view, were devoting themselves to 'the immoral writing that is rife amongst us'.

The harshest and most insulting words were reserved for Strindberg's publisher Albert Bonnier:

> The publisher; yes he is also a significant cause of our literature being enriched with these filthy stories and these vile opinions that are destroying our growing youth, and moreover his guilt is even greater than that of the writer (...) Herr Albert Bonnier, chair of the Swedish Publishers' Association, has the honour of bringing this literature into the light of day.

The antisemitic elements of the message were not something Personne sought to hide. He referred to the 'Moses' chapter in *The New Kingdom* and repeated the frequent accusation that Albert had more or less bribed Strindberg to stop writing negative things about Jews:

There is talk of a kind of agreement between Herr Bonnier and Strindberg, by virtue of which the former is said to have undertaken to be the publisher of the latter with relatively unlimited freedom for him to write what he likes as long as he leaves 'Moses' in peace. If this is the case, it would indeed explain the otherwise utterly inexplicable. *The publisher* Bonnier has martyred himself for the *Jew* Bonnier. But when that martyrdom is at the expense of growing youth and of society, its value is moderately great; as it is society that has to *pay* in any case. –

Were I briefly and generally to express my thoughts on those who publish morally wretched literature, the statement would read as follows: *for my part I cannot see the moral difference between such a publisher and a buyer of stolen goods or a madam of a bordello.*

Albert reacted to this unprecedented onslaught with lofty calm. 'I believe it is most sensible to answer the whole attack with the silence and contempt of indifference,' he wrote to a friend. Instead it was one of the representatives of 'Young Sweden', Gustaf af Geijerstam, who rushed to Albert's defence in public:

Even if one is inclined to object to some of the things Strindberg states, in this now indignant atmosphere the fact that Herr Bonnier has published Strindberg and other newer writers is a matter for which Herr Bonnier should be honoured. For a writer shall be countered with scolding but not brutally be prevented from speaking at all.

One would not like to comment on whether Personne truly realised the consequences but his intentional reference to Albert's position as chair of the Swedish Publishers' Association was like an explosive charge set under the professional organisation that Albert had belonged to almost from its first beginnings and in which he numbered some of his closest colleagues in the world of publishing.

In the association, Albert Bonnier was namely on the brink of open conflict with his most formidable opponent so far, Norstedts' managing director Gustaf B. A. Holm, who, in the words of Karl Otto Bonnier 'came to cause my father a wound so deep that it could never be healed'.

On top of this, another factor arose that made Albert more vulnerable to public attacks; the debate on morality that had been so heightened at the time of the publication of *Getting Married* suddenly gained a new lease of life.

* * *

The plans for a radical paper that August Strindberg had put to Albert Bonnier in early 1882 were never realised but in their eagerness to find new ways to disseminate liberal and progressive ideas, in the October of the same year a group of young radical graduates of Uppsala University founded a student association, 'Verdandi', with the aim of promoting freedom of opinion and freedom of expression. Its name was carefully chosen. In Norse mythology, Verdandi was one of the fates, the Norns, where she represented the present.

Leading names in the association included Karl Staaff and Knut Wicksell. Hjalmar Branting was involved in the preparations before he moved to Stockholm and a post as assistant at the Stockholm Observatory. Strindberg, on the other hand, was not interested in contributing to Verdandi, mainly due to the association's backing of female emancipation. Among its female sympathisers was Ann Margret Holmgren, later a central figure in the women's suffrage movement.

To begin with, Verdandi had the character of an internal debating society but as the association grew, its activities became more outward-looking, to the great anger of the university town's establishment.

On 2 April 1887 Verdandi arranged a debate in Uppsala on 'questions of morality'. Participants included Knut Wicksell, Gustaf af Geijerstam and the young socialist with anarchist tendencies, Hinke Bergegren. The meeting discussed topics such as extra-marital relations, family planning and prostitution. Several of those involved were connected with Albert and Karl Otto Bonnier, among them the fellow Jew Oscar Levertin, on the threshold of his breakthrough as a poet and especially as a literary scholar. Karl Otto had also gone to school with Karl Staaff.

It was a lively evening. Bergegren, who was not a member of Verdandi, pleaded for 'a healthy, natural sex life' as a counter-measure to prostitution in which vulnerable women were exploited by 'moral' married men. Wicksell argued for birth control, an idea that Geijerstam supported. The language and the messages, entirely unproblematic today, were at the time seen as an outrageous provocation against prevailing norms of love and sexuality.

The reaction to the event had features of a moral panic. The conservative press raged, with the Uppsala paper *Fyris* at the helm:

One might truly think oneself transported to ancient Rome in the days of Claudius or Caligula instead of being in nineteenth-century Sweden.

The university issued 'reprimands and warnings' to the entire Verdandi committee and two participants lost their chance of being awarded scholarships. Ann Margret Holmgren, who was married to a professor at the university, suffered so much vitriol for her contacts with Verdandi that she felt it safest to move to Norway for a few months.

First Strindberg and *Getting Married*, then Personne and Verdandi. The ground was shaking beneath Albert Bonnier's feet.

Two days after the Verdandi event, on 4 April, a short text written by Gustaf Holm was read out at the spring meeting of the Swedish Publishers' Association in Stockholm:

As we do not approve of the foundations on which the association is built, and as we do not see ourselves capable of achieving change in the direction that we desire, we find we have no other course open to us than to resign from the association, of which we hereby give notice.

The explosion had come but the fuse had been burning for a long time.

* * *

Albert Bonnier had been elected chair of the Swedish Publishers' Association on 19 September 1877. It was one of the high points of his publishing career. Barely two years later, the new manager of Norstedts, Gustaf Holm gained a place on the committee. Holm, a lawyer and deputy district court judge, was twenty-five years younger than Albert but considerably more old-fashioned in his values and his leadership style. In Sven Rinman's history of the association, an invaluable source of information about the state of the nineteenth-century Swedish publishing industry, he is described as follows:

> Holm was a tough, dominant character without any deeper erudition but with all the instincts of the conservative Oscarian lawyer. He always knew exactly what he wanted and with his iron will and his eminent practical skills he was also capable of achieving it.

Initially there was no major friction between Holm and Albert Bonnier on organisational and practical issues, although it was clear that the former was put out by the fact that the Publishers' Association was headed by the owner of a publishing house that was smaller than the one he himself represented. Albert does not even seem to have reacted when Holm made an independent attempt to rewrite the association's constitution after only a year or two on the committee.

However, Holm's proposed statute contained a paragraph that was a foreboding of the implosion to come.

Holm proposed that a member who engaged with texts 'of clearly immoral or otherwise criminal content' could be ejected from the association. In April 1881 the proposal was unanimously rejected, which may explain why Albert took the matter so calmly. His tolerant and liberal line still enjoyed strong support. Holm, whose publishing firm only published literature to a limited extent, saw himself, on the other hand, as the representative of a more moral high ground and of a view of the mission of publishing that contrasted with Albert's alleged commercialism.

In the years that followed, Holm tried to undermine the position of the chair through one attack or another. One such occasion was the meeting of Scandinavian booksellers in Copenhagen in July 1884. Holm and Albert disagreed on the approach to translations between the Scandinavian languages. Somewhat paradoxically considering his inclinations towards Scandinavianism, Albert argued for the importance of trans-lations. He pointed out that Hans Christian Andersen in particular had only become a famous name in Sweden once his works were translated from Danish into Swedish. Holm, on the other hand, considered that translation 'contributes towards preventing literature in its original form', before adding, his poison dart aimed straight at Albert, that 'in publishing one should also have idealistic goals in sight and not merely think of earning money'.

The discussion did not lead to any firm position being taken but the cracks were clear between two members who set the tone of the Swedish Publishers' Association.

The seizure and the prosecution of August Strindberg's *Getting Married* took place a few months later. The mood shifted in a conservative direction. Holm saw his chance, but his first target was not Albert but another Bonnier.

Isidor Bonnier, Albert's nephew, had been an appreciated editor of the Publishers' Association's publication *Svensk Bokhandelstidning* for some years. Immediately after the *Getting Married* trial he published a series of articles under the heading 'Our Freedom of the Press Act', in which he criticised the fact that the printer of a book could be prosecuted. It was unavoidably seen as a defence of his relative Albert, who was rumoured to be behind the piece, something that Isidor firmly denied.

Holm protested at what he saw as 'poor quality' articles and demanded that Isidor take sole responsibility for the opinions put out and cancel the series. This time he got other members on board. Humiliated, Isidor Bonnier had to resign his editorial post.

One Bonnier had fallen, but another, Albert, was still sitting as chair of the association – to Holm's great irritation. Determinedly, but in secret, Holm continued to gather support for his efforts to remove Albert too.

At the committee elections in September 1885, the first after the furore surrounding *Getting Married*, Albert encountered what was for him surprisingly strong opposition, apparently organised by Holm. Friends among the publishers advised Albert not to attend the meeting, but he did not heed their warnings.

At the meeting Erik Wilhelm Wallin was put forward as a candidate against Albert, a strange move as Wallin was a bookseller, not a publisher. Wallin was elected as chair but refused the post on the spot; clearly no-one had informed him in advance that he was to be part of a coup. The drama increased. A new vote had to be held, now with publisher Frans Beijer as the opposition candidate. Beijer and Albert received equal numbers of votes and the choice had to be made by drawing lots, which Albert won. Faith in him had been renewed by a hair's breadth.

Two camps faced each other in the Publishers' Association. Schematically they can be described as a liberal camp headed by Albert and a conservative camp headed by Holm, although the latter avoided putting himself forward as chair; he knew very well that he was not particularly popular in publishing circles.

The conflict's true basis in a disagreement on the role of literature and the job of the publisher is confirmed by the fact that in 1886 Holm took on responsibility for personally editing Norstedt's *Svensk kalendar*, a conservative response to *Svea*, Albert's literary annual.

The same year, however, a temporary ceasefire occurred between the factions in the association. This was caused by the question of how Sweden would react to the Berne Convention for the Protection of Literary and Artistic Works, an international agreement which afforded a certain amount of protection against unauthorised translations of foreign works. Both Holm and Bonnier, representatives of two of Sweden's largest publishing firms, were against Sweden signing up as they feared it would become more expensive to publish foreign books and that this would have a knock-on effect on Swedish literature. In an unholy alliance they jointly advocated a narrow commercial interest that in practice meant that foreign authors could not count on compensation when their works were translated into Swedish. They took a majority of the Publishers' Association with them. Sweden would not ratify the convention until 1904.

The fundamental conflict between Holm and Bonnier remained unresolved however – the question of morality.

* * *

That was where the front lines were drawn in early 1887 when John Personne's wild attacks on Strindberg and Albert made the situation untenable. The Publishers' Association was split and connections between Albert Bonniers Förlag and classic firms such as Hiertas and Gleerups were torn asunder. What Albert and Karl Otto were particularly hurt by was that after a little hesitation, publisher Hugo Geber joined Holm and the other opponents in the association. Born in 1853 and a former commercial partner of Joseph Seligmann, Geber was not only a fellow Jew with German and Danish family roots similar to those of the Bonnier family, but also a close friend of Karl Otto. To Albert and his son this was a huge betrayal.

The New Publishers' Association adopted its constitution on 27 April. Gustaf Holm was the chair. He was now able to push through the principled approach that more than anything else had defined his aversion to Albert Bonnier. Section 10 of the new association's constitution read as follows:

Where a member themselves or through another publication disseminated to the public, whose content *either* has been declared by the jury in question to be criminal following a public prosecution, *and/or* officially designated harmful to discipline and morality, this member, at the behest of two other members, *in the former case* shall be unconditionally expelled from the association and *in the latter case* shall be subject to a vote as to whether or not he is to be expelled from the association.

Barely a week later, on 21 April, Albert had given a speech to his decimated association. He regretted what had happened but also expressed his surprise that matters had gone so far. He referred to the explanation of the break-away contingent that they did not consider it possible to achieve the change they desired under the current constitution. Albert asked a justified question: 'When and how has any serious attempt been made on the part of those who had left the association to remedy these cited and alleged shortcomings?'

No such action had been taken after the discussion on the constitution at the start of the decade. There were no formal or practical grounds for the conflicts that ultimately led to the explosion. Instead they were due to different views on literary freedom and the responsibility of the publisher, fanned by the *Getting Married* feud and its side-effects, with Personne's pamphlet as a kind of peak. In other words, it was a revolt against a chair, Albert Bonnier, who was seen as being scandalous. This was Sven Rinman's view too: 'The action was (...) less directed at the cornerstones of the association than at the person of the chair.' The attempt to unseat Albert in 1885 bears this out.

Keen not to make the conflict worse, Albert sidestepped this aspect in his speech to the association:

> Whether any other, perhaps more personal, reasons might lie thereunder and have played a role – that is something that I do not consider I should investigate at this time.

Subsequently Albert explained that he had considered standing down immediately but had allowed himself to be persuaded by friends in the association who 'firmly advised me against further increasing the disorder in such a way'. Instead he announced that he would step down in September, when he would 'reach the round number of ten years during which I have had the honour of leading the association's negotiations'. And so he did.

* * *

It took a couple of weeks for the events in the Publishers' Association to become a hot topic in the press; the Verdandi debate overshadowed practically everything else. Once attention did start to be paid to the explosion in the association, the defenders of public morality were not slow to express their sympathies for the break-away members. In *Aftonbladet* a future court priest named Teodor Mazér was pleased that it had now become obvious 'which publishers feel themselves to have a moral obligation towards society' and linked this with a campaign to remove naked pictures from bookshop windows.

On 1 May the conservative *Stockholms Dagblad* went on the general offensive against the new literature that had lured young people into 'attacking our longstanding Christian moral teaching':

> Herr Strindberg has written, Herr Albert Bonnier has published and the Swedish public have received with curiosity one volume after the other of this new gospel which in fact consists of destroying the ten commandments.

Now a counter-reaction had finally arisen, said the paper, which viewed with satisfaction 'expressions of the self-defence of a wounded sense of morality' and referred particularly to 'the exit of the best Swedish publishing firms from the Swedish Publishers' Association'.

Gustaf Holm also entered the debate with a piece in *Handelstidningen* in which he explained that the purpose of the new association was 'the healthy development of the

Swedish book publishing industry (...) whereby one should particularly safeguard the extent to which the publication and dissemination of such literature as has damaged discipline and morality can be prevented'.

Holm's article was a response to one of Albert's few defenders, Karl Warburg, who on 28 April had written in the same paper:

> So the new association threatens to remove from a bookseller the right to sell its books if he disseminates any book that the association considers harms discipline and morality.
>
> *Herein* lies the very danger. As to what the gentlemen agree between them, that is up to them. But if they wish to exercise censorship over the range booksellers are allowed to sell, that is a dangerous move.

Rhetorically, Warburg asked which eighteenth-century publisher would have dared to publish Bellman under such terms.

Outwardly and towards the remaining members of the association, Albert was careful to behave in a calm and dignified manner so as not to fuel the conflict further, but he was bubbling with anger inside. This is shown by a letter to Karl Warburg in which he thanked him for his article in *Handelstidningen*:

> There is no doubt that among other nice motives, antisemitism and jealousy were involved and therefore it angers me most of all that the 'ignorant' Geber should run after them and beg his way in amongst them.
>
> My conviction is that both he and several of the

others will have reason to regret their haste. Those of us remaining should probably stick together and not allow ourselves to be frightened.

In the same letter, Albert stated that he had considered suing John Personne, but had not done so, partly because it would 'show the man greater honour than he deserves' and partly because he would prefer to 'live undisturbed and in peace'. Finally he conveyed the hope that 'this moral prudery and hypocrisy' would meet with growing resistance:

After all it does not only concern me and a couple of other publishers, but whether a kind of censorship is to be introduced against everything that is new and independent in our literature.

After a month or two the fuss surrounding the publishers' conflict started to die down. At the autumn meeting Albert Bonnier resigned as chair and was replaced by his colleague Sigfrid Flodin.

In purely practical terms, the split had no serious consequences for the industry, apart from the inconvenience that booksellers now had to negotiate with two parties instead of one. The booksellers and the publishers did, after all, have an overarching common interest in selling as many books as possible. The two associations merged in 1912.

* * *

Not long after stepping down as chair, Albert Bonnier had the chance, at least for a moment, to banish thoughts of everything he had been forced to endure during the year. On 22 October 1887 his friends arranged a magnificent party at Hotel Rydberg in Stockholm to celebrate the fiftieth anniversary of the publishing house; half a century had passed since Albert published his first book, *Bevis att Napoleon aldrig har existerat.* At it he was celebrated by Viktor Rydberg, Frans Hedberg and Rudolf Wall, among others. The praise rained down on a publisher who, it was said 'had always been a free-thinker and unafraid as few' and who possessed 'a guaranteed place in the annals of Swedish literature'.

The menu, which included salmon in hollandaise sauce, *Glace en Surprise*, cheeses and exclusive wines, was decorated with drawings by Carl Larsson, one of which depicted Albert with a firm grip on the reins of Pegasus, the winged horse of Greek mythology. The bust of his idol Albert Blanche, which had decorated Albert's private flat, was also shown in a corner.

Here a problem arises for the biographer of the life of Albert Bonnier in terms of sources. In his memoir, his son Karl Otto wrote that the party took place 'the day after my father's birthday'.

Karl Otto was clearly convinced, as was Albert himself, that Albert was born on 21 October 1820 and that he had therefore celebrated his sixty-seventh birthday the day before the party. Even such a reliable reference work as the Swedish biographical dictionary, in a text written in the 1920s, gives Albert's birthday as 21 October. In the genealogy of the members of the family published in the early 2000s, *Gerhard Bonniers ättlingar*, however, the date was changed to 22 October, which is also the date listed in the records of the Jewish congregation of Copenhagen where Albert was born.

Everything thus indicates that Albert Bonnier's birthday

was 22 October not 21 October, something that he seems to have been unaware of throughout his lifetime. The reason for this misconception is unclear but it might have been because his father Gerhard, who perhaps found it difficult to keep track of the dates of birth of all his children, had mixed his own birthday up with Albert's. Gerhard was born in Dresden on 21 October 1778.

* * *

All the conflicts around August Strindberg in the wake of *Getting Married* and then surrounding *The Son of a Servant* had quelled Albert's desire to fight any more battles, but he did not abandon his fundamental values. This is confirmed by the way he enthusiastically threw himself into a publishing project that was to develop into a Swedish classic of public education.

Back in 1886 Karl Staaff had raised the idea in the student association Verdandi of a series of small pamphlets 'intended to convey useful content in popular form'. After the uproar surrounding the night of discussions on morality in April the following year, Staaff and his friends felt an even greater need to make the idea a reality. So what could be more natural than for the controversial association to turn to a publisher who had also been painted as the enemy of morality?

In early 1888 Albert and Karl Otto were sought out by a group including Staaff and David Bergström, later a minister in Staaff's governments, asking whether they would help with publication. By this point Verdandi had five manuscripts waiting to be printed. Albert was more than happy to oblige. In April a contract was written and the very next month the first pamphlets were printed, designed by Carl Larsson, with

David Bergström as editor and Albert Bonnier as publisher. In this first year, ten Verdandi publications came out with titles such as *Om människans ursprung* (*On Human Origins*), *Dödlighetens aftagande i Sverge och orsakerna därtill* (*Falling Mortality in Sweden and the Causes Thereof*), *Koranen* (*The Koran*), *Skolans ställning till religionsundervisningen* (*The Position of the Schools on Religious Education*) and *Från människosläktets barndom* (*From the Childhood of Humanity*). The two latter titles were written by early feminists who were soon to become central figures in Swedish public life, the teachers Anna Whitlock and Ellen Key. They were followed by pamphlets on the right to vote and the French revolution and a translation of John Stuart Mill's classic *On Liberty*.

Until 1954, when the series was reworked, 531 issues of Verdandi's pamphlets were published, widely circulated in millions of copies. It was a huge enlightenment project which was enabled by Albert Bonnier's sympathies for the criticised Verdandi members from the organisation's very beginnings. The radical flames of his youth had not been entirely quenched but he was marked and exhausted by all the conflicts, as was also noted by the man who was the cause of so much of the stress that Albert had suffered, August Strindberg.

On the way home from a trip with Betty to Marienbad, Albert took the opportunity of meeting Strindberg in Copenhagen in June 1888. Strindberg wrote to Verner von Heidenstam – they were still friends at this point – and told him of the meeting: 'Yesterday I met Albert Bonnier, who has grown old and mild.'

And another trial, more private and personal, was waiting round the corner.

* * *

Betty Bonnier loved travelling, especially to the south, to France, Italy and Spain, but she also had a desire to travel in the opposite direction to experience the fjord landscape of Norway. In the summer of 1888 Betty, Albert and their daughters Jenny and Eva set off. The plan was to journey via Trondheim and Molde and then on to Hardanger by cariole, a type of two-wheeled horse-drawn carriage that could cope with Norway's bad roads. When they reached the small fishing village of Faleide in Nordfjord, Betty suffered a severe stroke. She died on 29 July.

For ten days Albert accompanied his wife's coffin all the way to Stockholm via Bergen and Christiania.

The same day as Betty's funeral, 11 August, August Strindberg's manuscript of *Miss Julie* arrived at the publishing house. According to Karl Otto this was a contributing factor to its refusal: 'No-one would be surprised that neither I nor my father were in the mood to read a tragedy by Strindberg.'

To an extent, though, this was said with hindsight. Even if Karl Otto had wanted to take the manuscript, Albert would have said no. With *Getting Married* and the battles over morality fresh in his memory, he was categorical: 'No, no question of it.'

Betty's sudden death came as a shock. Betty had largely been in good health since recovering from her severe bout of depression in 1876. The whole family were naturally devastated, but Karl Otto was particularly deeply affected. Karl Otto and his mother were especially close, with a warm relationship, not least since Betty in practice had acted as his personal nurse during his periods of illness and stays abroad in the late 1870s.

Albert handled his sorrow at the loss of his life partner as he usually did in dark times – by throwing himself into more work. His grandson Åke summed it up in his family chronicle thus:

> The loss of his wife became hard to bear for Albert but his capacity for work was undiminished; quite the opposite, his loneliness meant that his passion for work almost doubled. But the optimism and cheerful outlook that were so characteristic of Albert Bonnier throughout his life had taken a severe knock.

* * *

Work at the publishing business continued with the same intensity as before, with Albert as its obvious head, but now also with Karl Otto as an increasingly active partner.

One of the key projects in the transition from the 1880s to the 1890s was August Blanche's Collected Works in sixteen volumes illustrated by artists such as Jenny Nyström and Bruno Liljefors. Albert's idea was to follow up the success of the illustrated version of Zacharias Topelius' *The Surgeon's Stories*, where Carl Larsson had been responsible for the artwork. This had had a print run of 30,000, an amazing number at that time. Blanche's Collected Works were also a success, although Carl Larsson only found time to design the cover.

At least as important was the fact that Albert and Karl Otto signed up a writer who in many ways was to define the publishing firm – and Swedish literature in general – for the next decade.

In January 1888, about six months before Betty's death, two aristocratic ladies turned up at the publishing house wanting to buy a book that they insisted had been published by Bonniers. No member of staff had heard of such a book, however, and the ladies asked to meet 'Herr Bonnier himself'. Karl Otto was in the office and received them. He listened attentively as they explained that they had met the author in Switzerland and that he had definitely said that he had written a collection of poems for Albert Bonniers Förlag. Karl Otto answered: 'I know no author by that name, and I can assure you that no book by him has been published, neither by our firm or by anyone else's.' There must, he added, be some misunderstanding.

The next day Albert told Karl Otto that the night before he had had an unexpected visitor at home. This was an austerely elegant gentleman aged about twenty-five to thirty who briefly asked whether he might submit a manuscript to the publishing firm. The visitor said he was a good friend of August Strindberg and that Zacharias Topelius had read and liked some of his poems. Then he vanished as quickly as he had materialised at the door.

The following day a parcel was delivered to the publishing house containing a manuscript and a cover letter in which the author said he wished to avoid 'excessive pleading for his own work', but that he hoped to 'be able to return next week to discover the result' of the reading by the intended publisher.

The letter was signed:

'Respectfully,

Verner von Heidenstam'.

CHAPTER 9

THE NINETIES

**At the publishing firm. Verner von Heidenstam,
Oscar Levertin and Albert's last decade.
Some misjudgements. Revolution in the air.
Gustaf Fröding. The moral panic continues.
Another court case. Selma Lagerlöf.**

———

The environment in the publishing house's offices at Mäster Samuelsgatan 17, the firm's new address after a reform of Stockholm's street names in 1888, was both welcoming and spartan. A glimpse into life at Bonniers was provided much later by Herman Bergqvist, who was taken on as an assistant in 1889, before then advancing to office manager. After fifty years in the firm, Bergqvist published his memoirs, *I böckernas värld*, (*In the World of Books*), which he dedicated to Albert and Karl Otto Bonnier. Here he described Albert as a man 'incessantly at work, in the company of his constant companion, his cigar':

> Beneath what many perhaps saw as a gruff exterior, however, Albert Bonnier had a good heart and I will never forget the time when I had been out on an errand in the pouring rain and came walking across

the courtyard soaked to the skin, and Albert Bonnier, whose office was on that side of the building, caught sight of me and came out to offer me his coat.

Frans Hedberg, who was a frequent visitor in a professional as well as a private capacity has also described the atmosphere. The top boss, Albert Bonnier took pains to keep his door open:

It was only closed on special, serious occasions, but when it was closed, he shut it himself, as he did not like anyone else seeking to isolate him from his surroundings. When he sat there with the desk in front of him overflowing with pieces of paper, manuscripts, newspapers and telegrams, he could be quite brusque when one came in and interrupted him, but it did not take long for him to thaw and would share a joke and forget all the tasks awaiting his attention for a moment.

The office, which had moved to larger premises in the same property in 1880, consisted of seven rooms, while the staff comprised only seven or eight people. Books were transported by horse and cart; lorries were, as yet, an unknown phenomenon. Father and son had offices next to each other, Karl Otto's a little humbler than Albert's. The only phone, number 6609, was in a storage area called the 'cubbyhole'. When it rang, the person wanted had to be informed by messenger and then rush through the office to the apparatus. However, a certain amount of modernisation was on the march, Bergqvist remembers:

When I came to the company in 1889, there were no typewriters and all documents were written by hand. Gifted with legible handwriting, I was given the job of copying out publishing contracts, for example. The first typewriter, a Densmore, wasn't bought until the 1890s.

Another modernisation was even more important to the business at that time. Towards the end of the 1880s Bonniers had finally established itself as a publishing firm for the younger generation of authors. This was also seen in the literary annual *Svea*, which Albert continued to edit himself. Its columns had been opened for writers such as Victoria Benedictsson (under the pseudonym Ernst Ahlgren), Oscar Levertin, Albert Ulrik Bååth and Edvard Fredin, the latter best known for his translation of Alfred Tennyson's *Ring Out Wild Bells*. The same year that the ground-breaking artist Ernst Josephson, nephew of Ludvig Josephson, suffered mental illness, 1888, Bonniers published a selection of his poems under the title *Svarta rosor (Black Roses)*.

Openness to foreign novels remained a signature of the firm, which had introduced Tolstoy to a Swedish audience with *Anna Karenina* in 1885.

Albert, as we have seen, had an interest in travel writing and from the 1870s published a dedicated travel writing library, *Bibliotek för resebeskrifningar*. The same year as the publishing association showdown, 1887, a young explorer made his debut with a journey from Persia, Mesopotamia and the Caucasus. His name was Sven Hedin and he was to be of major commercial importance to the firm in the future. Popular non-fiction and handbooks, such as *Genom Sveriges bygder*, a guide to Sweden, and a home medical guide, *Hemläkaren,* also boosted profits in the 1880s.

And then there was that stylish visitor.

Born in 1859 into a noble family, Verner von Heidenstam mainly grew up in Stockholm, but saw Olshammar on Lake Vättern as his true childhood home. Olshammar was a stately home that had been owned by his mother's family and the sickly only child spent his summers there, developing a lifelong love for the area that left its mark on his poetry. In the 1920s he had a house, Övralid, built there on a slope overlooking Lake Vättern, which remained his home until his death in 1940.

Von Heidenstam was to be one of the Bonnier publishing firm's very biggest names, with early works such as the intricate novel of ideas *Hans Alienus,* a collection of poetry and *Karolinerna (The Charles Men).* His successes led to him becoming a member of the Swedish Academy in 1912 and to being awarded the Nobel Prize four years later for reasons that seem rather dubious today; he was rewarded more for his nationalism than for his poetry.

Besides writing books, Heidenstam was involved in reconstructing the daily paper *Svenska Dagbladet* when it suffered a crisis in the late 1890s. This was where he first published the suite of poems *Ett folk (A People),* which contains the lines by him that have perhaps become best known to posterity. These are in the poem 'Medborgarsång', (*Song of Citizenship*) written as part of the suffrage debate:

It is a shame, it is a stain on Sweden's banner,
that the name of citizenship is money.

Albert's faith in Karl Otto's literary judgment took many forms and the day after Verner von Heidenstam's unannounced evening visit in January 1888 he passed the manuscript over to his son. Karl Otto took it home and read it out loud to his wife Lisen. They were deeply moved:

> Right from the first word to the last, it was clear to us that here a new and great poet was revealed. That evening was one of those high points that a publisher never forgets but which are oh so rarely granted him.

Karl Otto's delight at his first encounter with Heidenstam's poetry is almost as easy to understand as his joy when he read August Strindberg's poems a few years earlier. Both writers – two friends who would later become irreconcilable enemies, their mutual hatred peaking in what was termed the Strindberg Feud of 1910–12 – presaged something new in Swedish literature, in von Heidenstam's case a stream of dreaming idealism with elements of national romanticism.

When reading out loud to Lisen, Karl Otto may have stopped at one particularly introspective passage, often quoted today:

> I have longed for home for eight long years.
> In sleep itself this longing have I known.
> I long for home. I long wherever I go
> – but not for men! I long for the earth,
> I long for the stones where I played as a child.

The manuscript, a collection of poems inspired by von Heidenstam's time in southern Europe and the Near East for health reasons when suffering from tuberculosis, was immediately accepted and was published with the title *Vallfart och vandringsår* (*Pilgrimage and Wandering Years*). The book was not a huge commercial success but the critics were fulsome with their praise. In *Handelstidningen* Karl Warburg wrote that 'a more beautiful, more original, more mature debut has not been seen in Swedish poetry in a long while'.

Almost overnight, the unknown Verner von Heidenstam had become a literary sensation, and the publishing firm had recruited yet another talent. That autumn Heidenstam delivered a novel, *Endymion*.

* * *

With his debut, Verner von Heidenstam, also a skilled watercolour painter, went to bat for the literary opposition against the 'grey eighties' as he put it in the pamphlet *Renässans* (*Renaissance*) in 1889.

The following year these ambitions were defined by Heidenstam and Oscar Levertin in their joint manifesto *Pepitas bröllop* (*Pepita's Wedding*), published by Albert Bonniers Förlag. The aim, they wrote, was 'a poetry of beauty, which is not harnessed before the load of utility'. At that point Levertin had broken away from the '*åttitalister*' (the writers of the 1880s) to join Heidenstam's cause. A new epoch in Swedish literature was dawning, synonymous with the new decade, the 1890s. Besides von Heidenstam and Levertin, this golden age was associated with names such as Gustaf Fröding and Selma Lagerlöf.

Swedish painting was also enjoying a creative upsurge, partly in the wake of Ernst Josephson, painter of *Näcken* (*The Water Sprite*), Anders Zorn, Carl Larsson, Prince Eugen, Hanna and Georg Pauli – and Eva Bonnier.

Several of the writers of the nineties became closely linked with Albert Bonniers Förlag, with one striking exception.

Karl Otto described the course of events in one of the many informative and entertaining footnotes that garnish his memoirs. Possibly this is an episode that says something about the confusion that could arise in Bonniers' office as a result of the literary helm being shared between an aging father and his ambitious son.

One day in 1895 a manuscript of poems arrived. It was left in a pile 'as can happen sometimes when you have a lot of other things to do'. After a few months, the sender sent a messenger to the firm to fetch the manuscript back and it was returned without 'any of us having looked at the poems for a second'. This was Erik Axel Karlfeldt's debut collection, *Vildmarks- och kärleksvisor*, (*Songs of the Wilderness and of Love*) which was instead published by Seligmanns.

Karlfeldt never became a Bonnier author, but he did become an appreciated poet, permanent secretary of the Swedish Academy and a posthumous winner of the Nobel Prize. Karl Otto sighed: 'In truth a warning to publishers not to get worn out and not to refuse unread manuscripts!'

Albert and Karl Otto were guilty of another couple of misjudgements in the 1890s. The first was when they refused to publish a collection of short stories by Per Hallström, as his debut, *Lyrik och fantasier* (*Lyrics and Fantasies*), had been a less successful deal for the firm. They had taken a risk with Hallström not simply because he was promising but also because he had been turned down by Albert's nemesis, head of Norstedts Gustaf Holm; getting one over on Holm was something they simply could not resist. After Bonniers said no to the short stories, Hallström turned to Wahlström &

Widstrand, where *Vilsna fåglar* (*Lost Birds*) became a wonderful success. He was elected to the Swedish Academy in 1908.

The other misjudgement concerned the Skåne poet Ola Hansson, who had moved to Germany. He offered a translation of Friedrich Nietzsche's *Also sprach Zarathustra* from 1883–5, a future classic in the world of philosophy, and said his aim was to introduce 'a completely new and unusually terrifying element into our culture'.

Albert, who had never heard of Nietzsche, asked Gustaf af Geijerstam and Karl Otto if they knew of a German writer and thinker by that name, but received vague answers. Albert turned it down, which Karl Otto later regretted. Part of the issue was probably that a few years earlier Hansson had been eviscerated by the critics for *Sensitiva amorosa*, a collection of prose poems that were considered erotic. Another complicating factor, particularly in contacts with Albert, was Ola Hansson's antisemitism.

The publishing house had a complicated relationship in general with the difficult and strange Ola Hansson, who considered himself misunderstood and opposed at every turn. Bonniers took pity on him at times, however, and published some of his books, including a collection of short stories, but neither the critics nor the book-buying public developed a taste for this odd character influenced by Nietzsche, who, despite his personal shortcomings, is now seen as one of the most forward-looking Swedish writers of the late nineteenth century.

Even the contact with Verner von Heidenstam could have gone wrong. This was not Karl Otto's fault but down to Albert, who worried that von Heidenstam's books were not selling better, despite critical acclaim. Once more, the father's financial caution collided with the son's literary enthusiasm.

In a bitter comment before the publication of *Hans Alienus* in 1892, Albert wrote to von Heidenstam that the book would be hard to sell because it was not 'an ordinary exciting novel that produces an effect in the reader through its plots etc.'. This kind of language, a little peevish in tone, became increasingly common from Albert after the *Getting Married* debacle and the battle at the Publishers' Association. These stresses – and the unavoidable effect of aging – meant he lost some of the social ease that had previously been so characteristic, an infallible ability to use his skills of persuasion to make authors feel special and chosen.

Von Heidenstam was not enraged by this response, possibly because Albert nevertheless offered a generous fee of 4,000 kronor, which is also the conclusion drawn by Per I. Gedin in his biography of von Heidenstam. As with Strindberg ten years earlier, Albert realised that despite everything, he was dealing with a unique talent.

Karl Otto was von Heidenstam's main contact at the firm but when von Heidenstam decided to write about Karl XII (Charles XII), a figure who had fascinated him since childhood, he turned directly to Albert. Von Heidenstam wanted to extract the highest possible fee and was well aware that in such situations it was Albert who had the last word.

The negotiations ended with a contract for an astonishing 16,000 kronor, the equivalent of a million kronor today, without von Heidenstam having allowed anyone in the publishing house read the manuscript.

Karolinerna (*The Charles Men*), the first part of which came out in 1897, was a series of tales from the era of Sweden's 'hero king' Karl XII which placed simple, suffering people in the centre and drew a more nuanced picture of the idealised military monarch. Von Heidenstam became so obsessed by the work that he claimed he had received nightly visits from the dead king, who had sat in an armchair and instructed the author.

A few lines from the section 'A clean white shirt' confirm Heidenstam's capacity to paint a scene in beautiful language even when depicting terrible conditions. We see before us the warm blood steaming in the bitter cold:

> Soldier Bengt Geting had got a Cossack's pike through his chest and his comrades laid him down on a pile of branches among the trees, where pastor Rabenius gave him communion. They were on the icefields outside the walls of Veprik and a whistling north wind tore the dry leaves from the bushes (...) Bengt Geting lay with his hands clasped and bled. His stony eyes were wide open and the stubborn, craggy face was so leathered with sun and frost that the blue paleness of death could only be seen on his lips.

Albert and Karl Otto took a significant risk when they bought *The Charles Men*, 'a pig in a poke', but it worked. Over time, the two volumes of the work would sell more than 120,000 copies.

Von Heidenstam's friend and loyal follower Oscar Levertin, another of the central figures of the 1890s, on the other hand was given a harder time, at least for as long as Albert was alive. Albert thought that Levertin's financial demands were too high, but there may also have been another reason: 'Paradoxically enough, the Jewish poet was too Jewish for the firm,' says literary scholar and Levertin expert Per Rydén.

Albert, always keen to maintain a clear Swedish profile in his publishing, seems to have reacted against the Jewish topics in Levertin's work, such as in the poem 'På judiska kyrkogården i Prag' ('At the Jewish Cemetery in Prague') in the collection *Legender och visor* (*Legends and Songs*) from 1891:

> These ancestors in exile who were driven
> from land to land with mockery and jibe,
> in the ghetto's age-long dark were given
> no view of dawn for our defeated tribe.

This did not affect Karl Otto's friendship with Levertin. 'None of my contemporaries have been dearer to me,' wrote Karl Otto in his memoirs. In the greatest of secrecy, he and Lisen donated 100,000 kronor of their own money to a professorship in literary history designed for Levertin personally.

When Albert found out about this at the very end of his life, he had no objections.

Oscar Levertin, one of the foremost essayists and critics of the turn of the century, died in 1906, at the age of only forty-four. His cause of death was rather bizarre. Ill with tonsillitis, Levertin happened to swallow a glass of gargling liquid that caused an allergic reaction. He was deeply mourned by his friends Karl Otto and Lisen Bonnier.

* * *

At the same time as new literary waves were breaking through, processes were under way that were to have wide-ranging consequences for the whole of Swedish society.

Emigration to America accelerated; by the start of the

next century, about a million Swedes would have abandoned the country.

The union with Norway was creaking at the seams and would finally be dissolved in 1905.

In political debate, universal suffrage was moving higher up the agenda with liberals and social democrats as the driving forces in the suffrage movement, which formed an organisation, the Suffrage Movement of Sweden (SARF) in 1890. The purpose of the organisation was 'in aid of working together for universal suffrage, to gather together everyone in the country striving for this goal'.

Agitation for social democracy was particularly met with repression, partly through what was known as the 'Muzzle Act' of 1889, targeting 'attempts to lead to disobeying the law or legal authorities'. The labour movement still continued to grow, however, and in 1896 Hjalmar Branting was elected to the second chamber of the Riksdag on a liberal list. Revolution was in the air.

Albert kept himself informed of these current events and the fact that he felt a certain amount of sympathy for them is shown by his support for Verdandi, but in his declining years, when he was worn down by both professional and personal troubles, his political and ideological leanings were probably better reflected by his conservative literary preferences.

Among all his publishing projects, besides *Svea*, he was most engaged in republishing old favourites such as August Blanche's writings and Viktor Rydberg's *Singoalla*.

One of the firm's major projects in the early 1890s was a new edition of Elias Sehlstedt's collected songs, impressively illustrated by Carl Larsson and selected by Carl Snoilsky, one of Albert's favourite poets and a good friend.

Larsson, who had become Albert's foremost illustrator following the success of Topelius' *The Surgeon's Stories*, was overjoyed when he saw the first sheets, which Albert and Karl Otto had had printed in Vienna using the latest technology. From his combined home and studio in Sundborn outside Falun, he wrote in June 1892:

> Oh, Lord how beautiful they are! (...) If one can get one's art works out into the world like this, I don't give a damn about painting pictures. This is true democracy! Jesus, how happy I am!

Albert Bonnier avoided taking a public stance on political issues. Even in this area, he was a cautious general. His faith undoubtedly was a contributory factor in his restraint. He had experience of the forces that were unleashed when he, a Jew, found himself in the centre of public controversies.

Albert's free-thinking, or liberalism if one might call it that, was of an older kind, with its roots in the ideas of 1848 and in politicians such as Johan August Gripenstedt. This approach became less important after the representational reform, which had turned out a disappointment to radical friends of reform; the right to vote in Sweden remained more circumscribed than in most comparable countries.

Albert did respect younger advocates of democracy such as Karl Staaff and Hjalmar Branting, but distanced himself from statements of opinion looking to overturn society. Back in 1884 he had declined to publish a play *Det angår ingen* (*It's No-one's Business*) by the ultra-radical Hinke Bergegren, with the damning rejoinder 'it's not our business'. A year or two later, the publishing firm was sought out by a 'peasant student' who offered a number of short stories. His answer was also 'no', possibly after some hesitation, as the slightly more tolerant Karl Otto said that the author 'had an unusually original and powerful style' and was 'definitely a man of the future'. The young man was Axel Danielsson, who founded the newspaper *Arbetet* in Malmö before going on to write Sweden's first ever Social Democratic Party manifesto.

Albert's unprejudiced attitudes for their time were manifested personally and professionally rather than politically, e.g. in his natural business relations with female writers and in promoting Gustaf Banck from servant to bookkeeper.

Sweden had no legislation on minimum working hours whatsoever, but thirty years before the act on an eight-hour working day was introduced, Albert adjusted the publishing firm's closing time so that staff could go home at 6 p.m. instead of having to work long into the evening. Previously they had had to stay until Gustaf Banck or another member of management let them go. 'I still remember the joy when I heard the news. It was like stopping work in the middle of the afternoon,' Herman Bergqvist remembers.

Moreover, Albert was virtually immune to pomp and formality. When, in an attack of flattery, August Strindberg offered to use his French contacts to get Albert awarded the *Legion d'honneur*, Albert refused politely but firmly:

I am and remain utterly cold-hearted to such decorations – and much as I love France and the French people, I would not consider myself to be entitled to bear such a mark of distinction – it would be far too lightly achieved.

Albert's political attitude can probably best be summed up by a passage in the first part of Louis De Geer's memoirs from 1892, the most impressive political memoirs in literary terms to be published in Swedish besides those of Ernst Wigforss:

> I am optimistic not merely on the question of the government of the world as a whole but also on the question of social development, and I set the ultimate goal of my ideal society quite radically in terms of liberty, fraternity and equality. But as convinced as I am that developments are moving towards this goal (...), I am equally certain that this development, in the main, must proceed extremely slowly and unevenly (...) The true art of statesmanship lies in pre-empting revolutions or, in detail, in never pursuing anything at a pace greater than that which the public mind will not react against, but also, with the aim constantly in sight, in never standing still, as without taking this risk one cannot move forwards; however, better to stand still than risk having to go backwards.

No, the old Albert Bonnier was no raging radical, but in what was to be his last decade, his instinctive tolerance was nevertheless interwoven with the social issue that was to dominate Swedish public life for the next quarter of a century.

When a thirty-year-old journalist and hopeful poet from Värmland received a prize from the Swedish Academy for his debut collection, published by Bonniers, Albert seemed to have nothing against the poet donating the money to the suffrage movement.

Gustaf Fröding had made his entrance.

* * *

In October 1889 a letter arrived at *Svea* sent from Die Nerven-Heilanstalt in Görlitz in Germany and signed with a name unfamiliar to Albert and Karl Otto. The letter made a humble offer:

> The undersigned hereby takes the liberty of sending some poems considering that the editors might be able to use one or more of them in the annual. Whether or not they are used, I would be grateful to you were you to return the manuscript at your convenience.
>
> I make no claim for a fee but would be grateful if you would send me a copy of the annual to the above address should one of my poems be so fortunate as to win a place in the same.
>
> Respectfully,
> Gustaf Fröding

Albert was interested but felt he only had room for one of the six poems 'Sol och pannkaka' ('Sun and Pancakes'). In his reply to Fröding, however, Albert made the effort to keep the door ajar; he would be pleased 'to hear from you, should you have any literary work to offer in the future'.

Fröding was unhappy with Albert's choice of poem as he did not think that 'Sol och pannkaka' was quite up to scratch. 'Bonnier should be whipped (...) all he had to do was choose', he wrote to a friend. Despite this, he took Albert at his word and in July 1890 sent a manuscript of poems 'for your perusal'. In the cover letter, Fröding wrote that he was not unaware of some deficiencies but that 'some is truly felt and reproduced' and that in any case it was the critic's job to judge 'if the book really will see the light of day'.

Gustaf Fröding can be seen as Albert Bonnier's last great discovery – Albert had less than ten years left to live when Fröding made his debut – and in his memoirs Karl Otto Bonnier was careful to point out that it was his father who immediately realised that they had found 'a poet of truly great dimensions'.

The background to Karl Otto's clarity on this point was a strange exchange in the press that took place shortly after Fröding's death in 1911.

From the start, Fröding had expressed a desire for his debut book to be published in autumn 1890 but Albert wanted to wait until the following year and referred to 'pure material grounds', adding the not entirely diplomatic phrase that it might perhaps be an advantage for Fröding were he to allow his poetry to 'mature further during that time'.

Twenty years later, once Karl Otto had published some early letters between Fröding and Albert at the request of *Dagens Nyheter*, critic and peace activist Mia Leche, later a writer and the wife of politician Eliel Löfgren, went on the offensive against Bonniers and especially against the late Albert claiming that he had rejected Fröding. In *Stockholms Dagblad* she wrote:

When Gustaf Fröding, in broken health and with barely a penny to his name, decided to send his poems out into the world, he was met by the one who in the first instance held his fate in his hands, with the same dry and schoolmasterly strictness that is usually the bitter experience of every young debutant on the road to Parnassus.

Karl Otto, incensed, answered that Mia Leche was attempting 'to twist the matter completely' and quoted long sections of letters to Fröding in which Albert had assured him how much he appreciated his poems.

According to Karl Otto, the reason why publication was delayed, Albert's 'material grounds', was that Bonniers' old printworks had been demolished in spring 1890 and that a new, more modern facility was being built. It would not be ready until around Christmas. In other words, capacity was severely limited and 'accepting new manuscripts under such conditions was obviously impossible'.

Fröding, however, grew uncertain of Albert's intentions. 'Your delay has made me suspect that my verses set your head crawling with ants,' he wrote in August. If Albert had decided not to print the poems, Fröding asked him to send them back to 'the above address' in Malmö, in other words the public hospital where he was staying due to 'temporary ill-health'.

Whatever the reasons for publication taking longer than Fröding had hoped, his debut collection *Guitarr och dragharmonika* (*Guitar and Concertina*) finally came out in May 1891, a year of note in Swedish literary history which also saw Selma Lagerlöf's debut with the novel *Gösta Berling's Saga* (*The Saga of Gösta Berling*).

The poetry collection was well received. The mighty Carl Snoilsky capitulated completely: 'Yes, *I* cannot write poetry at all.' Sales were initially poor but that was to change over time. With their light springiness and folk themes, several of the poems in *Guitar and Concertina* have become eternal classics, constantly reprinted. The rhythms are irresistible:

They danced by the roadside on Saturday night,
And the laughter resounded to left and to right,
With shouts of 'Hip, hip!' and of 'Hej!'
Nils Utterman famed as a queer old freak,
Sat there and made his accordion squeak
With doodely, doodely, day!

Whether Albert reacted to the address of the sender in Fröding's early letters is unknown, but they were sent from a nerve clinic in Görlitz and then from a hospital in Malmö whence Fröding informed Albert, rather cryptically: 'My stay in Germany was somewhat cut short due to certain unforeseen circumstances.'

Gustaf Fröding had, as they say, problems.

After having been discharged from the clinic in Görlitz, he made his way to Dresden where he soon drank himself to destruction. His older sister Cecilia, who did all she could to help him, arranged for him to come home to Sweden and be taken into hospital in Malmö.

These were Fröding's 'unforeseen circumstances'.

* * *

Born in 1860, Gustaf Fröding came from a relatively well-off landowning family in Värmland with links to the cultural elite. His maternal grandfather was the famous naturalist, writer and bishop Carl Adolph Agardh, who was involved in founding the Academic Society at the University of Lund. However, the Fröding family fell on hard times, and combined with young Fröding's tendency towards alcohol-related and sexual excess, led to him failing his studies at Uppsala in the 1880s, where he was in the Verdandi circle and passionately admired Georg Brandes and Henrik Ibsen. One of his best friends was the liberal journalist and politician Mauritz Hellberg, who chaired the notorious morality debate in Uppsala.

Instead Fröding took to journalism and in 1887 he gained a permanent post at the radical pro-suffrage *Karlstads-Tidningen*, where Hellberg became the editor a few years later. Besides reviews and columns, the paper also published poems by Fröding. A certain amount of normality entered Fröding's chaotic life but he never felt at home in the role of journalist. His behaviour became increasingly self-destructive and was to tip over into mental illness in the years that followed.

It was in the middle of this downward spiral that he established contact with Albert Bonnier, which seems to have slowed the destructive process, at least temporarily. Mauritz Hellberg wrote that with *Guitar and Concertina* Fröding finally gained the 'consoling sense that he would do'.

Three years after his debut came *Nya dikter* (*New Poems*), where Fröding's social and political engagement shone through in the depiction of the exploitation of human labour by industrial capitalism:

Millrace bellowed and sledgehammer thundered,
drowning the voices of rage and fear.
Still not a word of the downtrodden, plundered
Mill worker's injuries
After a century's
Brandy comfort and cold despair.

Guitar and Concertina and *New poems* brought Gustaf Fröding a prominent position in the literary nineties. His friendship with Verner von Heidenstam was also significant. With the cartoonist and writer Albert Engström, the painter J. A. G. Acke and the writer Count Birger Mörner and others, they formed a colony of artists and writers that revolved around Sandhamn in the Stockholm archipelago. Pictures of the three gentlemen, Fröding, von Heidenstam and Engström, energised by snaps for breakfast and wearing nothing but laurel wreaths, are classics in their self-assured, laid-back hedonism.

The photographs were taken in 1896, the same year that Fröding, with Albert Bonnier, was dragged into another battle on press freedom that was to be at least as intense and dramatic as the one that surrounded August Strindberg's *Getting Married*. This concerned Fröding's third major poetry collection, *Stänk och flikar* (*Splashes and Patches*), and particularly the poem 'En morgondröm' ('A Morning Dream').

The conflict was preceded by a couple of introductory skirmishes that confirmed that the moral panic was still raging. Albert Bonniers Förlag was involved in both of them.

* * *

When the restaurant Operakällaren moved into new premises in Stockholm in 1895 artist Oscar Björck was hired to decorate it. His paintings, taking their themes from the ancient world, depicted naked bodies, much to the horror of the guardians of public morality. The discussion went as far as the Riksdag, where member of the second chamber Paul Peter Waldenström, founder of the Mission Covenant Church of Sweden, was particularly agitated. His voice shaking, he warned that the paintings might awaken salacious fantasies in the restaurant's diners. Questions were raised in the Riksdag and in his response Minister for Finance Claes Wersäll expressed the hope that the Opera Consortium, who had commissioned the paintings, would ensure that they were removed.

The Consortium then turned to the Royal Swedish Academy of Fine Arts for an opinion. The Academy in turn passed the question on to Viktor Rydberg, professor of art history at Stockholm Högskola. Rydberg rejected the criticism of Björck's paintings. Morality and immorality, purity or licentiousness lay entirely in the eye of the beholder, said Rydberg, who produced a small publication on the subject entitled *Om Nakenhet och klädselsätt* (*On Nudity and Ways of Dressing*). It was published by Rydberg's old friend Albert Bonnier.

This was Viktor Rydberg's last intervention in public life. 'The weaponsmith of Swedish culture', Oscar Levertin's name for Rydberg, died in September the same year.

For many writers, not just Fröding, being published in *Svea* could be the gateway to a more lasting relationship with Albert Bonniers Förlag. One such writer was a journalist on *Kristianstadsbladet* who in 1892 sent in a small observation, *Ur glömskan* (*Out of Oblivion*), which Albert printed. The journalist, who was soon to move on to *Dagens Nyheter*, was Hjalmar Söderberg, born in Stockholm in 1869. In autumn 1895 Bonniers published his debut novel, *Förvillelser* (*Delusions*), on the keen recommendation of Oscar Levertin.

Söderberg had not been convinced that the book would see the light of day. 'It cannot be assumed that the publisher will pay anything and it cannot be assumed that I will find a publisher,' he wrote to his sister Frida.

One reason for Söderberg harbouring certain doubts can be seen in the letter to the publisher that accompanied the manuscript. The book was, he wrote, 'titillatingly moral'. But the novel was accepted for publication and when he signed the contract, Söderberg was relieved and happy. He bought a cigar and went to Hasselbacken in Stockholm. Outside the restaurant, he took some dance steps with such enthusiasm that a couple of gentlemen stopped and applauded, as Jesper Högström relates in his biography of Söderberg, *Lusten och ensamheten*.

Albert and Karl Otto seem not to have feared that Delusions would cause a storm, but there they were wrong. Theatre director and playwright Harald Molander went on the violent attack in his review in *Aftonbladet*, somewhat surprisingly considering that Molander was one of the otherwise unprejudiced writers of the 1880s:

> One could hardly say that this novel, read by older, sensible folk, is immoral in its tendencies but it might be one of the most wanton works by a Swedish pen to have sneaked its way onto the book market without a sealed wrapping these days.

Along the same lines as the debate on 'filthy literature' of the 1880s, Molander particularly warned of the effect of the book on 'young people lacking in judgement'.

In the magazine *Nordisk Revy*, Hjalmar Söderberg replied with a magnificent broadside:

> I once read of a shower of rain that was so heavy that all the pigs became clean and all the people became dirty. It might be natural, yes, very natural, to assume that Herr Molander's approach in this matter had precisely the intention of stirring up such a storm

to benefit himself – perhaps under the influence of that longing for cleanliness that not uncommonly assails an old roisterer, when he nears the border of man's estate.

What weighed heaviest, however, was that seven well-known cultural figures, including Verner von Heidenstam, Ellen Key and the journalist Edvard Alkman, defended Söderberg and urged Molander to withdraw his insults. They seem to have had a certain effect. Molander changed his focus and attacked the publishing firm instead. It had, he said, made 'commerce' out of a debut novelist 'who had shown himself to lack self-criticism':

Did the publisher that published 'Delusions' not previously voice any doubts or reservations whatsoever and if he did, what was the author's response?

Karl Otto also wrote a defence in *Nordisk Revy*. There he stated, perhaps a little harshly, that although Söderberg's book 'was not a successful work in every respect', it also contained 'much clear evidence of talent'.

Once Karl Warburg had written a more favourable review in *Handelstidningen*, the firm put together a newspaper advertisement with a selected quote, which made *Aftonbladet* comment that the book nevertheless was 'so boring that it was not even capable of winning any of the "succes de scandale", that might have been intended'.

Albert only came into fleeting contact with the debate on Söderberg's novel. To avoid too much fuss over his seventy-fifth birthday, he left Sweden that autumn on what was to be his last trip abroad, to Austria and Italy with his daughter Jenny.

In any event, the row, which soon evaporated, became the start of a lasting relationship between Bonniers and Hjalmar Söderberg, who was to become one of the most outstanding figures in Swedish twentieth-century literature, in many people's eyes the most outstanding, with works such as *Doktor Glas* (*Doctor Glas*) and *Den allvarsamma leken* (*The Serious Game*), books that also caused moral outrage.

The next conflict was to be considerably tougher.

* * *

After his two first poetry collections, Gustaf Fröding had established himself as one of Sweden's most popular poets. Albert and Karl Otto therefore looked forward eagerly to his next collection and made several proposals to Fröding. Finally, in early summer 1896, Fröding delivered a manuscript to the firm, via Karl Staaff, with the title *Dagar och nätter* (*Days and Nights*), which was then changed to *Stänk och flikar* (*Splashes and Patches*). Staaff, a lawyer engaged in union issues and on his way into national politics, acted as an ombudsman in the Swedish Writers' Association, where he helped members who, like Fröding, preferred to avoid negotiating with publishers on their own.

Fröding was worried how Albert might react to some of the poems and wrote to Staaff: 'It may be that Herr Bonnier finds that some pieces are too indigestible and if that is the case, I am willing to cut the most difficult ones or make one or two amendments.'

Nothing indicates that Albert reacted negatively on

receiving the manuscript. It was not until late August, at the proof stage, that he grew uneasy. His concerns were about the poem 'En morgondröm' ('A Morning Dream') and primarily its fifth song or section.

Albert wrote a letter to Fröding with a courteous enquiry:

Far from wishing to practise any censorship upon you in the mildest degree, I venture, however, to request for your consideration as to whether you might not find there might be reasons – in your otherwise so highly excellent poetry collection – to allow some lines in the poem 'A Morning Dream' to undergo a reassessment and potential retouching.

By this point Albert had realised that 'A Morning Dream' contained a depiction of the purely physical act of love between a man and a woman, basically a sex scene:

And with heartbeats racing, whole,
Breath for breath and soul to soul
Bodies twined in rhythm twin
Closely held,
Rose and fell
Down and up and in
Back and forth as one
Til at once burst forth in need
From his loins a stream now freed
Forged father-life in mother-seed
As two rivers both converging
Father, mother, surging, merging
Joined then in a son.

Fröding was in Sandhamn in the company of his writing and artist friends. When he received Albert's letter he consulted them, especially Verner von Heidenstam, whom he admired. He replied to Albert on 3 September:

> After consulting Herr v. Heidenstam I think it is hardly advisable to exclude the parts commented on. The book cannot be family reading in any case and can well be kept out of sight in a corner.

Four days later, Fröding sent final proofs back to Albert: 'I wanted to see the whole thing one more time and then I won't argue any more.'

Splashes and Patches reached the bookshops in late September. It caused a scandal. Numerous book buyers contacted the publishers in protest at 'filth' and the Swedish Academy's Carl David af Wirsén raged against Fröding's 'shamelessness'.

The right-wing press began to rumble with demands for legal action. The influential Alfred Hedenstierna who wrote as 'Sigurd' in *Smålandsposten* called for 'public examination (...) in a court of law' and launched into an almost mindless attack on Albert:

> The commerce of publishing that offers the filthy works of such a poor being's confused imagination for sale evokes revulsion and contempt. Herr Bonnier, the worthy seventy-seven-year-old bordello poet publisher has carried the entire dung heap to the bookshop counter.

Sigurd considered that *Splashes and Patches* made Strindberg's *Getting Married* look like 'snow-white innocence', and wondered whether the Minister of Justice was asleep.

Even *Aftonbladet* turned against Albert. In a leader with a brief headline 'Shame!' the newspaper blamed him for 'forgetting his duty to and his responsibility for Sweden's reading public'.

Unusually, Albert composed a reply. In it he emphasised that Fröding had wanted to keep the criticised section 'on consulting other writers':

> Under such circumstances, the publisher – who ultimately is merely a subordinate assistant in the service of literature – must bend to the author's will. Or does one wish him to exercise censorship or impose a printing ban entirely on prominent geniuses like this poet in question or others of his rank and importance? To what consequences (...) might this not lead.

Ludvig Annerstedt, Minister of Justice in Erik Gustaf Boström's government, initially refrained from intervention, but when the scandal sheet *Budkaflen* reproduced 'A Morning Dream' – to the accompaniment of gross insults against Fröding – Annerstedt realised that the poem's spread had to be halted. Possibly the fact that even King Oscar II was agitated over 'an openly filthy text' had a part to play.

On 12 October two issues of *Budkaflen* were seized, as was Fröding's poetry collection. Gustaf Fröding and Albert Bonnier, the printer of the book, were prosecuted but clearly having learned from his experience in the *Getting Married* trial, Albert had asked Fröding for an affidavit well in advance, which the author immediately provided. Albert could thus be discharged from legal responsibility.

When some constables tramped into the publishing firm on Mäster Samuelsgatan, they only found seventeen copies from an edition of 4,200; the rest had disappeared out to the shops. The apostles of morality criticised the police and the Minister of Justice for their slowness, but above all, they continued to attack Albert, sometimes with antisemitic overtones. In the comic *Nya Nisse* he was depicted as a peddler wearing a skull-cap. Sigurd in *Smålandsposten* went further than most with expressions such as 'old Jew' and 'bordello poet publisher':

An elderly Jewish publisher, teetering on the edge of the grave, who is already a multi-millionaire and has the honour of counting a large proportion of what the heights of Swedish genius are capable of achieving among his published works, publishes this Song of Songs of the bordello to allow him to increase his fortune by yet another thousand kronor note or possibly two; however the book is such that none of the kingdom's *better* publishing firms would have wished to soil their hands with it, even were the potential profits ten times that amount.

In a comment that he sent to *Aftonbladet* Fröding reacted against these attempts to 'quite unjustifiably (...) shift part of the responsibility for my poems *Splashes and Patches* to people other than their author'.

Albert appreciated Fröding's upright approach and wished him 'bon courage' to which Fröding replied with fine irony over all the fuss about the poem:

Thank you for the letter and for urging courage! I am not exactly lacking courage, more indifferent. I find it nigh on impossible that one could be condemned for pages 110 and 111. Sexual intercourse is no *vice* and in any case, if it were, the passage contains no aim to spread this 'vice' − it is sufficiently widespread in any case, not least in marriage proscribed by God.

Fröding also agreed to be interviewed in *Östergötlands Dagblad*. The interview was spread further by *Dagens Nyheter* and other major newspapers. When asked whether he expected prosecution, Fröding answered arrogantly:

I have made myself conversant enough with the possibility of it but it did not matter to me (...) The book was not written to be prosecuted, nor was it written with anxious consideration to avoid that eventuality.

Albert Bonnier and Gustaf Fröding did not ever become close personally and never dropped their titles but their mutual respect became clear during the freedom of the press trial against *Splashes and Patches*. Fröding did what he could to take full responsibility while Albert paid the cost of a lawyer and the advance payments, for which he did not demand repayment. Certain of an acquittal, Albert wrote soothing letters to the labile Fröding and brought Fröding's sister Cecilia to Stockholm so she could support her brother on the spot.

At the same time, Albert and Fröding were able to rely on loyal friends in the press. One of them was Hjalmar Branting in *Social-Demokraten*, the main organ of the Social Democratic Party, which had been formed in 1889. When the case was brought, Branting urged 'an educated jury to rectify this blunder' and praised Fröding as a poet whose name 'shall be remembered when the bureaucrat Annerstedt's is long forgotten'. *Dagens Nyheter*, the leading liberal organ of the press, also took Fröding and Albert's side. The newspaper pointed out the unreasonableness of forcing the publisher to be the 'judging authority'. It was almost an echo of Albert Bonnier's own motto: the publisher is a disseminator, not a judge.

One person who kept his head down, however, was Verner von Heidenstam. He had played a part in convincing Fröding to publish 'A Morning Dream' but when the case was brought, Heidenstam grew afraid that this would come out and damage his public position. On top of that, the highly self-obsessed von Heidenstam was jealous of Fröding's popularity. He talked about Fröding behind his back in letters to Oscar Levertin and other mutual friends, sought to avoid finding himself on the freedom of the press jury at any price and took offence at having been directly pointed out as sharing the blame for 'A Morning Dream' by Albert's reference to 'other writers'.

This was not the 'national poet's' finest hour. Or as Per I. Gedin puts it in his biography of Karl Otto Bonnier: 'Heidenstam is grandiose when he can be the leader (...) When matters are against him, he is spineless.'

Fröding defended himself in a written submission to Stockholm's City Court and the jury in which he rejected accusations of having devoted himself to 'promoting a pernicious lifestyle':

> The pages prosecuted contain, as everyone can find,
> a depiction of the innermost embraces of sexual love
> between a young man and a young woman, belonging

to a poetic people of nature who are conceived as living in an original state of innocence where nakedness is customary and where the relationship between man and woman is less bound by certain formalities as it is in contemporary society.

As an appendix Fröding submitted *On Nudity and Ways of Dressing* by the recently deceased and highly admired Viktor Rydberg.

The jury included Carl Snoilsky, appointed by the prosecutor, and the liberal suffrage fighter David Bergström, chosen by Fröding. How much weight the jury gave to Fröding's carefully worded document is unclear but on 27 November they only took two hours to acquit him. The publisher of *Budkaflen* had been acquitted a day earlier.

Even if the decision was expected, there was great relief in the radical circles that felt an affinity with Fröding. From Lund came a congratulatory and celebratory telegram from the student association Den yngre gubben, D Y G, a little in the future to be the cradle of future social democratic politicians such as Ernst Wigforss and Tage Erlander:

Before our eyes dawned an Aryan land
With roses wild, without a thorn,
Where Venus bravely was reborn
In foam and splashes on joyful strand.
That poem the wave that mirror-clear
Gently carried the goddess here.

Despite such praise, Fröding was deeply depressed after the trial and accused himself of having defiled pure love. When the second edition of *Splashes and Patches* was published before

Christmas 1896 the fifth song of 'A Morning Dream' and an additional two poems had been cut. This was partly on Albert's initiative, but Fröding was once more careful to take on the responsibility, despite Albert's protests. The poems had been removed, wrote Fröding in a self-critical explanation 'less due to the disapproval that they suffered and perhaps even less due to their openness than due to the fact that I myself view them as not particularly successful in execution and unclear in terms of content'.

For decades, until at least the 1970s, the fifth song of 'A Morning Dream' was cut from some editions of Fröding's poetry.

A sick and anxious Gustaf Fröding was admitted to Uppsala mental hospital. He never recovered.

* * *

One of the publishing firm's greatest popular successes towards the end of Albert Bonnier's life was the Swedish publication in 1897 of the Norwegian polar explorer Fridtjof Nansen's *Fram öfver polarhafvet*, the story of his three year-long dramatic and adventurous journey across Svalbard and Frans Josef Land. On his return Nansen and his men enjoyed hero status around the world. Bonniers paid a riskily high fee, a move that paid off. The book was a huge success.

However, the most important contact the publishing firm made for the future in the 1890s was with Selma Lagerlöf, then a teacher at the Elementary School for Girls in Landskrona.

The association between Bonniers and Lagerlöf was to blossom in earnest only after Albert's death with works such as *Jerusalem, Herr Arnes penningar (Lord Arne's Silver), Nils Holgerssons* underbara resa genom Sverige (Nils Holgersson's Wonderful Journey through Sweden), Körkarlen (translated into English as Thy Soul Shall Bear Witness in 1921 and as The Phantom Carriage in 2011) and Kejsarn av Portugallien (The Emperor of Portugallia).

Still, it was Albert who first took the initiative. As was so often the case, he asked Selma Lagerlöf for a contribution to Svea. Lagerlöf answered that naturally she would like to participate in 'the old, respected annual' and in 1892 sent in a story with the title 'De fågelfrie' ('The Outlaws'). It was printed in Svea, with illustrations by artist Georg Pauli. For it she received a fee of 150 kronor, more than what she was used to from Ord och Bild, the weekly magazine Idun and other publications. She wrote to Albert:

Hereby may I with the greatest of thanks accept the receipt of the fee for 'de fågelfrie'. It is of course entirely too high, but I am so much more grateful. Naturally I had worked a great deal on the story but I dared not estimate it at even a hundred kronor. It gives me great happiness that you were pleased with it.

The reason behind Albert's request for a text for Svea was that the previous year Lagerlöf had made her debut with another publisher with a novel that attracted attention, though of the negative kind. The literary critics, including the otherwise open Karl Warburg, virtually massacred Gösta Berlings saga (The Saga of Gösta Berling), first published as an award-winning serial in Idun.

The reactions to a novel whose first sentence – 'At long last the minister stood in the pulpit' – is now part of Sweden's literary canon, must naturally also be viewed in the light of the patriarchal and even blatantly misogynistic attitudes of the day; female authors were not deemed to possess the same innovative capacity as male ones. This was a prejudice that the socially and politically aware Selma Lagerlöf was to run into time and time again over her long career as an author. At the same time, she became an early symbol of the fact that women authors also firmly deserved a place on the literary heights of Parnassus. She was the first woman to be awarded the Nobel Prize for literature, in 1909, despite the attempts of Carl David af Wirsén, the permanent secretary of the Swedish Academy, to prevent it.

The Saga of Gösta Berling made Albert Bonnier curious about the teacher in Landskrona who wrote, but, like many other judges of literature, he found this novel with a difference quite alien, founded as it was in the oral storytelling tradition with which Lagerlöf had grown up on the small farm of Mårbacka in Värmland. 'My father never really understood the book, which was unique in so many respects,' admitted Karl Otto.

However, Albert was to change his opinion on Selma Lagerlöf's skills. Once she had sent in another contribution to *Svea*, published in the fiftieth anniversary issue for 1894, he decided to make their connection more permanent. He offered to publish Lagerlöf's next book, which she eagerly accepted. The result was the short story collection *Osynliga länkar* (*Invisible Links*), whose first edition sold out.

Lagerlöf and Albert soon started to discuss another book, but when this did not materialise, Karl Otto instead offered that they take over the rights to publish *The Saga of Gösta Berling*. Lagerlöf asked for a concrete offer, because she was in great need of money: '...Both my mother and another elderly relative have to live from my work and thus I have to place great importance on being able to obtain for them a position free from cares.'

By the time Selma Lagerlöf received the offer from Bonniers, the situation had been complicated by another publisher having offered not only to republish *The Saga of Gösta Berling* and for a higher fee, but also to buy the rights to new books by her.

Albert and Karl Otto did not know at the time who this publisher was. Only later did they find out that it was the Dane Ernst Bojesen, who had Scandinavian ambitions. His interest in Lagerlöf made sense; in Denmark *The Saga of Gösta Berling* had been praised by no less than Georg Brandes. Bojesen had also had success with *En roman om förste konsuln (A Novel about the First Consul)*, written by another female Swedish writer, living in Copenhagen. Her name, which was originally kept secret, was Mathilda Malling. She had made her debut in 1885 under the pseudonym Stella Kleve.

Selma Lagerlöf felt she was unable to turn down Bojesen's offer and explained her decision in a letter to Albert that was both apologetic and a little beseeching:

> For the sake of my finances I cannot do anything other than be pleased at the deal, but, on the other hand, it has taken much hesitation to resist having my book published by you. I have acted as I have been forced to, but I do not know if I have been truly intelligent and forward-thinking.
>
> In all events, the matter is decided now and all that remains is for me to thank you for the great kindness you have shown me and hope that you may not entirely withdraw it from me in the future.

Bojesen worked closely with Bonniers, for example through the joint top-seller *Fransk-tyska kriget* (*The Franco-German War*) published in 1895 on the twenty-fifth anniversary of the outbreak of war. Therefore it was natural for Bojesen, businessman to his fingertips, to allow Albert Bonniers Förlag to buy the rights to publish both Malling and Lagerlöf's books in Sweden, while he himself retained the other rights in Scandinavia and was compensated by Bonniers for making the books available to the firm. It was a clever system, in which Bonniers had to pay more to Bojesen than he had paid to the authors. 'We were forced to accept these terms,' sighed Karl Otto in his memoirs.

Selma Lagerlöf was happy to be able to retain the connection with Albert Bonniers Förlag. When Albert was still living, she managed after *Invisible Links*, to also publish *Antikrists mirakler* (*The Miracles of Antichrist*), *Drottningar i Kungahälla jämte andra berättelser* (*The Queens of Kungahälla and Other Sketches*) and *En herrgårdssägen* (*The Tale of a Manor*), but she never felt entirely comfortable with the arrangement between Bojesen and Bonniers, as is shown by the letters and Anna-Karin Palm's major Lagerlöf biography *Jag vill sätta världen i rörelse* (*I Want to Set the World in Motion*): 'It is not good to stand up to the gentlemen.' She asked Bojesen to release her from the contract and he agreed. The pieces were in place by summer 1900. That was when Selma Lagerlöf, in full flow with the preparations for her great work *Jerusalem* became a Bonnier author for real. Relieved, she wrote to Albert that this felt 'much more suitable and pleasant than the arrangement hitherto'.

It was one of the very last letters that Albert Bonnier opened. A week later he was dead.

CHAPTER 10

JEWISH HERITAGE

A private matter.
The unwilling 'Israelite'. The Jewish high bourgeoisie.
Western Jews and Eastern Jews.
From Central Europe to Sweden.

———

In Copenhagen, Albert Bonnier had spent his childhood in a large family in which Jewish customs were a natural part of daily life, but as an adult he generally had quite a relaxed attitude to this background. When Albert had attended a Jewish service, he might say that he had been 'at church' not at the synagogue, and he referred, rather vaguely to his 'confession' rather than more explicitly to his Jewish faith.

Jewish friends and relatives were sometimes invited to Shabbat dinners in the Bonnier home where traditional dishes such as *Gefilte Fisch* and *Butterkuchen* were served. During the conversation at table Yiddish terms such as *chutzpah*, *unser Leut* (in other words, 'fellow Jews'), and *Mensch* were used.

These references to Judaism, however, were more in the nature of reminiscences from the past. The atmosphere surrounding Albert was essentially secular and liberal and the majority of the Bonnier family's circle was made up of Christians, which reflected the desire that ran throughout Albert's life and work; without in any way denying or minimising his Jewishness, Albert Bonnier wanted to be seen – and accepted – as Swedish. His identity was inexorably characterised by his Jewish origins, but he viewed religion as a private matter, entirely in line with the individualistic, free-thinking values that, in the words of Karl Otto Bonnier, were 'in his blood'.

He could be upset by the antisemitic prejudice with which he was constantly confronted. In some cases, as in that of August Strindberg, this could cause a personal aversion to a prominent author. In others, as in the case of Zacharias Topelius, it made no matter. Literature came first.

Albert avoided public comment on topics related to Judaism, well aware of the reactions this could arouse at a time when antisemitism was rife, but privately and professionally he expected special loyalty from other Jews. He was furious when Ludvig Josephson suddenly abandoned Adolf's bookshop and hurt when Hugo Geber failed him in the festering battle in the Swedish Publishers' Association in 1887. However, these were emotions he kept to himself or those close to him.

The member of Albert's family who seems to have found it hardest to tolerate antisemitic attacks was his hot-tempered daughter Eva, but even she tried to bite her lip.

In December 1883 when Eva was in Paris studying art, she had attended a party with several Swedish guests. One of them spoke condescendingly about the 'Moses' Albert and Adolf Bonnier. The person behind the comment was apparently acquainted with Albert. Eva wrote home about 'this intermezzo of the most unpleasant kind', but said that she had avoided 'getting into a fight with the old man' because 'howling dogs like that are better ignored'.

But she asked Albert for a favour: 'Perhaps daddy might have occasion to give the copyright holder what he deserves.'

* * *

Of the Bonnier brothers it was Adolf, the oldest, who kept most closely to the traditions from Dresden and Copenhagen. In early 1841, the younger members of the Jewish elite gathered in an association, Israelitiska Intressen (Israelite Interests), abbreviated to I I. The founders included music publisher Abraham Hirsch, who was to become Adolf's brother-in-law a few years later. The purpose of this society was to lobby for the emancipation of the Jewish minority as citizens and to modernise religious life. Older Jews were dubious about the latter aim; they viewed I I as a gang of radicals.

Adolf Bonnier joined a month or two after the organisation was founded and in the years that followed contributed to the emancipation efforts by publishing brochures such as *Judarne i deras närvarande ställning* (*The Jews in their Current Position*) and *Förtjena judarne politiska rättigheter?* (*Do the Jews Deserve Political Rights?*).

Albert was more cautious. He did not join the association until 1847. According to Karl Otto Bonnier, who must have discussed such matters with his father, Albert's doubts were due to him 'being reluctant to show solidarity with an organisation that only had emancipation on its programme, where instead he wanted to place assimilation'. When Albert did become a member, he was welcomed with open arms and immediately voted in as chair for the next three months; the role rotated on a quarterly basis.

Albert thanked the organisation for its confidence in him

and then gave a speech about 'intelligent Jewry that performs with the pen in its hand and with caution in its breast, which demands equality because it has the right to demand it, and safeguards itself by its actions, its knowledge, its education and not by its chests of money'.

He continued:

True emancipation should come from the inside outwards, we must start by striving to improve ourselves, our moral as well as our social person, and then mix ourselves among the Christians, without, out of false fears, choosing the circles in which we socialise, preferably among the better and most educated among them, and, where we find someone worthy, seek to win and retain his friendship, his respect (...) Every such relationship of friendship is a greater, a more important gain than were it to succeed in conquering the whole Land of Canaan.

A straight line runs from this proud declaration to Albert's work as a book publisher, where setting up lasting bonds of friendship with authors was his prime distinguishing feature, and what made him unique in the early phases of the industry.

Despite his initial doubts, Albert became one of the more active members of the Israelite organisation. Later on he also served on the building committee for the Great Synagogue on Wahrendorffsgatan in Stockholm. But throughout his life, Albert Bonnier remained sceptical about ideas of Jewish distinction. He was Swedish and that was that. This attitude was passed on to his son and heir, who was, if possible, even clearer than his father on this point. On Karl Otto Bonnier,

Hugo Valentin wrote: 'He took (...) an extremely negative view not only of Jewish orthodoxy but also of the positive Jewish movements of his time.'

* * *

Albert Bonnier's insistence, as early as 1847, on the importance of intelligence, knowledge and education in the Jewish emancipation and assimilation process can be seen as an expression of what he and his brothers represented. It is true that they were born in Copenhagen, but through their father Gerhard and the family's roots in Dresden they were connected to a cultural tradition in Central Europe – Vienna, Prague, Budapest – that towards the end of the nineteenth century and the early twentieth century was to blossom into what was in many ways an innovative golden age, deeply embedded in Jewish experiences: Gustav Mahler, Sigmund Freud, Franz Kafka, Stefan Zweig, Arnold Schoenberg, to name but a few. It was as if compulsory professional and social exclusion had in turn forced out unparalleled artistic and intellectual creativity, which also had an impact in remote Sweden.

On Swedish soil, the Bonnier brothers were early exponents of this tradition, with which Albert had also come into direct, and practical contact when learning the bookshop trade in Leipzig, Vienna and Budapest. But they were not alone by any means.

Anyone studying the cultural and intellectual life of late nineteenth-century Sweden cannot be anything but impressed by the contribution made by a small and often persecuted minority.

Besides publishers like Albert Bonnier, Joseph Seligmann

and Hugo Geber, here were artists such as Ernst Josephson, Hanna Pauli, Hugo Salmson and Eva Bonnier, literary scholars such as Karl Warburg and Henrik Schück, men of the theatre like Ludvig Josephson, writers like Oscar Levertin, economists like David Davidson and, a little later, Eli Heckscher, patrons like Pontus Fürstenberg and philanthropists like builder Isaak Hirsch, the man who created so much of Stockholm's cityscape – Kungsbropalatset, Oscarsteatern, and the imposing facades on Strandvägen. Their numbers also include financier and art collector Ernest Thiel, Karl Otto Bonnier's brother-in-law, with a Walloon father and a German Jewish mother.

Jewish over-representation in the field of culture and education had to do with these families, who had established themselves relatively early in Sweden, being shaped by the restrictions that surrounded them. Because Jews, in Sweden as in other parts of Europe, were long excluded from a long line of occupations, it was natural to seek less restricted ways of earning a living in trade, finance – and the arts. Among the Jews who contributed to Sweden's rapid economic and material development at this time, banker and industrialist Louis Fraenckel and department store pioneer Josef Sachs, the founder of NK, stand out.

This group, mainly with German roots, are often called 'Western Jews' in Sweden and were characterised by an ambition to integrate into Swedish society as quickly as possible. Many became successful, not least in sectors where they were able to benefit from international contacts. In this way a top layer of high bourgeoisie was created in Sweden's Jewish community, what economic historian Rita Bredefeldt has described as a 'minority within the minority', characterised not only by entrepreneurial zeal and openness to innovation but also by social engagement, cultural interests and 'imposing residences with imported influences from buildings in the cities of contemporary Europe'.

Albert Bonnier, a hardworking book publisher with an impressive home in Norrmalm, was definitely in this category.

* * *

In the 1860s when passport freedom and freedom of enterprise had been introduced, a new group of Jewish immigrants started to settle in Sweden in the aftermath of pogroms and other antisemitic attacks in what was then the Tsarist Empire. Between 1870 and 1900, Stockholm's Jewish population doubled. The newly arrived Jews, who came to be called 'Eastern Jews' were as a rule less highly educated and practised their religion in line with more orthodox patterns. They often earned a living as peddlers. In Stockholm there was sometimes also talk of the well-established 'Northern Jews' and the new 'Southern Jews' denoting the fact that these groups lived in different parts of the city.

The Eastern Jews challenged the self-image of the Swedish Jews, often second or third generation, who considered themselves to be integrated and assimilated. This led to friction, which was not only cultural and religious but also financial; until 1899 the mosaic congregations were obliged to take care of their own poor. In Stockholm the community attempted to 'solve' the problem by insisting on Swedish citizenship.

It was now that Sweden's Jews started to spread across the country to a much greater extent than before, to Kalmar in the south and Östersund and Sundsvall in the north. In Malmö the

'Eastern Jews' became the dominant group and in Lund, the poor district of Nöden was known as 'Sweden's only ghetto'.

Over time, the antagonism faded and even Jews with Eastern European roots were to be thoroughly integrated and contribute to Sweden's cultural development. One example was the artist Isaac Grünewald, whose mother came from Courland in what is now Latvia.

* * *

In 1900 when Albert Bonnier died, the Jewish population of Stockholm in Sweden amounted to 3,912 people. This was a small percentage, 0.076 percent of the population, but in Albert's lifetime the presence of Jews in Sweden had been transformed from being an exception to being taken for granted.

This does not, however, mean that antisemitism was at an end, and in Albert's last years it moved into an even more toxic phase. The English writer Houston Stewart Chamberlain, active in Germany, and other 'racial theorists' wanted to give antisemitism a scientific sheen, where the 'Semitic' Jews were seen as being biologically inferior to the 'Aryan' Germans. One of Chamberlain's Swedish followers was the otherwise progressive Bengt Lidforss, a botanist from Lund. These ideas were to have horrific consequences for the continental and Jewish-dominated cultural heritage from which Albert and his brothers had sprung.

Perhaps though, their contribution should be understood in a greater Jewish and European context: that through their work in safe Sweden, they helped to rescue this heritage.

CHAPTER II

THE END

**Albert's last days.
Slowing down. A parallel family.
Death. Obituaries.
The Albert Bonnier Stipend Fund.**

———

After Albert Bonnier's return from his final trip abroad in 1895, his son Karl Otto and others in his immediate circle noticed a growing tiredness in him. Albert had made it to the age of seventy-five, a respectable age in those days, and the years were taking their toll. There was nothing wrong with his work ethic or interest in the business, however.

Alongside the names that will be most associated with the literary nineties to posterity – von Heidenstam, Levertin, Fröding, Lagerlöf – Albert Bonniers Förlag also published books by other authors who helped to define the golden age of the late nineteenth century, such as Tor Hedberg, Gustaf af Geijerstam, August Bondeson and Anne Charlotte Leffler, and Karl August Tavaststjerna from Finland.

Albert also concluded what was to be his last major deal; a contract with Zacharias Topelius' heirs for his collected works. There were several interested parties and so Albert sent Karl Otto to Finland to negotiate with the heirs, who were represented by Eva Acke, one of Topelius' daughters, married to the Swedish artist J. A. G. Acke and, handily, a good friend of Karl Otto. The instructions from Albert were clear; he was to have the rights to his old friend's works, 'whatever it costs'. He got them. Zacharias Topelius' collected works started to be published in late 1899 in what was to be a total of thirty-four volumes.

Albert Bonnier had once and for all established himself as Sweden's biggest and foremost publisher of literature, but his energies were fading and now perhaps he wanted to enjoy his success. In the second half of the 1890s Albert developed the habit of spending extra-long summer weekends at his country home on the island Dalarö, where he would sit on the veranda reading proofs, the Danish paper *Politiken*, his regular reading since his youth, and *Revue des Deux Mondes*, a French magazine for literature and social debate published since 1829, all while puffing on his cigar.

As Albert slowed down, Karl Otto increasingly took on the central role in the publishing firm, although his father retained the last word on major undertakings and deals. Fully aware of the responsibility that awaited him, Karl Otto started to build up a broad network in the Swedish cultural scene, with the same sense for bonds of friendship and loyalties that set its stamp on Albert's work as a publisher.

One example, almost mythical in Bonnier family history, was 'Juntan', which in Swedish means a group or circle, a small group formed in 1890 on the initiative of Ellen Key. The circle met regularly in the homes of its members for conversation, discussion and reading out loud. Karl Otto and his wife Lisen Bonnier were the hub of this community, which also included the artists Georg and Hanna Pauli and Nanna Bendixson, daughter of the late liberal journalist August Sohlman, who had been one of Albert's close friends.

* * *

At the same time, a certain amount of friction had arisen in the family circle, particularly between Albert and his older daughter Jenny. After Betty's death in 1888 she had become the strict and determined manager of the Bonnier home. Albert, namely, had a secret, which he did not reveal until the trip to Italy and Austria he made with Jenny in 1895.

The unavoidable end was near and Albert Bonnier clearly felt a need to put his affairs in order with the help of his son and heir. He wrote home to Karl Otto and told him that for some years he had been living a kind of double life.

> In the event that it were to be God's will that I do not return alive (...) I particularly pray to your care and also to the kindness of your sisters, to open your hearts to two children – two boys that I have brought into the world in recent years, the oldest of whom 'Nils' (now 5 ½ years old) promises to become a kind and lovable creature. The younger 'Sven', is now just 1 ½ years old – but also healthy and with God's help he too can also become a good person.
>
> I have already assigned a suitable annual amount for maintenance to them and their mother in my will and as God has blessed us with worldly Goods it would have been wrong to leave them wanting.

Six years earlier – in other words, the year after Betty's death – Albert had begun a relationship with a woman forty years younger than he was, the actress Ebba Herván. This resulted in two children who were given the ultra-Swedish names Nils and Sven. As a widower, Albert had formed a parallel family.

The relationship with Ebba Herván, who later changed her surname to Hennings, was no secret to Albert's closest relatives. Jenny, in particular, did not approve. In his memoirs, Karl Otto's son Tor related an incident that he had found awkward:

> My grandfather had not come home for Sunday dinner – served at 4 p.m. on the dot. We waited a few minutes and then Aunt Jenny wrote something on a bit of paper, folded it up and told me to go down to Berns Salonger and ask a waiter where Patron Bonnier was sitting – 'because he will be sitting there with that dreadful woman' – and give grandfather the note. I was ten or eleven and following the directions from the waiter, had to cross my way between the tables all the way to the platform where grandfather was sitting with his friends Frans Hedberg and Malström the painter, and yes, quite right, a lady. Grandfather read the note and came back with me, while his friends around the table smiled. It was not a pleasant expedition. I did not know then that the 'dreadful woman' was the person who had brightened his last decade.

Tor Bonnier was born in 1883 so if he remembers his own age correctly, this must have taken place in 1893 or possibly 1894. But it was not until a year or two later that it became known that Albert had also had children with the lady in question.

Despite Jenny, especially, feeling uncomfortable with the situation, both Ebba and the two boys Nils and Sven, were well taken care of with an annuity, maintenance and large lump sums.

However, Ebba Herván was not the only woman with whom Albert had had an intimate relationship after Betty's death. Karl Otto was therefore instructed to 'lend a deaf ear to begging that might come from other female quarters'. This particularly referred to a lady in Nice who had become poor 'through her own foolishness'.

* * *

Just after the turn of the century, in February 1900 Albert started to feel that something was not quite right. He felt worse and worse and consulted a friend and doctor, Ernst Fogman, who initially calmed Albert, saying it was unlikely to be anything serious, perhaps just a stubborn cold.

Karl Otto was given different news; according to Fogman, Albert Bonnier's symptoms indicated that he had cancer of the pylorus, the lower opening of the stomach. There was only one possible outcome.

Whether Albert was informed in detail of how bad the prognosis was is unclear but his condition deteriorated week by week. Nevertheless, he continued to spend some time each working day in his office at the firm almost to the very last. As late as 14 July, he sent his last letter, which by a touching coincidence was about his favourite project, his beloved annual *Svea*.

Barely two weeks later, on the morning of 26 July 1900, Albert Bonnier died, according to his son Karl Otto, calmly and peacefully and without having suffered severe pain. On the bed lay a copy of *Revue des Deux Mondes*.

* * *

The news of Albert's death was received respectfully in the press. *Dagens Nyheter*, the newspaper he had helped to father and which had often supported him in his battles, praised Albert's capacity for work and 'free-thinking' the next day:

> Throughout his long and hardworking life, he has managed to accomplish much more than many. Complaints about his activities are only to be expected. However, the Swedish book world, the literary world and the general public have vastly overwhelming reasons to remember the old man with recognition and respect.

What otherwise, with hindsight, seems most interesting about *Dagens Nyheter*'s obituary is that it confirms that Gerhard Bonnier's invention of a revolutionary ancestor, Antoine Bonnier d'Alco, and the myth of the family's French roots, also nurtured by Albert, stubbornly lived on: 'The Bonnier family, as the name indicates, is of French origin.'

Even newspapers that had been wildly critical of Albert, e.g. in the Gustaf Fröding trial, paid their respects, although in the case of *Aftonbladet* this took some great effort:

> There is a multitude of things that could be said about the principles of our country's publishing industry, but this is not the place. As B. was, in any case he

stood far above his colleagues in terms of the keenness of his eye.

At Albert's burial the liberal rabbi Gottlieb Klein said:

> If you want to know the value of a human life, measure it against the yardstick of work. By this shall Albert Bonnier's life be measured!

The reactions of the authors who were on close terms with him perhaps shed more light on what Albert Bonnier had achieved. Selma Lagerlöf wrote to Karl Otto:

> He was such an admirably clever man, that it was always a great joy to me to listen to him – and I have fond memories of the kindness with which he treated me from the first moment to the last.

Even August Strindberg, seized by momentary and atypical generosity, wrote to Karl Otto: 'The news of your father's death has reawakened the memory of all the good he did me and my children.'

Hardly surprisingly, Frans Hedberg went the furthest in his praise, in a long obituary in *Svea*, unavoidably coloured by Hedberg's close friendship with Albert, but with a grain of truth when it came to all the writers, dead and living, on whose behalf Hedberg wrote:

> Without such an intermediary between us and the public, where would we be, us men of the pen? We would probably not spin silk from 'self-publishing' and

we should preserve in grateful recollection the memory of our old publisher, of the man who was a faithful friend to some of the best of those who have gone before, an often kind helper to the young and untried, and a never failing support to the old and tired.

That he *was able* to do this was thanks to his work, that he *wanted* to, was thanks to his heart.

Albert Bonnier lies buried beside Betty, at the Jewish cemetery in Norra kyrkogården in Solna.

* * *

When Albert Bonnier had departed this world, his children Jenny, Karl Otto and Eva were determined to institutionalise their father's memory in some way. This led to the formation of the Albert Bonnier Stipend Fund, a foundation whose charter was drawn up by Karl Staaff. The awarding committee was to comprise seven people, six of whom were to be authors and the seventh to represent the family. The very first members included Oscar Levertin, Ellen Key and Verner von Heidenstam. Karl Otto, now alone as head of the publishing firm, was the obvious representative of the donors.

The fund was partly a riposte to the Swedish Academy, appointed for life and controlled by the puffed-up backstabber Carl David af Wirsén, a poet of dubious quality who used his position as permanent secretary to promote his own reactionary preferences, a factor that had irritated both Albert and Karl Otto. To counteract such calcification, it was decided that the author members of the awarding committee could not be older than fifty-five.

Since 1901 the fund has awarded generous grants, rewarding new, Swedish literature every year.

Albert Bonnier, the old radical, would have loved it.

AUTHOR'S NOTE

Albert Bonnier, founder of the publishing firm, has been dead for more than a hundred years. Yet he still makes his presence felt in practically every Swedish home that owns a bookcase. Classic novels by August Strindberg and Selma Lagerlöf, and books by popular contemporary authors like Kerstin Ekman and Björn Ranelid all have one thing in common – they all bear the name of the imprint Albert Bonnier.

In a way this is paradoxical. On the one hand, Albert Bonnier had no interest in being seen as a public figure in his own right; he wanted to promote the reputation of his authors, not his own. On the other hand, he was central to the modern Swedish public sphere that started to emerge in the nineteenth century and which was highly defined by the literature he had printed and published.

I was struck by this thought while browsing my parents' library in my family's summer cottage while working on this book. Because, as I learned at an early age, there are some books that one *has to* read. I have been assailed by memories of the first, tentative experiences of the magic of literature from my childhood, and by an observation that seems relevant at a time when nationalist sentiments are rife and there is talk far and wide of Sweden's 'literary canon', in other words a set of works that are considered normative for Swedish culture.

If there really is such a thing as a blue and yellow canon of Swedish literature, then it came about largely thanks to an immigrant Jew from Copenhagen whose family roots lay in Dresden.

* * *

Some of the books are ones I read when I was young; others I came to as an adult. Some I gobbled down, others I skimmed. But it was not until I was writing a book about Albert Bonnier that I started to think about how important he – and his brand – had been for my educational journey and that of many others. Because it says 'Albert Bonnier' on almost every other book on these sagging shelves.

Right in the middle, as if in pride of place, shine a set of bound volumes containing Viktor Rydberg's most famous works – including *Singoalla*, the poems and *The Weaponsmith* – in a beautiful 'anniversary edition' from the 1930s. A similar set of Gustaf Fröding's collected works contains not just the poetry collections such as *Guitar and Concertina* and *Splashes and Patches*, but also a selection of Fröding's letters. Rydberg's beautiful but slightly ponderous language took some grappling with, while Fröding danced straight into your heart.

Verner von Heidenstam's *The Charles Men* was a book I found incredibly exciting as a young man, but the volume next to it, his debut *Pilgrimage and Wandering Years*, did not interest me at the time. I didn't read it until much later, and was surprised by the timelessness of a poet who was sometimes rejected as being hopelessly out of date.

What Swedish journalist doesn't have some kind of relationship with the Titan August Strindberg, the Bonnier firm's most talked-about and in his day the most contentious writer who combined the knife-sharp eye of a reporter with the storytelling delight of literature: *The Red Room*, *The New Kingdom*, *The People of Hemsö*.

A dozen artistically elegant covers – black, red, golden text – not only encase prose works such as *Getting Married* and *Swedish Destinies and Adventures* but also Strindberg's dramas, including *Master Olof*, *Easter*, *Gustav Vasa* and *A Dream Play*.

A well-thumbed copy of Selma Lagerlöf's *Nils Holgersson's Wonderful Journey Through Sweden*, mended with tape, evokes especial nostalgia; it was my reading book in primary school in Malmö. I was deeply fascinated by the story of the tiny little boy who flies over the country on the back of a goose, not least because one of the most dramatic scenes, Nils Holgersson's encounter with the fox, takes place by the lake in Skåne where I learned to swim.

By the time *Nils Holgersson's Wonderful Journey* came out and became a sensation Albert Bonnier had departed this life, but the relationship between Lagerlöf and the publisher had come about due to his curiosity about her debut novel, *The Saga of Gösta Berling*, which stands in line beside it. It was a book that Albert never quite understood. Despite that, he wanted to recruit Lagerlöf, a clear example of the way that Albert Bonnier did not let his own literary preferences stand in the way when he sensed a talent.

I was less fascinated by Zacharias Topelius' *The Surgeon's Stories*, which I picked up when I was about thirteen or so, on the firm advice of my father because he'd have me know he'd read them at that age. Now I understand that Topelius was Albert's good friend and one of the publishing firm's greatest assets, a Herman Lindqvist of the nineteenth century, one could say, popularising history for a wide audience. As a teenager, I gave up on the first volume.

All these writers from the golden age of literature in Swedish – Rydberg, Strindberg, Heidenstam, Fröding, Topelius, Lagerlöf – had a connection with Albert Bonnier. So did my personal favourite Hjalmar Söderberg, though his writing is mainly linked with the genius and taste of Albert's heir Karl Otto Bonnier. I literally feel a shiver down my spine when I take the books out; as a nineteen-year-old on military service I sat hunched up in the freezing cab of a terrain vehicle at Skillingaryd shooting range reading *Doctor Glas* and *The Serious Game*, completely entranced.

The shelves are also crowded with translated novels by foreign authors who Albert Bonnier helped to launch to a Swedish audience. In one corner is Émile Zola's *Nana*, which concerns prostitution – a phenomenon that Albert was accused of in a literary and commercial sense, often with antisemitic undertones. At the other end there is a long row of fifteen volumes of Charles Dickens, including *A Tale of Two Cities*, set in Paris and London at the time of the French Revolution, the after-effects of which had a major impact on the young radical Albert. The masterly first sentence is still relevant today: 'It was the best of times, it was the worst of times.'

* * *

One of Albert Bonnier's characteristics as a publisher was his tolerance, encapsulated in a few words to him from August Strindberg: 'I took you because you were the most fearless.'

This deep tolerance was passed on to his son Karl Otto and could sometimes tip over into something that with hindsight seems naive, manifested in a Jewish-owned publishing business making Sven Hedin, a fan of Hitler, one of its poster boys.

The traces can even be seen here in this rural idyll.

My father was especially keen on caricatures and cartoons. A book collection that contains anthologies from *The New Yorker* and titles like *Comic Drawing* and *Best Cartoons* bears witness to that. The legendary nineteenth-century Swedish cartoonist Oskar Andersson, 'O. A.', is represented by *Mannen som gör vad som faller honom in och andra historier*, (*The Man Who Does Whatever Springs to Mind and Other Stories*) compiled by Hasse Z and published by Bonniers.

More problematic are eight volumes of Albert Engström's collected drawings, printed in 1943–4.

My father enjoyed Engström's slightly burlesque humour and characters such as the alcoholic tramp Kolingen, but the antisemitism made him uncomfortable. A lover of Duke Ellington, his attitude was deeply entrenched, formed by experiences in the period between the wars: 'Anyone who likes jazz can't ever become a Nazi.'

I flick through the Engström books and realise that you can't even open them at random without being confronted with swarthy, corpulent figures with huge, hooked noses and a speech impediment.

It feels bizarre to see Albert Bonnier's name in the same company as these antisemitic stereotypes. But 'humour' of this kind, unacceptable today, was part and parcel of Albert's existence, making his efforts for Swedish literature seem even more generous.

* * *

Albert Bonnier did not lack failings. He could be overly cautious about financial matters and worry unnecessarily about his financial position. In old age he could be gruff and brusque with those around him when he disapproved of something. And over time his literary priorities became quite conservative, although he was intelligent enough to balance this with Karl Otto's more radical, liberal approach.

Nevertheless, Albert Bonnier emerges as strikingly modern.

When Per I. Gedin terms him 'the first modern publisher', he is mainly referring to Albert's capacity to forge close and lasting ties with his authors. Albert Bonnier was alone in this for a long time. But he was also modern in other respects.

He was open to new literary trends, although not always enthusiastic about them. He immediately recognised the opportunities that the new inventions of the day would open up, particularly the railways. He helped female authors who found forces ranged against them in a patriarchal age, not least the Swedish Academy, an institution which rarely impressed him.

Consequently he became an object of hate for the guardians of conservatism and of 'morality'. Their hostility placed him under great strain at the time. Now it is a confirmation of how forward-thinking he was.

* * *

Albert Bonnier's main interest was literature, and at his death in 1900 he was the leading Swedish publisher in the field, but he also published vast quantities of non-fiction and devoted himself, like his father and his brothers, to the publication of periodicals, from the short-lived newspaper *Stockholms Figaro* to his 'baby' *Svea*, and the cash cow, his Swedish trade directory *Sveriges Handelskalender*. He printed *Dagens Nyheter* in the newspaper's very first months.

As for the mass media revolutions of a later age – radio, television, the internet – Albert Bonnier naturally knew nothing of those, but he laid the first building blocks of a large and open media house, the cornerstone of which is a principle of journalism that he introduced in his new homeland against what were at times difficult odds – disseminate, don't judge.

BIBLIOGRAPHY

Aftonbladet

Albert Bonniers Förlag 100 år, 1837–1937 (Stockholm: 1937)

Albert Bonniers Förlag. Ett familjeföretag 1837–1962. Etthundratjugofem år (Stockholm: 1962)

Alm, Göran et al, *I världsutställningarnas tid. Kungahus, näringsliv & medier* (Stockholm: 2017)

Andersson, Lars M, *En jude är en jude är en jude ... Representationer av 'juden' i svensk skämtpress omkring 1900–1930* (Lund: 2000)

Bergqvist, Herman, *I böckernas värld. Minnen och anteckningar från en femtiotreårig verksamhet i Albert Bonniers bokförlag* (Stockholm: 1950)

Bergsten, Staffan, *Gustaf Fröding* (Stockholm: 2016)

Biografiskt lexikon för Finland (blf.fi)

Bonnier, Eva, *Börs och katedral – sex generationer Bonniers* (Albert Bonnier family archive (Centre for Business History)

Bonniers Förlag/Stockholms universitetsbibliotek: 2003)

Bonnier, Karl Otto, *Bonniers. En bokhandlarefamilj. Anteckningar ur gamla papper och ur minnet, I och II* (Stockholm: 1930)

Bonnier, Karl Otto, *En bokhandlarefamilj. Anteckningar ur gamla papper och ur minnet, III* (Stockholm: 1930)

Bonnier, Karl Otto, *En bokhandlarefamilj. Anteckningar ur gamla papper och ur minnet, IV* (Stockholm: 1931)

Bonnier, Karl Otto, ed. *Minnen från Rom. Utdrag ur brev till hemmet* (Stockholm: 1928)

Bonnier publishing archive (Centre for Business History)

Bonnier, Tor, *Längesen. Sammanklippta minnesbilder* (Stockholm: 1972)

Bonnier, Åke, *Bonniers – en släktkrönika 1778–1941* (Stockholm: 1975)

Bredefeldt, Rita, *Ekonomi och identitet: de svenska judarnas ekonomiska verksamheter och självbild från 1800-talets andra hälft till 1930, Nordisk Judaistik – Scandinavian Jewish Studies, Vol. 18, No 1–2, 1997, 22–9*

Cavalli-Björkman, Görel, *Eva Bonnier – ett konstnärsliv* (Stockholm: 2013)

Dagens Nyheter

Dagligt Allehanda

Forsgård, Nils Erik, *I det femte inseglets tecken. En studie i den åldrande Zacharias Topelius livs- och historiefilosofi. Skrifter utgivna av Svenska litteratursällskapet i Finland, nr 616* (Helsinki: 1998)

Franzén, Nils-Olof, *Hjalmar Branting och hans tid* (Stockholm: 1985)

Freja

Fröding, Gustaf, *Brev. Skrifter av Gustaf Fröding* (Stockholm: 1937)

Fröding, Gustaf, *Dikter. Bonniers folkbibliotek* (Stockholm: 1955)

Furuland, Gunnel, *Romanen som vardagsvara. Förläggare, författare och skönlitterära häftesserier i Sverige 1833–1851 från Lars Johan Hierta till Albert Bonnier* (Stockholm: 2007)

Gedin, Per I., *Litteraturen i verkligheten. Om bokmarknadens historia och framtid* (Stockholm: 1975)

Gedin, Per I., *Litteraturens örtagårdsmästare. Karl Otto Bonnier och hans tid* (Stockholm: 2003)

Gedin, Per I., *Verner von Heidenstam. Ett liv* (Stockholm: 2006)

Göteborgs Handels- och Sjöfarts-Tidning (Handelstidningen)

Gripenstedt, Johan August, *Tal, anföranden och uppsatser, I-II* (Stockholm: 1871–1872)

Gustafsson, Karl Erik, Rydén, Per, ed. *Den svenska pressens historia. II. Åren då allting hände, 1830–1897* (Stockholm: 2001)

Gustafsson, Lars, ed. *Swedish Från trollformler till Frostenson* (Stockholm: 1995)

Gynning, Margareta, ed. *Pariserbref. Konstnären Eva Bonniers brev 1883–1889* (Stockholm: 1999)

Hadenius, Stig, *Dagens Nyheters historia. Tidningen och makten 1864–2000* (Stockholm: 2002)

Hammarlund, Bo, *Den aristokratiske rebellen. Magnus Jacob Crusenstolpe i 1800-talets offentlighet* (Falun: 2017)

Hansson, Svante, *Den förste Bonnier* (Stockholm: 2004)

Hasselberg, Gudmar, *Rudolf Wall. Dagens Nyheters skapare* (Stockholm: 1945)

Hedin, Marika, Holmberg, Håkan et al., *Karl Staaff. Arbetarvän, rösträttskämpe och socialreformator* (Stockholm: 2015)

Heidenstam, Verner von, *Karolinerna, I, II. Med vinjetter av E. v. Strokirch* (Stockholm: 1946)

Heidenstam, Verner von, *Vallfart och vandringsår. Verner von Heidenstams samlade verk utgivna av Kate Bang och Fredrik Böök* (Stockholm: 1943)

Hellberg, Mauritz, *Frödingsminnen* (Stockholm: 1925)

Herberts, Carola, publisher, *Zacharias Topelius korrespondens med förlag och översättare. Svenska litteratursällskapet i Finland* (Helsinki: 2015/topelius.fi)

Hermele, Bernt, *Firman. Bonnier – Sveriges mäktigaste mediesläkt* (Stockholm: 2015)

Hjorth, Daniel, Attius, Håkan, ed. *Excelsior! Albert Bonniers Förlag 150 år. En jubileumskavalkad i brev* (Stockholm: 1987)

Hägg, Göran, *Den svenska litteraturhistorien* (Stockholm: 1999)

Idun.

Ilshammar, Lars, *Hjalmar Branting, Sveriges statsministrar under 100 år, Vol 6*, ed. Mats Bergstrand & Per T Ohlsson (Stockholm: 2010)

Lagercrantz, Olof, *August Strindberg* (Stockholm: 1979)

Lagerlöf, Selma, *Brev, 1, 1871–1902 i urval av Ying Toijer-Nilsson* (Lund: 1967)

Lagerlöf, Selma, *Gösta Berlings saga* (Stockholm: 1948)

Lauritzen, Monica, *Karl Warburg. Den varsamme vägvisaren* (Stockholm: 2018)

Levertin, Oscar, Heidenstam, Verner von, *Pepitas bröllop. En litteraturanmälan* (Stockholm: 1890)

Lindorm, Erik, ed. *Ny svensk historia. Carl XIV Johan–Carl XV och deras tid 1810–1872. En bokfilm* (Stockholm: 1942)

Lindorm, Erik ed. *Ny svensk historia. Oscar II och hans tid. En bokfilm*

(Stockholm: 1936)

Litteraturbanken

Lundqvist, Åke, *Kultursidan. Kulturjournalistiken i Dagens Nyheter 1864–2012* (Stockholm: 2012)

Lönnroth, Ami, Mattsson, Per Eric, *Tidningskungen. Lars Johan Hierta – den förste moderne svensken* (Stockholm: 1996)

Lönnroth, Lars, Delblanc, Sven ed. *Den Svenska Litteraturen, 2. Genombrottstiden* (Stockholm: 1999)

Michanek, Germund, *Skaldernas konung. Oscar II, litteraturen och litteratörerna* (Stockholm: 1979)

Modéer, Kjell Å, *Land skall med lag byggas. Sex rättshistoriska uppsatser* (Lund: 1980)

Myrdal, Jan, *Johan August Strindberg* (Stockholm: 2000)

Nationalencyklopedin

Nerman, Ture, *Crusenstolpes kravaller. Historiskt reportage från Stockholm sommaren 1838* (Stockholm: 1938)

Nordisk familjebok

Odelberg, Axel, *Vi som beundrade varandra så mycket. Sven Hedin och Adolf Hitler* (Stockholm: 2012)

Ohlsson, Per T, *100 år av tillväxt. Johan August Gripenstedt och den liberala revolutionen* (Stockholm: 1994)

Ohlsson, Per T, *Konservkungen. Herbert Felix – ett flyktingöde i 1900-talets Europa* (Stockholm: 2006)

Ohlsson, Per T, *Svensk politik* (Lund: 2014)

Ord och Bild

Palm, Anna-Karin, *'Jag vill sätta världen i rörelse'. En biografi över Selma Lagerlöf* (Stockholm: 2019)

Personne, John, *Strindbergs-litteraturen och osedligheten bland skolungdomen. Till föräldrar och uppfostrare samt till de styrande* (Stockholm: 1887)

Projekt Runeberg

Retzius, Gustaf, *Biografiska anteckningar och minnen, II* (Uppsala: 1948)

Riksdagens protokoll

Rinman, Sven, *Svenska bokförläggareföreningen 1843/1887. En historisk översikt utarbetad med anledning av föreningens 100-årsjubileum* (Stockholm: 1951)

Rydberg, Viktor, *Romerska sägner, Romerske kejsare, Singoalla m.m. Jubileumsupplaga* (Stockholm: 1932)

Rydberg, Viktor, *Dikter, Vapensmeden. Jubileumsupplaga* (Stockholm: 1932)

Rydén, Per, *Sveriges National-litteratur är inte bara historia* (Stockholm: 2012)

Schön, Lennart, *En modern svensk ekonomisk historia. Tillväxt och omvandling under två sekler* (Stockholm: 2007)

Sjöberg, Birthe, *Dialog eller dynamit. Viktor Rydberg och August Strindberg – förtryckets fiender* (Halmstad: 2018)

Solomon, Nina, *Strindbergiana. Eflte samlingen utgiven av Strindbergssällskapet*, ed. Boel Westin (Stockholm: 1996)

Stockholms Figaro

Stockholmskällan

Strindberg, August, *Dikter på vers och prosa and Sömngångarnätter på vakna dagar. Samlade skrifter av August Strindberg 13* (Stockholm: 1913)

Strindberg, August, *Det nya riket. Skildringar från attentatens och jubelfesternas tidevarv. Samlade skrifter av August Strindberg 10* (Stockholm: 1913)

Strindberg, August, *Giftas I–II. August Strindbergs Samlade Verk 16* (Stockholm: 1982)

Strindberg, August, *Röda rummet. Skildringar ur artist- och författarlivet. Samlade skrifter av August Strindberg 5* (Stockholm: 1912)

Strindberg, August, *Strindbergs brev, III. Strindbergssällskapets skrifter. April 1882–1883. Utgivna av Torsten Eklund* (Stockholm: 1952)

Strindberg, August, *Strindbergs brev, IV. Strindbergssällskapets skrifter. 1884. Utgivna av Torsten Eklund* (Stockholm: 1954)

Strindberg, August, *Strindbergs brev, V. Strindbergssällskapets skrifter. 1885–juli 1886. Utgivna av Torsten Eklund* (Stockholm: 1956).

Strindberg, August, *Strindbergs brev, VI. Strindbergssällskapets skrifter. Augusti 1886–januari 1888.* Utgivna av Torsten Eklund (Stockholm: 1958)

Strindberg, August, *Strindbergs brev VII. Strindbergssällskapets skrifter. Utgivna av Torsten Eklund* (Stockholm: 1961)

Svanberg, Ingvar, Tydén, Mattias, *Tusen år av invandring. En svensk kulturhistoria* (Stockholm: 1992)

Svea

Svedjedal, Johan, *Bokens samhälle. Svenska Bokförläggareföreningen och svensk bokmarknad 1887–1943, I* (Stockholm: 1993)

Svenning, Olle, *Hövdingen. Hjalmar Branting. En biografi* (Stockholm: 2014)

Svensk uppslagsbok

Svenska Dagbladet

Svenskt biografiskt lexikon

Sundin, Staffan, *Viktor Rydberg och hans förläggare Albert Bonnier* (Veritas 26/2010)

Söderholm, Gundel, *Svea. En litterär kalender 1844–1907* (Uppsala universitet: 2007)

Söderström, Göran, *Strindberg. Ett liv* (Stockholm: 2013)

Thorsell, Elisabeth, ed. *Gerhard Bonniers ättlingar* (Stockholm: 2004)

Tigerstedt, E N, ed. *Ny illustrerad svensk litteraturhistoria. Fjärde delen. Åttiotal. Nittiotal* (Stockholm: 1957)

Topelius, Zacharias, *Fältskärns berättelser, I* (Stockholm: 1937)

Valentin, Hugo, *Judarnas historia i Sverige* (Stockholm: 1924)

Valentin, Hugo, *Judarna i Sverige. Från 1774 till 1950-talet* (Stockholm: 2004)

Valentin, Hugo, *Urkunder till judarnas historia i Sverige* (Stockholm: 1924)

Vasenius, Valfrid, *Zacharias Topelius. Hans lif och skaldegärning. Sjette delen* (Helsinki: 1930)

Vegesack, Thomas von, *Stockholm 1851. Staden, människorna och den konservativa revolten* (Stockholm: 2005)

Västerbro, Magnus, *Svälten. Hungeråren som formade Sverige* (Stockholm: 2018)

Warburg, Karl, *Viktor Rydberg. En lefnadsteckning, I–II* (Stockholm: 1900)

IMAGE SOURCES

The pictures in the plate section, unless stated below, are in the Bonnier family archive / Centre for Business History, and photographed by Nina Ulmaja.

Gerhard Bonnier: unknown artist from *Albert Bonniers Förlag 100 år, 1837–1937* (Stockholm: 1937).

Illustration from *Stockholms Mode-Journal*, No.1, 1843.

Cover of *Stockholm's Figaro*, No. 1, 29 December 1844.

Pages from *Svea*, 1845.

Cover sketch for Strindberg's letter.

From the newspaper *Fäderneslandet*. Photographed from Per I Gedin, *Litteraturens örtagårdsmästare*, (Stockholm: 2003).

Cartoon of Fröding and Bonnier: Per I Gedin, *Litteraturens örtagårdsmästare* (Stockholm: 2003).

Painting by Eva Bonnier, 1890. Photo: Nationalmuseum.

INDEX

ABOUT THE AUTHOR

Per T Ohlsson (1958–2021) was a multi-award-winning author, journalist and Senior Columnist for the Swedish paper *Sydvenskan*. His previous publications include biographies of nineteenth-century politician Johan August Gripenstedt and grocery pioneer Herbert Felix, and books on Swedish politics and the year 1918. Per T Ohlsson was awarded an honorary doctorate by Lund University in 2017.